A Guide to Post-classical Narration

A Guide to Post-classical Narration

The Future of Film Storytelling

Eleftheria Thanouli

BLOOMSBURY ACADEMIC
NEW YORK • LONDON • OXFORD • NEW DELHI • SYDNEY

BLOOMSBURY ACADEMIC
Bloomsbury Publishing Inc
1385 Broadway, New York, NY 10018, USA
50 Bedford Square, London, WC1B 3DP, UK
29 Earlsfort Terrace, Dublin 2, Ireland

BLOOMSBURY, BLOOMSBURY ACADEMIC and the Diana logo are trademarks of
Bloomsbury Publishing Plc

First published in the United States of America 2024

Copyright © Eleftheria Thanouli, 2024

For legal purposes the Acknowledgments on p. ix constitute an extension of this copyright page.

Cover design: Yannis Mazarakis

All rights reserved. No part of this publication may be reproduced or transmitted in any form or by any means, electronic or mechanical, including photocopying, recording, or any information storage or retrieval system, without prior permission in writing from the publishers.

Bloomsbury Publishing Inc does not have any control over, or responsibility for, any third-party websites referred to or in this book. All internet addresses given in this book were correct at the time of going to press. The author and publisher regret any inconvenience caused if addresses have changed or sites have ceased to exist, but can accept no responsibility for any such changes.

A catalog record for this book is available from the Library of Congress

ISBN: HB: 978-1-5013-9306-8
PB: 978-1-5013-9307-5
ePDF: 978-1-5013-9308-2
eBook: 978-1-5013-9309-9

Typeset by RefineCatch Ltd, Bungay, Suffolk

To find out more about our authors and books, visit www.bloomsbury.com and sign up for our newsletters.

For Anastasia

CONTENTS

Acknowledgments ix
Preface x

Introduction 1
    0.1 Cutting Up the Past 2
    0.2 Opening Historical Poetics 21
    0.3 *A Guide to Post-classical Narration* 30

1 Post-classical Narrative Logic 37
    1.1 Introduction 37
    1.2 Post-classical Compositional Motivation 38
    1.3 Post-classical Realistic Motivation 60
    1.4 Post-classical Generic Motivation 79
    1.5 Post-classical Artistic Motivation 85
    1.6 Conclusion 95

2 Post-classical Space 97
    2.1 Introduction 97
    2.2 Intensified Continuity 98
    2.3 Graphic Frame 113
    2.4 Spatial Montage 140
    2.5 Conclusion 157

3 Post-classical Time 159
    3.1 Introduction 159
    3.2 Mediated Time 160
    3.3 Complex Chronology 162
    3.4 Elastic Duration 164
    3.5 Conclusion 182

4   Post-classical Narration 185
    4.1 Introduction 185
    4.2 Self-consciousness, Knowledgeability, and
        Communicativeness 186
    4.3 Levels of Narration 189
    4.4 Conclusion 214

5   The Post-classical Auteur: Quentin Tarantino 217
    5.1 Introduction 217
    5.2 *Pulp Fiction* (1994) 220
    5.3 *Kill Bill: Vol. I* (2003) 223
    5.4 *Inglourious Basterds* (2009) 229
    5.5 *Once Upon a Time in Hollywood* (2019) 233
    5.6 Conclusion 238

6   Conclusion: On Modes and Boundaries 241
    Dunkirk: Two Readings 243
    Evaluating Principles: The Dominant and the
        Necessary/Sufficient Conditions 247
    Towards More Historical Poetics 251

Appendix A: A List of Suggested Post-classical Films 255
References 259
Filmography 265
Index 267

ACKNOWLEDGMENTS

I would like to thank the students at the School of Film at Aristotle University of Thessaloniki who became fascinated by post-classical storytelling, offering me ever more film examples over the years, and thus validating the gist of my theory. Among them, Nikolas Lund became one of the most avid enthusiasts and offered to read the first draft of the manuscript, helping me render it as student friendly as possible. Giorgos Dimoglou also lent a helping hand with several tables and other technical issues. Above all, I am indebted to Yannis Mazarakis for patiently designing several versions of the book cover before finalizing the one that is currently used. From the start, it was of utmost importance for me to have this book published in color, so that the textual analysis based on hundreds of stills would be effective and convincing for the reader. I am indebted to Onassis Culture, which so eagerly funded the reproduction of images in color.

On a more personal level, I am grateful to Stamatis Valasiadis for faithfully discussing post-classical narration for almost twenty-two years. Without a doubt, this book is also the result of my editor's unwavering support; thank you, Katie, for believing in me. Finally, I would like to thank my family, and particularly my kids, Giorgos and Anastasia, for infusing joy and purpose into my life every day.

This publication is supported by Onassis Culture.

PREFACE

This book is the culmination of my research on post-classical narration, which began as my doctoral thesis and later developed into the publication of *Post-classical Cinema: An International Poetics of Film Narration* back in 2009. The project was formulated clearly in my mind from the very start: I wanted to add another chapter to David Bordwell's *Narration in the Fiction Film* (1985), describing the "post-classical" mode of narration as a full-blown historical mode that emerged in the 1990s and featured in films across the world. My mentor and supervisor, Thomas Elsaesser, detected a "Trojan Horse logic" in this endeavor and characterized my strategy as a "scenario worthy of Greek tragedy or at least Greek epic." Why? For reasons he explicated with his own unique talent: "At first glance, a demurely modest project: add merely another chapter to an existing work. But then, what boldness, what truly Greek hubris, when you consider that the chapter to be added was to a book, written by no lesser God than David Bordwell. An act of homage or of parricide? Of homage as parricide or parricide as homage?"[1]

As much as I still enjoy Thomas's dramatic tone, his flair for melodrama and, above all, his love for paradoxical wordplay, I believe that the purpose of my work on post-classical narration was never meant to inflame great passions. It was, and remains, a painstaking attempt to extend the research of historical poetics to the study of contemporary cinema and revive the interest in formalist analysis as the basis for any further theoretical explorations in the field of film studies. In the years since the 2009 edition, I was glad to observe the spreading of the post-classical mode in new territories and in more mainstream films, reinforcing its place in the poetic history of cinema. This book is my latest attempt to describe and refine the creative norms of the post-classical mode in a detailed and accessible manner, using new films from the period 2005–22. It also hopes to address head on a range of methodological issues in the analysis of film form, acquainting students and scholars with the relevant concepts and tools. Studying and understanding the narrational process through post-classical fiction films is an exemplary way of not only grasping the historical origins of storytelling, but also for sensing its future prospects.

Note

1 Excerpt from Thomas Elsaesser's speech on the day of my PhD defense in Amsterdam, June 21, 2005.

Introduction

In order to become an object for discussion and inspection, time has to be transformed into a causal sequence. The only way in which this can be done is by narration.

MUNZ 2006: 85[1]

Narration will be the focus of this book on two different levels: on the one hand, I will be studying the latest narrative developments in a series of films made across the globe in order to examine how the post-classical mode of narration[2] continues to hold sway in more and more popular segments of filmmaking. On the other hand, the very process of narrating cinema's poetic history will be placed center stage so that both scholars and students will be able to understand how the terms we deploy, the questions we ask, and the lines we draw on the calendar are not givens that we, as historians, discover simply by digging. Rather, they are choices that we make based on a wide range of motivations, from personal idiosyncrasies to political ideology.

When David Bordwell, Janet Staiger, and Kristin Thompson wrote the history of the classical Hollywood cinema up to 1960, focusing on issues of style and mode of production, they aptly drew on George Kubler and his advice that one should not try to determine a country's network of railroads by studying the itinerary of every traveler (Bordwell et al. 1985: xvi). From Kubler, what I would also like to keep in mind is this: "The narrative historian always has the privilege of deciding that continuity cuts better into certain lengths than into others. He never is required to defend his cut, because history cuts anywhere with equal ease, and a good story can begin anywhere a teller chooses" (Kubler 1970: 2). My goal here is to tell a story about the emergence of a new mode of narration that appeared in the early 1990s and continues to this day, expanding into new territories and affecting diverse types of filmmakers and film practices that follow in its wake. Yet my story does not stand alone; it intersects, intercuts, and often collides with many others in the process of carving up and explaining the cinematic past.

In this introductory chapter I would like to describe the theoretical context in which my account of post-classical narration is situated by giving a general and selective overview of some of the most influential positions regarding the periodization of the history of American cinema, with a particular emphasis on the methodological and conceptual assumptions of the historians in question. My argument about the existence of post-classical narration as a distinct historical paradigm is not a self-evident truth. It is a carefully crafted theoretical construction based on the observation of historical data, i.e., specific films that are chosen, categorized, and described according to a number of theoretical principles that fall under the scope of "historical poetics." These principles will be elaborately explained in the coming pages but we need to begin by finding an entry point into the discussions that have demarcated and explained the phases in American cinema, especially Hollywood, so far.

0.1 Cutting Up the Past

0.1.1 Cinema and Classicism

It has been well over a century since the moment that we tend to consider as the birth of cinema—that is, December 28, 1895, when the Lumière Brothers unveiled their new invention.[3] From those first moments until roughly the early 1950s, thinkers pondered the nature of this new medium, wondering whether it should be regarded as an art form, and (if so) why. It is customary to consider André Bazin as one who tackled these questions with most insight, providing us with observations regarding cinema's "mummy complex" or its tendency to satisfy our "obsession with realism" (Bazin 1967). Yet it is his views on the idea of classicism that should be deemed as equally influential since they inspired Bordwell's own work on classical Hollywood. In fact, it was Bordwell himself who relatively recently paid a tribute to his mentor, underlining Bazin's value as a poetician (Bordwell 2018). Bazin, as Bordwell explains in the same work, should be discussed not only with regard to his philosophical deliberations, but also in light of his penchant for the analysis of "shots and scenes in exquisite detail," the solidification of the analysis according to specific concepts (depth of field, long take, classical narration) and the careful balancing of the microscopic and the macroscopic take on the history of the medium (Bordwell 2018).

Bazin's work is, indeed, a milestone in the discussion around classicism for all the reasons that Bordwell highlights, including the following famous definition of cinema as a classical art:

> In seeing again today such films as *Jezebel* by William Wyler, *Stagecoach* by John Ford, or *Le Jour se lève* by Marcel Carné, one has the feeling that in them an art has found its perfect balance, its ideal form of expression, and reciprocally one admires them for dramatic and moral themes to which the cinema, while it may not have created them, has given a grandeur, an artistic effectiveness, that they would not otherwise have had. In short, here are all the characteristics of the ripeness of a classical art.
>
> BAZIN 1967: 29

In arguing that the film production in the United States and France had reached a stage of maturity immediately prior to the start of the Second World War, Bazin makes a typical use of the biological metaphors that proliferate in the art history tradition (Kubler 1970: 4). "Death," "birth," and "maturity" are recurring words in his vocabulary, illustrating a constant need for marking historical beginnings and endings that shape cinema's history into certain periods. His historical analysis, however, does not establish a solid middle ground; he selects specific films, like those mentioned above, in order to substantiate broad organicist arguments about the nature of the cinematic art. When reading his countless essays,[4] one cannot help noticing the fluidity of the statements and the ambiguities inherent in the poetic patterns that he tentatively identifies.[5]

Bordwell, on the other hand, clearly proved to be a more efficient disciple. In the formidable history of Hollywood as style and mode of production mentioned above, Bordwell and his two co-authors launched the most expansive investigation to date into the economic, technological, and formal mechanisms that built the gigantic film enterprise that we call "classical Hollywood cinema" (Bordwell et al. 1985). Their meticulous study showed that from 1917 to 1960, Hollywood cemented a unified mode of film practice that relied on the mutual interdependence of aesthetic norms and production practices. These norms will be discussed regularly throughout this book, but it is important to explain here why Bordwell considered the label "classical" to be the most appropriate. As he notes,

> It seems proper to retain the term in English, since the principles which Hollywood claims as its own rely on notions of decorum, proportion, formal harmony, respect for tradition, mimesis, self-effacing craftsmanship, and cool control of the perceiver's response—canons which critics in any medium usually call "classical."
>
> BORDWELL et al. 1985: 3

Although the dialogue with Bazin is very open and respectful, Bordwell's definition of classicism refrains—as becomes obvious from the direct comparison of the two quotes—from referring to specific films or filmmakers and, above all, to the concept of art. In fact, the choice of the word "medium" signals a marked difference, despite the references to the notions of "harmony" and "proportion" that echo Bazin's "balance." What also comes from this quote is that Hollywood as a whole, at least from 1917 to 1960, is equated with classicism. Every film that was produced in a Hollywood studio during that period was a "classical film," which means that it was an instance of the unified group style that developed within this specific film practice. This is a powerful, all-encompassing thesis that has raised a series of questions over the years[6] but is painstakingly backed by a plethora of empirical evidence to which all three authors contributed, each in their own domain: Bordwell on style, Thompson on technology and style, Staiger on technology and economics. Their example, among other things, showcases a historiographical model where a powerful theoretical argument dictates the organization, the ordering, and the interpretation of the historical data. As they confess, as early as the *Preface*, "For rhetorical purposes, our argument is cast chronologically, but the idea of a 'classical Hollywood cinema' is ultimately a theoretical construct, and as such it must be judged by criteria of logical rigor and instrumental value" (Bordwell et al. 1985: xviii).

An equally self-conscious historical argument was put forward by Robert B. Ray in his book *A Certain Tendency of the Hollywood Cinema, 1930–1980*, which was also published in 1985. In fact, the comparison between Bordwell and Ray's accounts of Hollywood cinema is particularly intriguing, as they seem to constantly converge and diverge from each other in ways that only the latter would acknowledge.[7] From my point of view, drawing a lineage from Bazin to Bordwell and, finally, Ray on the topic of classicism and Hollywood is most enlightening for the role that our concepts play in the shaping of cinematic history. For Ray, the "classic" Hollywood years extend from 1930 to 1945, while two consecutive breaks occur in 1946 (the post-war period 1946–66) and in 1967 (the contemporary period 1967–80). The coming of sound is viewed as a turning point in history, as it "saw Hollywood reach the peak of its narrative and commercial success" (Ray 1985: 25). The aspect of popularity is crucial in Ray's theory, as he chooses to discuss films with a commercial or critical impact instead of adopting more scientific criteria, such as biased or unbiased sampling. His argument goes like this: during the classic period, Hollywood produced narratives with certain "formal" and "thematic" paradigms in order to perform a specific ideological function, namely, to conceal from the audience the necessity for a choice (32). In terms of the formal paradigm, which relies on the invisible style, Ray's observations are astonishingly close to Bordwell's description of the classical *mise-en-scène* and the continuity editing. What differs though is that Ray moves further into an interpretation of those formal elements drawing on terms from Barthesian mythology, Freudian psychoanalysis and Althusserian ideology. The same applies to the thematic paradigm as well. Ray identifies three types of Hollywood heroes (the outlaw, the official, and the reluctant) that embody the contradictions of American mythology and perform their ideological role by concealing from the audience the necessity for choosing one side over the other. In Ray's words:

> We can begin to describe this mythology by observing that, like the invisible style, it concealed the necessity for choice. As the formal paradigm depended on consciously established rules for shooting and editing, Hollywood's thematic conventions rested on an industry-wide consensus defining commercially acceptable filmmaking. This consensus's underlying premise dictated the conversion of all political, sociological, and economic dilemmas into personal melodramas.
>
> RAY 1985: 56-7

According to Ray, the classicism of Hollywood has very little to do with art, harmony, or balance and a great deal to do with an industry that cares to produce popular films that perpetuate the core principles of the American mythology, while helping the audience negotiate the external political and economic troubles with personalized stories that tell them "they can have it all." Despite the terms "myth," "dream," and "ideology" that inform Ray's account, his take on classicism converges with Bordwell's when it comes to Hollywood's enduring stability. Regardless of the chronological breaks in 1946 and 1967, Ray believes that the core ideological effects of the classic Hollywood film were barely affected by the technological developments or the political/historical conditions. To the question: "is there a dissident paradigm in American cinema until the 1980s?," Ray's answer, like Bordwell's, is an unequivocal "No."[8]

0.1.2 Cinema and Postmodernism

Apart from the notion of classicism as a historical and qualitative marker in the history of cinema, thinkers have brought forward several other concepts in their efforts to identify and explain epochal shifts. The one that stands out in the literature from the 1990s onwards is that of postmodernism. The passionate and belligerent discussions about the passage from modernity to postmodernity, as a new phase in our historical, cultural, and economic life soon emigrated to the study of film. The result was a very mixed assortment of arguments that either favored ideological elements over stylistic/narrative ones or meshed them indiscriminately. In their midst, the terms classical Hollywood, New Hollywood, and postmodern cinema exist in a very ambiguous relationship. As Peter Kramer notes,

> Since the mid-1970s, then, critical debates about the New Hollywood have been characterised by a confusing proliferation of contradictory and

shifting definitions of the term, and by different attempts to conceptualise the development of mainstream American cinema in the post-war era with reference to modernism and postmodernism.

KRAMER 1998: 305

These different and contradictory attempts to map American cinema from the 1960s onwards in the continuum between modernism and postmodernism have woven a very rich theoretical tapestry that I could not fully describe here.[9] I would like, however, to juxtapose some key positions from two distinct perspectives: one stems from prominent literary scholars, like Fredric Jameson and Linda Hutcheon, who adapt a wide humanistic agenda to the analysis of film, while the other comes from a film scholar, Yvonne Tasker, who imbues the postmodern discourse with a number of popular concepts from contemporary film theory.

In the classic volume *Postmodernism, or, The Cultural Logic of Late Capitalism* (1991), Jameson sought to describe a phase in our history and culture that is distinct from anything that went on in the past. The stakes in this enterprise are, however, particularly high, for the reasons that he explains right from the start: "Postmodernism theory is one of those attempts: the effort to take the temperature of the age without instruments and in a situation in which we are not even sure there is so coherent a thing as an 'age,' or zeitgeist or 'system' or 'current situation' any longer" (Jameson 1991: xi). Yet his efforts in this book and other writings proved to be fruitful, as they formed a wide range of observations that established postmodernism as an overarching "periodizing concept" that could perform a rather traditional Marxist function, namely the connection of changes in the economy with those in culture. In his words,

> It is not just another word for the description of a particular style. It is also, at least in my use, a periodizing concept whose function is to correlate the emergence of new formal features in culture with the emergence of a new type of social life and a new economic order—what is often euphemistically called modernisation, post-industrial or consumer society, the society of the media or the spectacle, or multinational capitalism.

JAMESON 1983: 112

The postmodern style is thus a formal manifestation of the deeper social changes that took place in the phase of late capitalism after 1945 in the United States and Western Europe. The principal characteristic of this style is a sustained reaction to and a critical rejection of what was considered "grand" in the past: from the styles of high modernism established in the universities, museums, and art institutions to the traditional boundaries between high and popular/mass culture, as well as other long-standing hierarchies and values (Jameson 1983: 112–13). The key formal vehicle for this postmodern enterprise is the use of pastiche. For Jameson, pastiche is blank parody; it is the imitation of dead styles and the re-cycling of dead signifiers in a creative world where the possibility for creating something "new" does not exist (114).

In the cinema, the manifestation of this postmodern symptomatology is found in what Jameson labels the "nostalgia film." The nostalgia film is obsessed with the past but not always in a literal sense. In fact, there are four variations of nostalgia films that include the following:

1. Films that portray life in various historical periods and try to recapture the atmosphere of older eras, as in *American Graffiti* (1973), *Chinatown* (1974), and *Il Conformista* (1970).

2. Films that evoke the past metonymically by trying to reinvent "the feel and shape of characteristic art objects of an older period" and by reawakening "a sense of the past associated with those objects" (116). The example here is *Star Wars* (1977), a film that makes older generations long with nostalgia for the popular Saturday afternoon serials from the 1930s–50s.

3. Films that combine the previous two strategies and evoke the past both literally and metonymically, with *Raiders of the Lost Ark* (1981) as a prime example.

4. Films that, despite their contemporary settings, try to conceal discreetly their contemporary references and their connections to the contemporary social reality. They create an archaic feeling and invite a nostalgic viewing experience, as if they took place in an eternal past somehow "beyond history." The classic example of this apparently broad category is *Body Heat* (1981).

Both the term "nostalgia film" and the idea of pastiche as a symptom of creative dead-end in the age of late capitalism have had remarkable impact on the writings of film scholars who were eager to cut the history of cinema along the lines of modernism and postmodernism and classify contemporary films according to their adherence to the postmodern agenda (Corrigan 1991; Denzin 1991; Landy and Fischer 1994; Sharrett 1990).

Those who followed Jameson's positions about the predicaments of our postmodern economic and cultural life were likely to interpret postmodern films with pessimism and disappointment regarding their inability to address the past in "real" terms. However, the negative attitude towards nostalgia represents only one side of the critics' stance. To Jameson's grievances against the loss of historicity in the postmodern world, Hutcheon counterposes the postmodern awareness about history's own ontological and epistemological limitations. As she writes, "Jameson laments the loss of a sense of his particular kind of history, then, while dismissing as nostalgia the only kind of history we may (honestly, in good faith) be able to acknowledge; a contingent and inescapably intertextual history" (Hutcheon 1990: 129).

What underlies the opposition between Jameson and Hutcheon on postmodern cinema is a more fundamental discrepancy between their respective notions of history; where the former defends a Marxist model of history with a firm belief in the "real referent" of the historical discourse, the latter endorses the postmodern realization that "there is no directly and unproblematically *accessible past* 'real' for us today: we can only know the past through its traces, its texts" (128 (emphasis in original)). Postmodern films, as all postmodern art, epitomize the postmodern approach to history through two different expressive strategies: parody and self-reflexivity. Where Jameson sees blank irony and pastiche, Hutcheon discovers the workings of a Bakhtinian parody that can be "constructively and deconstructively critical, challenging the monologic dominant discourse with a second voice, a second level of meaning that destabilises prior authority and unexamined power" (129).

In terms of archetypical postmodern films, Hutcheon's sample is quite varied. Woody Allen is featured with many examples (*Zelig* [1983], *Play it Again, Sam* [1972], *The Purple Rose of Cairo* [1985]), while other case studies include American and European fiction films and documentaries (*Brazil* [1985], *Carmen* [1983], *Desert Hearts* [1985], *The Return of Martin Guerre* [1982], *Cotton Club* [1984], *Marlene* [1984]). What they all share in common is their self-conscious tendency to "use and abuse" the formal, narrative, and ideological conventions of all previous art forms, both classical and modernist. Thus, postmodernism in the cinema signals "a fundamentally contradictory enterprise" that, according to Hutcheon is particularly welcome: the films dare to openly destabilize all types of conventions in parodic ways and to point to their own inherent paradoxes (Hutcheon 1988: 23).

Although the "dialogue" between Jameson and Hutcheon mostly concentrates on the issue of historicity and the ability of postmodern films to address the past in what each of them considers "proper" terms, the discussions about postmodernism in the cinema extend to numerous other concepts, such as identity, ideology, gender, race, and nationality, while the notions of "decenteredness," "incoherence," "fragmentation," and "surface" become common catchwords (Collins 1989; Degli-Esposti 1998). Admittedly, in all these discussions the overall framework of postmodernism appears to be too broad or fragmented to provide a solid and consistent explanation for the entire spectrum of contemporary cinema. As Yvonne Tasker aptly notes:

> Using postmodernism as a framework within which to position the contemporary popular cinema, rather than particular examples of it, has proved problematic. (...) Yet if the framework of postmodernism does have a value for an analysis of contemporary cinema, it must also be involved in thinking beyond individual films as "postmodern" or as symptoms of postmodernity.
>
> TASKER 1996: 225

The common strategy to search for postmodern symptoms in contemporary films is particularly illustrative in the case of *Blade Runner* (1982), which has been treated as the epitome of postmodern cinema for the following five reasons:

1. The setting, the *mise-en-scène*, and the mixture of architectural styles in the representation of urban space.
2. The references and the borrowings from the cinematic past, especially the *film noir* vocabulary.
3. The questioning of categories of identity and particularly the boundaries between humans and non-humans.
4. The exploration of the different time/space experiences.
5. The exploration of the relation between images and the construction of identity and personal history.

TASKER 1996: 225

This is a checklist that corroborates the film's postmodern nature by collating elements from a range of disciplines, from philosophy and architecture to literature and film theory. This exercise always runs the risk of being tautological, but I no longer believe that it is entirely futile.[10] It is true that the lengthy debates on cinematic postmodernism did not result in a unified and rigorous methodological framework by which one could "accurately measure" the qualities of postmodern films. But to expect that this is something that should or could happen is rather disingenuous. The interpretation of films from the 1970s onwards in relation to major economic, historical, and social developments may be imperiled by possible overstatements or faulty simplifications, but the tendency to consider films as cultural products that bear the marks of their times is no less important in our efforts to understand cinema and its complex relation to the world. In this sense, the extended literature on postmodern cinema and the wider periodization along the axis of modernity and postmodernity add another significant layer in the history of the medium.

0.1.3 Thomas Elsaesser: From Classical Hollywood to Unmotivated Heroes and Mind-game Films

Why does Thomas Elsaesser deserve his own sub-chapter in these debates? Because the breadth and depth of his work is such that, combined with his unique talent to identify breaks and ruptures almost at the time of their happening, render him an exceptional case of a film historian/theorist who pioneered all the discussions about Hollywood cinema: from the classical years to the New Hollywood of the 1970s, the post-classical blockbusters of the 1980s and 1990s, and the "mind-game" films of the 2000s. In his copious writings, Elsaesser struggled to fathom the dynamics between stability and change in the history of American cinema and to maintain a balance among various methodological tools that ranged from formal aesthetics to psychoanalysis and ideology.

Unlike Bordwell and Ray, Elsaesser did not produce large comprehensive volumes on Classical Hollywood and, yet, when one reads his lesser-known article "The American Cinema: Why Hollywood" published in *Monogram* in 1971, the feeling is clear: he was there first, pinning down all those aspects of Hollywood filmmaking (style, narration, industry, culture) that transformed it into a classical art and a classical system that could regulate repetitions and variations in terms of form, authorship, and generic construction. Notice, for instance, how he describes what Bordwell would eventually codify as "classical narration":

> To put it schematically, Hollywood rigorously respects and adheres to a first-level verisimilitude, in which any change of time, of place and action, as well as of a protagonist's goal or purpose is internally motivated, and communicated to the audience through a cinematic language primarily destined to follow, as closely as possible, the dramatic, causal and psychological exigencies of the action.
>
> ELSAESSER 1971: 7

I find it truly fascinating that several years later, when Bordwell described in painstaking detail the workings of Hollywood narration, he did not acknowledge the passage above but chose to quote the very next sentence following it, which contains a minor example about Raoul Walsh's filming style (Bordwell et al. 1985: 29). I am not writing this to defend Elsaesser as the "first" to discover the essence of classical cinema, especially knowing how he scorned the very idea of "firsts." The purpose is to illustrate how the history of classicism in the cinema has different genealogies[11] and different timelines that sometimes intersect, while often remain (deliberately or not) disconnected.

In Elsaesser's account, the representative period of classical Hollywood extends from the 1940s to the mid-1960s. Then, in the 1970s, a new generation of filmmakers begin to challenge the core principle of classical narration, namely character motivation. In the closing lines of "Why Hollywood," Elsaesser passes on the baton to his subsequent article "The Pathos of Failure. American Films in the 1970s: Notes on the Unmotivated Hero," which also came out in *Monogram* a few years later in 1975. There, the idea of "the unmotivated hero" and the "motif of the journey" seek to detect and explain a series of formal and ideological changes in films like *Easy Rider* (1967), *Bonnie and Clyde* (1969), *Five Easy Pieces* (1970), *Two-Lane Blacktop* (1971), and *The Conversation* (1974). The New Hollywood of Robert Altman, Sidney Pollack, Alan J. Pakula, Bob Rafelson, Monte Hellman, and Hal Ashby, according to Elsaesser, deploys nostalgia, pastiche, and loose causality in order to turn classical agency on its head; the protagonist is no longer a psychologically defined individual with a clear sense of motive. Instead, as he writes, "Today's heroes are waiting for the end, convinced that it is too late for action, as if too many contradictions had cancelled the impulse towards meaning and purpose" (Elsaesser 1975: 19).

Neither this phase nor Elsaesser's interest in the "pathos of failure" lasted very long; Hollywood in the 1980s moved on to spectacular blockbusters and Elsaesser, as a prompt cartographer, followed along with new concepts to meet the new conditions.[12] In his chapter "Classical/Post-classical," which appeared in a volume he co-authored with Warren Buckland, Elsaesser seeks to circumvent the aforementioned debates on postmodernism in the cinema by putting forth a theory of "post-classicism" and a method for a post-classical reading of Hollywood blockbusters. Using *Die Hard* (1988) as a case study, Elsaesser argues that a film can be both classical and post-classical depending on the analyst's theoretical and conceptual agenda. If one deploys Bordwell's neo-formalist poetics or a Proppian/Levi-Straussian structuralist methodology, then the film can be easily construed as classical thanks to its three-act structure, the goal-oriented hero, the continuity editing, the enigmas and the functions, the repetitions, and the resolutions (Elsaesser and Buckland 2002: 43–60). If, however, one wishes to detect what differentiates *Die Hard* from Hollywood films of the classical years, then their questions need to change. Specifically, a post-classical reading follows the following five steps:

1 It scrutinizes the apparent canonical story format for additional elements or layers that could facilitate the transfer of the film to other media platforms, such as video games.
2 It probes the heuristic distinction between surface and deep structure to see if the film takes it more literally, thus revealing a kind of "knowingness."

3   It examines the representation of the body, race, and gender, which is no longer constrained by censorship or cultural taboos.
4   It asks questions about the ties of the film and its storyworld to the transnational/post-colonial/globalized world.
5   It searches for "sliding signifiers," verbal and visual puns both at the textual and extra-textual level that denote the sophistication and professionalism of the industry. (66)

In this five-tier grid, Elsaesser strives to contain a comprehensive methodological toolkit that combines formal and narrative analysis with film interpretation, while taking as his object of study not only the film itself but its extratextual/industrial setting as well. In other words, Elsaesser's strategy, inaugurated in his 1971 article on the classical Hollywood and sustained through the 1975 report on New Hollywood, remains the same; the examination of form and content, of text and context, in order to explain the means by which Hollywood handles stability and change. Thus, the conclusion about post-classical Hollywood in the period 1980–90 could not be very different. Post-classical cinema, according to Elsaesser, has not made a radical break with the classical nor has it created something entirely new. Instead, it should be viewed as "classical plus." Hollywood blockbusters, like *Die Hard*, are distinguished by an excessive classicism, which exults at its mastery of the classical rules and invites a wide range of viewers in a reflexive play with "sliding signifiers" and multiple access points (78–9).

The Persistence of Hollywood (2012), Elsaesser's most recent volume comprising old and new pieces, will be my next stop in this brief overview for two reasons: firstly, it carries on with the discussion that he launched in "Why Hollywood" (reprinted for this collection), using the forty-year vantage point to evaluate the historical developments in Hollywood cinema; secondly, because its title to me signals a definitive concession. By echoing the famous chapter in Bordwell, Staiger and Thompson's magnum opus entitled "Since 1960: the persistence of a mode of film practice," the scales begin to tip towards continuity rather than change. Admittedly, this is not something that Elsaesser would easily concede. Notice, for instance, how he separates himself, once again, from Bordwell:

> On the other hand, if "classic/al" is a retronym from the start, then the very sign of the post-classical would be that it aspires to the "classical" as its dominant effect: each term would name the other, and be dependent on the other, which might explain why historians like David Bordwell see a continuation of the "classical Hollywood cinema" without a notable break, whereas others (myself included) have argued not only for the existence of a "post-classical" Hollywood, but for the epistemic necessity of placing oneself outside the classical, in order to understand

the classical. Both positions would be "correct" and "untenable" at the same time.

ELSAESSER 2012: 331–2

Due to Elsaesser's penchant for oxymora and self-contradicting statements, the necessity of a "post-classical Hollywood" sounds more like a rhetorical strategy rather than a historical reality. The reflexivity, the recursiveness (or the "feedback," as he calls it) in terms of narration, production, and promotion of Hollywood films, all become processes that ultimately keep the Hollywood enterprise firmly in place instead of disintegrating it. As he notes, "its robustness and persistence may actually be due to these unresolved tensions, which seem to energize the system overall rather than paralyze it" (328).

The same energizing function seems to be performed by a special category of films, the "mind-game" films. In two pieces, one published in 2009 and the other in 2018, Elsaesser identifies "a certain tendency" in contemporary cinema in the 1990s, though not exclusively in Hollywood, which bears specific narrative traits and raises important psychological and philosophical (ontological, epistemological) issues (Elsaesser 2009; 2018). The list of films extends from more traditional narratives like *The Silence of the Lambs* (1991) to more complex cases like *Lost Highway* (1997), *Fight Club* (1999), *Memento* (2000), *Donnie Darko* (2001), *Eternal Sunshine of the Spotless Mind* (2004), to the more recent Hollywood crop, such as *Inception* (2010), *Interstellar* (2014) and *Arrival* (2016). The common thread of all these films is the "game-playing" either at the diegetic level (characters playing games with each other) or the extra-diegetic one (the film playing games with the audience). Apart from the key narrative elements of the mind-game film, such as unreliable narrators, temporal loops, and multiple storylines, Elsaesser is most interested in how this new "tendency," "phenomenon," "prototype," or "thought experiment"—there is a range of terms, each with their own implications—aims at challenging a series of established ontological and epistemological givens in our relation to the cinema and the world around us. Particularly on the topic of character agency and motivation, he notices that the protagonists of the mind-game films are not characterized by "the pathos of failure," as their 1970s counterparts had been, but of "productive pathologies," i.e., personality disorders that nonetheless manage to work for them within the context of the storyworld (Elsaesser 2018: 13).

Elsaesser's contribution of the "mind-game" film was the last in a series of invaluable observations on Hollywood films and practices from the 1970s to his death in 2019. In his lengthy discussion of the mind-game examples, he exercised his unique ability to analyze the form and interpret the content of the films always in conjunction with larger industrial/institutional developments as well as the wider social, political, and even epistemic conditions of our current age. Do, however, mind-game films constitute a "break" in Hollywood filmmaking? Again, the answer is a "yes" and a "no," with the "no" eventually winning over the argument when looking at the bigger picture. In other words, films like *Memento* or *Shutter Island* may be considered as "the contemporary variants, extensions and transformations of classical cinema into post-classical and beyond" but seen through a wider lens, they can also be viewed as "the research-and-development arm of the ever evolving, self-differentiating conglomerate that is Hollywood picture making" (7–11).

0.1.4 Cinema and the Present: Complex Storytelling and (Impossible) Puzzle Films

Given that the workings of narration constitute the centerpiece of this book, I would like to conclude my brief history of the different periodizations and conceptualizations of Hollywood cinema with the approaches that examine new trends from a narratological perspective. It is impressive how the new millennium has brought a truly vibrant interest in film narratology, as more established and younger thinkers alike attempt to map the narrative options across a range of contemporary filmmaking traditions, with the issue of "narrative complexity" drawing the most attention (Branigan 2002; Staiger 2006; Lavik 2006; Berg 2006; Cameron 2008; Klecker 2013; Panek 2014; Buckland 2009, 2014a; Poulaki 2014; Campora 2014; Kiss and Willemsen 2017; Brütsch 2018; Schlickers and Toro 2018). Chronologically, the term "contemporary" is an expansive time frame that spans nearly three decades. Most scholars tend to bracket as "contemporary" the period from the 1990s to the present, often signaling Quentin Tarantino's *Pulp Fiction* (1994) as a turning point (Cameron 2008; Kiss and Willemsen 2017). Indeed, *Pulp Fiction* is a fascinating converging point that puts several theories to the test,[13] including Bordwell's "persistence of the classical" and my new mode labeled "post-classical" (Bordwell 2006; Thanouli 2009a). As I will be comparing and contrasting these two positions throughout the book, I would like here to discuss other voices and bring out the main points of discussion in regard to complex storytelling.

In this terrain, it is Warren Buckland's work that stands out with his two edited volumes, *Puzzle Films: Complex Storytelling in Contemporary Cinema* (2009) and *Hollywood Puzzle Films* (2014), offering a rich selection of writings that shed light not only on the narrative particularities of certain films, but likewise on the prospects for new terms and concepts in the way we approach film narrative. In his introduction to the first book, Buckland writes of a "new storytelling epoch" and characterizes contemporary "puzzle films" as a popular cycle that "rejects classical storytelling techniques and replaces them with complex storytelling" (Buckland 2009: 1). In this last sentence, Buckland makes clear from the start that a puzzle film is opposed to the classical narrative conventions and, as he explains later, it is "made up of non-classical characters who perform non-classical actions and events" (5). What are these non-classical elements, though? His list includes the following: nonlinearity, time loops, fragmented spatio-temporal reality, gaps in the plot, deception, labyrinthine structures, ambiguity, overt coincidences, schizophrenic/dead characters, and unreliable narrators. In other words, the complexity of puzzle films can either be traced in the narrative (plot) or the narration (the telling) or in both (6). Where do we find puzzle films? In American independent cinema, in European and international art films and even in some avant-garde filmmaking (6). What are the prototypes of this complex storytelling? The introduction closes with a list of thirty films that include the following: *21 Grams* (2003), *Abre los Ojos* (1997), *Being John Malkovich* (1999), *Chungking Express* (1994), *Dark City* (1998), *Donny Darko* (2001), *Fight Club*, *Inland Empire* (2006), *The Hours* (2002), *The Matrix* (1999), *Mulholland Dr.* (2001), *Oh!, Soojung!* (2000) and, of course, *Pulp Fiction*. The inclusion of films as diverse as *Inland Empire* and *The Hours* indicates that Buckland's initial mapping of the puzzle film is only tentative. He encompasses all possible variations as a first step towards exploring the rich diversity of the puzzle films.

Five years later, Buckland came back with another anthology, this time on the Hollywood puzzle film. He examines the "few" Hollywood filmmakers who have "actively appropriated" the conventions of the puzzle film in order to "inject novelty but also unpredictability and uncertainty into the stringent economic conditions of Hollywood filmmaking" (Buckland 2014a: 2). This reasoning is evidently in line with Elsaesser's aforementioned idea of the mind-game film as Hollywood's "research-and-development arm," even though Buckland maintains his focus on narrative and narration. Thus, he avoids the pitfalls of an overarching argument that collates film form and mode of production, a common predicament that I will explore in detail below. The new terms that this volume introduces, though not strictly of a narratological nature, are ontological pluralism, ambiguity, and cognitive dissonance. Put plainly, according to Buckland, puzzle films present a plurality of worlds that are not clearly distinguished, leaving the viewers cognitively challenged. Although the description of the puzzle film remains highly inclusive, the collection seems to be divided on the perennial question: is the Hollywood puzzle film a rupture from the classical narration or it is a diluted form, which domesticates, on behalf of the industry, a number of experimental techniques? Buckland's personal predilection for a break from the Bordwellian classical reading of complex films, as illustrated in his analysis of *Source Code* (2011) as a narrative with a video-game logic (Buckland 2014b), is not shared by all the contributors, leaving the discussion open for further reflection.

The broadness of the term "puzzle film," as defined in Buckland's work, is amended in two other notable monographs, Allan Cameron's *Modular Narratives in Contemporary Cinema* (2008) and Kiss and Willemsen's *Impossible Puzzle Films* (2017). Cameron argues that popular cinema since the early 1990s has displayed a preference for stories that express a "modular conception of time." Specifically, he writes, "'Modular narrative' and 'database narrative' are terms applicable to narratives that foreground the relationship between the temporality of the story and the order of its telling" (Cameron 2008: 1). The focus on temporality allows him to map and categorize complex narratives according to the axis of time and narrow down the issue of complexity to four distinct types: 1) anachronic narratives that involve the use of flashbacks and/or flashforwards (*Pulp Fiction*, *Memento*, *Irreversible* [2002], *21 Grams*); 2) forking paths that invoke divergent or parallel narrative possibilities (*Groundhog Day* [1993], *Run Lola Run* [1998]); 3) episodic plots organized as an abstract series or as a narrative anthology (*A Zed and Two Noughts* [1985], *32 Short Films About Glenn Gould* [1993], *Magnolia* [1999]); and, 4) split screen narratives that divide the narrative flow into parallel, spatially juxtaposed elements (*Time Code* [2000], *Pretend* [2003]). All of these categories contain films that can no longer be deemed as classical. In a head-on disagreement with Bordwell's "business as usual" argument, Cameron contends that these cases distance themselves significantly further from the classical norms, more so than other "deviations," such as the film noirs of the 1940s or the art cinema-influenced films of the 1960s (5). But this is not the only point of contention between Cameron and Bordwell's accounts. In a move that Bordwell would, in all likelihood, find objectionable, Cameron suggests that "modular narratives are a particular instance of narrative in the postmodern era," while they also "display strong connections with the formal and thematic concerns of the modernists" (16). In other words, building a detailed taxonomy of modular narratives is not the only purpose of his work; instead, Cameron, like many others before him, wishes to connect the formal manifestations of temporal complexity with broader technological and cultural developments, employing the umbrella terms "postmodernism" and "modernism" as guiding frameworks.

On the other hand, Kiss and Willemsen seek to narrow down the notion of complexity by concentrating on what they call the "impossible puzzle film" and by steering the discussion not outwards, i.e., in the direction of societal forces, but rather inwards, to the mechanisms of the mind that are called upon to tackle complex stories and puzzle films. According to Kiss and Willemsen, narrative complexification has proven to be a significant and enduring tendency in contemporary mainstream film and television that need not, however, be linked to the discussion of classicism or post-classicism (Kiss and Willemsen 2017: 22). Within this tendency, one can find varying degrees of complexity that sometimes bring the films closer to the classical conventions and other times further away, as is the case with the impossible puzzle films that constitute their focal point. This category contains all those complex narratives that deny coherent story construction and "create not only lengthy, but even permanent confusion through seemingly irresolvable puzzles" (59). Therefore, the list becomes shorter; *Chasing Sleep* (2006), *La moustache* (2005), *Lost Highway*, *Mulholland Drive*, *Inland Empire*, *Donnie Darko*, *Miraq* (2006), *Primer* (2004), *Source Code*, *Enter Nowhere* (2011), *Enemy* (2013), *Reality* (2014), *Triangle* (2009), *Timecrimes* (2007), *Loop* (2016), *Dark Country* (2009), *Predestination* (2014), and *Coherence* (2014) are the prototypical impossible puzzle films. Kiss and Willemsen's goal is to study these cases from a "cognitive poetics" approach, aiming to identify the narrative impossibilities and incongruities that they entail and to understand how their continuous "hermeneutic bait" keeps the viewers struggling in vain to establish a single unambiguous reading (63).

Despite their disputable effort to avoid taking sides on the question of whether these films are classical or post-classical by always placing the prefix "post" in brackets, what I find intriguing is how the question of art cinema as a relevant mode of narration also comes into play. In a chapter entitled "Impossible Puzzle Films: Between Art Cinema and (Post-)Classical Narration," Kiss and Willemsen explore the formal similarities and the common strategies of narrative complexity that impossible puzzle films share with the European art films of the 1950s and 1960s, concluding that there is a considerable overlap (152). On the other hand, the authors feel compelled to underline how the films in hand are also in close contact with the classical storytelling conventions. Thus, a Solomonian solution is reached when they conclude that "it is through a combination of formal and stylistic tactics, derived from both the art-cinema and classical narrative tradition, that impossible puzzle films achieve their distinct viewing effects" (181).

This idea of "betweenness" is not new, however. From the New Hollywood of the late 1960s and 1970s to the American independent cinema of the 1990s, scholars have regarded European art films/filmmakers as a source of "influence" or as a reservoir of film techniques from which American filmmakers could "borrow" or "pay tribute to," if they wished to break away from the classical norms (Kramer 1998: 295–300; Tzioumakis 2006: 26–78). The long-standing opposition "Hollywood versus Europe," as an antagonism between two distinct modes of narration, film practices and audience expectations, has offered for many years a solid framework for interpreting narrative developments, using the two poles as a point of reference. And, of course, when a film cannot clearly fit within either side, we can easily argue that it is situated in the space between. Despite the fact that globalization and the rise of world cinema has somewhat challenged this binary,[14] the symbolic power of classical vs. art cinema still holds sway, as is evident in the discussions about narrative complexity. When a film like *The Sixth Sense* came out in 1999, flaunting a major plot twist, "art cinema" readily came to mind, as we see in Erlend Lavik's reading of the film (Lavik 2006). Lavik explains that his intention is not to characterize *The Sixth Sense* as an art film, and rightly so. Yet, why should any trace of self-consciousness in a narrative mobilize a comparison with art cinema, if we are to conclude that this mode does not apply in this case after all? Similarly, in his analysis of *Eternal Sunshine of the Spotless Mind* Matthew Campora discusses how the film combines elements of the art cinema tradition with more classical conventions to generate a hybrid narrative. As he notes,

> The narrative complexity and aesthetic innovations of these complex hybrid films offer challenges not simply to audiences but to critics and scholars as well as they problematize existing generic and narrative categories and push the boundaries of the conceptual frameworks and vocabularies employed to analyze screen texts.
>
> CAMPORA 2009: 130

Indeed, this is a very insightful observation because, as I also believe, one of the key benefits of studying complex narratives is the realization that some of the long-standing narrative categories may no longer suffice to describe the current narrative forms. But the concept of "hybridity" cannot but be a provisional solution. Neither can we hold on to the argument about the "combination" or "betweenness" forever. Notice, for instance, the conceptual dead-end in another recent scholarly attempt, namely Cornelia Klecker's article "Mind-Tricking Narratives: Between Classical and Art-Cinema Narration." On the one hand, Klecker seeks to embrace novelty by replacing the terms "complex storytelling" or "puzzle film" with "mind-tricking narratives" as if they were something new. These narratives, on the other hand, cannot really be particularly novel if they remain trapped within the same old "between classical and art cinema" boundaries (Klecker 2013).

The idea of betweenness is not erroneous in itself. There are film examples that cannot fit within certain heuristic categories and, therefore, our only option is to leave them hanging in the joining room. What is a mistake, however, is the deliberate decision to categorize entire trends in filmmaking as "something in-between." And this mistake, admittedly, stems from an almost metaphysical belief that the only two narrational modes that can ever exist are the classical and the art cinema. The fact that the entire community of film narratologists still clings to this binary is both Bordwell's triumph as well as his failure. Or to put it differently, historical poetics became the victim of classical Hollywood's success; for it blocked any further theorization of the formal and narrative norms and it transformed what was initially conceived as a historical category (classical cinema) into a nearly ontological one.

The only way to amend this situation is to go back to the beginning, i.e., to the initial questions that historical poetics was supposed to ask and to discuss the possible directions that these questions may take. By re-opening historical poetics, I will be able to position my work on post-classical narration in a framework that should welcome change and innovation without compromising theoretical and methodological rigor. Besides, there is not a single unique way to categorize films nor is there only one possible historical mapping of the cinematic past. As Charts 0.1 and 0.2 illustrate, in the history of our discipline different thinkers have suggested different periodizations and taxonomies, each capturing a different facet of cinema, depending on whether we focus on narrative or mode of production, or both. It is also evident in these tables that the same film can be categorized in different ways, depending on the research questions and the tools that are deployed in each analysis. This pluralism should be welcome in our field and the discrepancies between different theorists should not lead to fanatical oppositions and fierce controversies,[15]

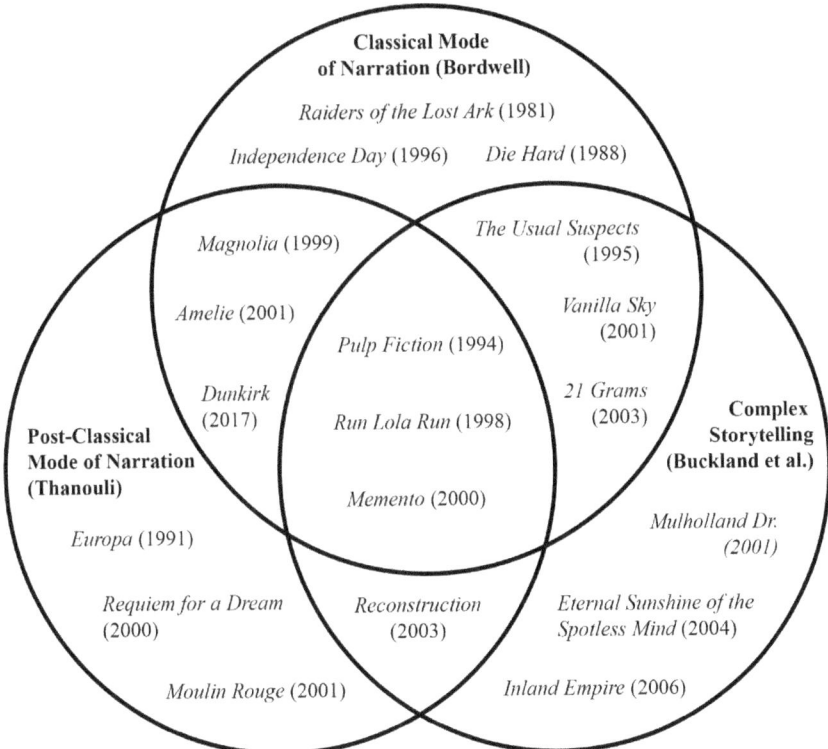

CHART 0.1

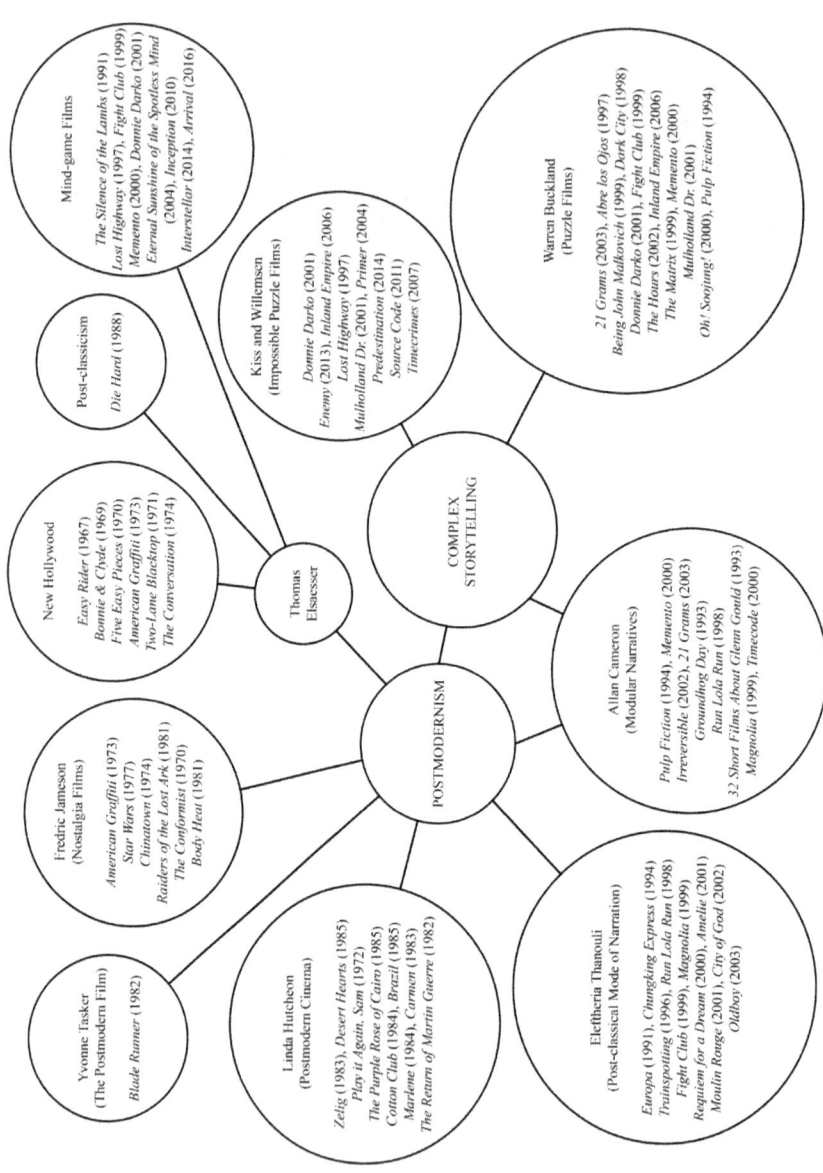

CHART 0.2

especially as we are summoned to face relentless changes in our ever-evolving media landscape.

0.2 Opening Historical Poetics

0.2.1 The Research Project: Neither a Theory Nor a Method

To meet the challenges that contemporary films present, we need to have a solid grasp not only of film history and film practice, but also of the history of the discipline that seeks to theorize the cinematic medium. In film studies, historical poetics and Bordwell's narrative theory stand out as a powerful model of research into cinema, which, in the latter's words, "offers the best current hope for setting high intellectual standards for film study" (Bordwell 1989b: 392). Leaning back on historical poetics for inspiration in the year 2023 should not be deemed as regressive or conservative. The need to talk about new films and filmmakers does not necessarily require entirely new tools and concepts. As I will explain, the umbrella of historical poetics always already contains the possibility of expanding its own research questions and updating its findings.

In the 1980s Bordwell introduced historical poetics into the study of cinema to invigorate the nascent academic field with a research platform that could counterweigh what seemed to be the dominant trend at the time, namely the interpretation of films through the use of Grand theories nurtured in other areas, such as psychology, literature, and cultural studies. In fact, in his seminal piece "Historical Poetics of Cinema," he fiercely criticizes what he acronymically calls "SLAB theories" (Saussurean semiotics, Lacanian psychoanalysis, Althusserian Marxism and Barthesian textual analysis) and he rejects their oversimplistic readings of films based on ready-made propositions (Bordwell 1989b). Instead of applying a general social or cultural theory to a film and looking for the manifestations of certain concepts like "Oedipal trajectory" or "mirror stage" on the screen, Bordwell prefers to ask specific low-scale questions about the construction of films that will potentially lead to broader theoretical or historical observations. His dismissal of the "interpretative school" was further elaborated in the book that came out the same year, *Making Meaning: Inference and Rhetoric in the Interpretation of Cinema* (1989), where he meticulously explains his reservations regarding the reading of films in search for a higher and/or deeper meaning. The remedy for this scholarly malaise is the growth of historical poetics described as follows,

> Poetics is thus not another critical "approach," like myth criticism or deconstruction. Nor is it a "theory" like psychoanalysis or Marxism. In

its broadest compass, it is a conceptual framework within which particular questions about films' composition and effects can be posed.

BORDWELL 1989a: 273

With Aristotle's *Poetics* in one hand and the Russian formalists' *Poetics of Cinema* (1927)[16] in the other, Bordwell developed a wide theoretical framework, which is neither limited to one method nor constitutes a cohesive "theory," i.e., a series of propositions that explain a totality of cinematic phenomena. Instead, historical poetics becomes a platform for asking questions. Which questions, though? The following:

(1) What are the principles according to which films are constructed and by means of which they achieve particular effects?

(2) How and why have these principles arisen and changed in particular empirical circumstances?

BORDWELL 1989b: 371

These two primary questions put under the microscope several issues, ranging from the institutional background of a film to the analysis of its stylistic features and its public reception. As I will argue below, the ordering of this research agenda should be reconfigured to avoid several theoretical missteps. For now, however, I would like to present Bordwell's application of historical poetics, as he developed it across numerous publications from the 1980s to the present. What remains a constant feature of historical poetics throughout this work, whether it focuses on narration, style, or production values, is that it constitutes a data-driven approach, aiming to study facts and concrete elements and to formulate arguments and inferences that are corrigible and falsifiable. It poses concise questions of a varied level of generality (small-, middle-, or large-scale), forms open hypotheses that are not committed to a priori conclusions, and originates answers and concepts that can be constantly re-defined through an encounter with the films and their surrounding evidence (381).

But what is the object of study and how far does it extend? Bordwell reformulated his answer to this question in his most recent publication on the topic, *The Poetics of Cinema* (2008). Here, he suggests a clever way of remembering the main concerns of historical poetics by calling them the 6 Ps: *particulars, patterns, purposes, principles, practices, and processing* (Bordwell 2008: 24). The particulars refer to any detail in the form of a film, ranging from a simple cut to a camera angle or a prop in the setting. All these details add up to certain patterns of narrative and visual style. For instance, a line in the dialogue (particular) is part of a character's behavior (pattern) or the lighting of one scene (particular) may be part of the film's general lighting scheme (pattern). Given that a film consists of thousands of details that build numerous patterns, we need to narrow down our attention to those patterns that seem to fulfill certain purposes.[17] A pattern in the character's behavior may serve the development of the plot, while a lighting pattern may obey the film's generic affiliations. These purposes may appear unique in each film, yet experience tells us they are not. Therefore, as we move from the particulars to the patterns and then on to the purposes, we reach the level of principles, which is a crucial level of generality for those who wish to work under the aegis of historical poetics. The repetition of particulars, patterns, and purposes across a variety of films gradually allows the scholar to observe overarching principles that we could also label as "norms" (26). Norms can exist at various scales (small/large) and can operate at various geographical lengths (local, transnational). Bordwell aptly describes the task of the poetician as follows:

> (...) studying norms is an exercise in extrapolation. By trying to chart the range of constructional options open to filmmakers at various historical moments, we come up with results that are always open to revision. In practical research terms, attention to historically changing devices, patterns, principles, functions, and norms moves us beyond the single film to groups of films.
>
> BORDWELL 2008: 27

"Extrapolation" and "revision" are two key aspects of historical poetics that justify my abiding faith in this research tradition. But let's stay with the P-words, for now. Thus far, the first four (particulars, patterns, purposes, and principles) pertain to the first question of historical poetics, namely the study of the form itself. Yet this research project aims higher than this by asking questions about two more Ps—practices and processing. The former refers to the technological and institutional parameters that affect the shape of the film form; the latter takes us to the realm of the spectators and the ways they cognitively engage with film narrative (44). Practices and processing are entwined in both primary questions, as the investigation of the practices seeks to explain "why" film form develops and changes in the way it does, while the processing concerns the "particular effects" that films achieve through their form.

The issue of effects, i.e., the cognitive side of Bordwell's poetics, is explicitly outside the scope of this book. Yet the questions of practices and causations (why things are as they are and why they change in the course of time) are not as easily circumvented. Bordwell claims that historical poetics is not a priori committed to any particular model of causation and change (16). This means that a poetician may explain formal changes with a broad teleological argument, as is the case with Bazin, or using an intentionalist model that centers on the filmmakers' personal initiative, as is the case with various auteurist approaches. Of course, Bordwell has repeatedly opted for a functionalist model of explanation, "whereby the institutional dynamics of filmmaking set up constraints and preferred options that fulfil overall systemic norms" (16).

The preference for functional explanations in Bordwell's poetic analyses, especially when it comes to Hollywood cinema, is not as flexible as he presents it in his introduction to historical poetics whether in the earlier article or the more recent overview (Bordwell 1989b; 2008). Broadly speaking, historical poetics was inaugurated as a framework for asking questions. But, in practice, Bordwell's towering figure overshadowed the openness and the corrigibility of the answers. In his unequivocally unique academic career, he painstakingly asked and answered questions about thousands of films and it was precisely this formidable body of work[18] that—sometimes inadvertently and other times more consciously—narrowed down the options for anyone else who wished to conduct poetic analysis and do research within historical poetics.[19] For that reason, I would like to suggest that the general conceptual platform of historical poetics, as proposed by Bordwell and presented here in a nutshell, should be gradually separated from the way he served it in his own projects and from his own answers to the two primary questions. These questions can continue to operate as templates for invaluable research into cinema, but the way Bordwell has explored them so far should not block the way for other scholars, like myself, who disagree with *some* of his findings. Separating Bordwell from historical poetics may not be an easy venture, but it is essential, if historical poetics is to remain relevant within film studies.

0.2.2 Bordwell's Application of Historical Poetics

0.2.2.1 Narrative Theory and Concepts

Working at the broadest level of generality, Bordwell's initial concern was to formulate the first comprehensive definition of film narration that would do justice to cinema's inherent characteristics instead of squeezing film features into molds that were crafted for other arts, whether literature or theatre.[20] As a result, the narration in the fiction film was defined as "the process whereby the film's syuzhet and style interact in the course of cueing and channeling the spectator's construction of the fabula" (Bordwell 1985: 53). Evidently, narration is viewed as a formal activity that comprises three building blocks: the *fabula* (story), the *syuzhet* (plot), and the *style*. The fabula/syuzhet distinction, descending from the Russian Formalists, aims to specify the dual nature of what an average viewer vaguely calls "the story of a film." This story is, in fact, two fairly separated entities; the fabula is the *mental* re-construction of a series of events portrayed in the film, while the suyzhet is the *actual* arrangement and presentation of those events on the screen (49–50). The third element, the style, also refers to the on-screen manifestation of these events but it is limited to the technical choices that are employed to represent them.

The film narration can be analyzed at three levels of generality: 1) the micro-level of the *devices* (technical elements like *mise-en-scène*, framing, lighting editing); 2) the middle-level of the *systems* (the system of narrative logic, cinematic time, and cinematic space); and 3) the macro-level of the *relations of systems* (how the three systems intertwine) (Bordwell et al. 1985: 5–6). For each system, Bordwell has crafted a meticulous taxonomy, which is impressively thorough and remains unparalleled to this date. For instance, the system of narrative logic is further distinguished into four types of motivation (compositional, realistic, generic/intertextual, and artistic), while the system of narrative time is broken down to the categories of order, duration, and frequency. All these analytical terms will be presented in detail in their respective chapters, and they will be deployed throughout the textual analyses in this *Guide to Post-classical Narration*. They are essential formalist concepts that form the basis for any study on film poetics.

Similarly, the concept of the "mode of narration" is another major contribution of Bordwell's work. This is the cornerstone of the book *Narration in the Fiction Film* (1985), whose aim is nothing short of impossible: to map all the key narrative options that have historically appeared in all the filmic traditions across the globe. The introduction of the "mode" as a conceptual category allows Bordwell to handle this impossibility and enables him to classify thousands of films within a limited number of narrative paradigms. He defines the mode as "a historically distinct set of norms of narrational construction and comprehension," arguing that it transcends genres, schools, movements, or national cinemas because it is "more fundamental, less transient, and more pervasive" (Bordwell 1985: 150). The flexible construct of the mode contains all the four Ps (particulars, patterns, purposes, and principles) but it rises to a higher level, acquiring a greater degree of stability. As we move from the particulars to the modes, the number of available options is narrowed down; there can be endless configurations of the particulars but (possibly) not endless modes. The possibility for multiple modes is key. Back in 1985, Bordwell was inclined to acknowledge not only the prospect of various modes but also the usefulness of "the notion of plurality" because it "allows us to grasp things differently" (Bordwell 1985: 150). To me, this is the most important tenet of historical poetics: the constructional principles of the films may be theorized and categorized in different ways, without one necessarily discrediting the other.

0.2.2.2. *The Mode of Classical Narration*

I have already mentioned *The Classical Hollywood Cinema* with respect to the idea of classicism and the compound argument that unites the Hollywood film style and the mode of production as the two sides of a coin. There is another reason why this publication is fundamental for historical poetics. Bordwell's account of classical narration is an exemplary study of poetics, setting the ground rules for any further research. One of its key statements is this: "Hollywood films constitute a fairly coherent aesthetic tradition which sustains individual creation" (Bordwell et al. 1985: 4). As the analysis of an extensive sample indicated, Hollywood films seem to adhere to consistent stylistic and narrational conventions that are not reducible to the personal initiative of individual filmmakers. These conventions form an overarching "aesthetic norm," which is not viewed as a stringent rule that limits creative freedom but rather as "a regulating energetic principle" that allows the artwork to come into being (Mukařovský 1978: 49).[21]

The minute dissection of the narration in Hollywood movies led Bordwell to a seemingly paradoxical observation; on the one hand, a film is governed by multiple norms in terms of how it handles its devices and systems, while, on the other, it is impossible for the same film to contain *all* the norms that develop within Hollywood filmmaking. In Bordwell's words, "no Hollywood film *is* the classical system; each is an 'unstable equilibrium' of classical norms" (Bordwell et al. 1985: 4). The idea of an unstable equilibrium led him to the concept of the "paradigm" as a "set of elements which can, according to rules, substitute for one another" (4). The paradigm as a concept can complement that of the mode to tackle the element of the creative range. Classical narration as a mode consisting of several alternative norms presents filmmakers with a range of choices, while it also binds them with limitations. Bordwell illustrates the open play between creative freedom and constraint with the following example:

> If you are a classical filmmaker, you cannot light a scene in such a way as to obscure the locale entirely (cf. Godard in *Le gai savoir*); you cannot pan or track without some narrative or generic motivation; you cannot make every shot one second long (cf. avant-garde works). Both the alternatives and the limitations of the style remain clear if we think of the paradigm as creating *functional equivalents*: a cut-in may replace a track-in, or colour may replace lighting as a way to demarcate volumes, because each device fulfils the same role.
>
> BORDWELL et al. 1985: 4–5 (emphasis in original)

The classical narration consists of a very detailed inventory of stylistic and narrative principles, such as character-centred causality and continuity editing, that developed in tandem with Hollywood studio practices that crystallized around 1917. However, Hollywood's success with spectators across the world soon transformed the American norms into global ones. As Bordwell puts it, "The accessibility of Hollywood cinema to audiences of different cultures made it a transnational standard" (620). This argument, admittedly, puts some strain on the functionalist model of explanation, while it also oversimplifies the issue of influence and cultural hegemony. Above all, the idea that almost all "ordinary" films—be they from the United States or France or Japan—are *basically classical* puts the first nail in the coffin of historical poetics. By generalizing beyond the geographical limits of the classical mode, Bordwell muddled up the causal forces that explain how forms evolve and compromised the strength of his otherwise formidable account of Hollywood filmmaking.

0.2.2.3 Other Historical Modes of Narration

In *Narration in the Fiction Film* Bordwell presented four historical modes, accentuating further the descriptive power of the concept of the narrational mode. Alongside the classical, he identified the *art cinema*, the *historical-materialist*, and the *parametric* mode as historically distinct sets of paradigmatic options for the construction of narration. For the first three modes, there is a specific chronological and geographical range: the classical, as we have seen, is primarily found in Hollywood between 1917–60; art cinema is situated in Europe from the late 1950s up to the early 1970s; while the historical-materialist is located in the Soviet Union during the years 1925–33. The only mode that lacks historical specificity is the parametric, as it applies only to "isolated filmmakers" such as Bresson and Ozu and their "fugitive films" (Bordwell 1985: 274). The characteristic trait of the parametric mode is that it allows the films to develop a stylistic system that works separately from the plot. This is a rare case in fiction cinema that can occur whenever and wherever a filmmaker wishes to explore the possibilities of the cinematic form, while staying nonetheless within the narrative tradition.[22]

Of the three "alternative" modes, as he called them,[23] Bordwell returned to art cinema only in his recent *Poetics of Cinema*, and even then with a brief afterword to his 1979 piece.[24] Aside from the classical, art cinema is indeed the most important historical mode of narration, and the one that has helped other theorists elaborate on the opposition between Hollywood and European filmmaking. However, Bordwell's latest update on art cinema is fraught with the same methodological problems that have plagued his "persistence of Hollywood" argument that will be discussed below. In fact, the problem is even greater in this case, as the mode of art cinema was tremendously spacious to begin with. Under the rubrics of "objective realism," "subjective realism," and "authorial commentary," Bordwell had classified a very extensive range of constructional norms, which largely included anything that was not classical. From neorealism to Fellini, from Dreyer to Bergman, and from Godard to Resnais, Bordwell handpicked the films that made these auteurs famous across film festivals and then sought to categorize their extremely varied narrational choices into a singular mode. Despite claims to the opposite, art cinema was delineated as a concrete mode in a top-down fashion; the films of the great European filmmakers *had* to be included in one category that *had* to contain all the "deviations" from the classical norms.

The same line of argument persists in the recent take on art cinema with respect to the films made from the 1980s onwards. Bordwell begins by listing the institutional factors that are currently at force outside Hollywood (state funding, film schools, and festivals) and then surveys various "New Waves" around the world, singling out the most celebrated auteurs: Wong Kar-wai (Hong Kong), Chen Kaige (China), Park Chan-wook (South Korea), Abbas Kiarostami and Mohsen Makhmalbaf (Iran), Aleksandr Sokurov (Russia), Béla Tarr (Hungary), and Lars von Trier (Denmark). Their films are *made* to fit within the same category, i.e., the art cinema mode, despite the blatant discrepancies in their narrational features. The only revision that he deems as necessary concerns a stylistic device, a type of image called "planimetric" (Bordwell 2008: 163). At the level of the mode, however, everything has to remain the same. With the historical-materialist mode dead and the parametric in the margins, the art mode becomes the only receptacle for the non-classical film in the whole world film production. If that is the case, where is the bottom-up approach where precision and attention to details is treasured? By preserving the mode of art cinema as it was almost fifty years ago, Bordwell adds another nail in the coffin of historical poetics, whereby both "the historical" and the "poetic" become empty vessels.

0.2.2.4 Contemporary Cinema

The church is so broad that heresy is impossible.

COWIE 1998: 178[25]

Although the sample in *The Classical Hollywood Cinema* included films from the period 1915–60, Bordwell was already eager to argue about the classicism of New Hollywood as well. With the title "Since 1960: the persistence of a mode of film practice," he opened an oft-quoted chapter, arguing that the American cinema from the 1960s onwards maintained the same principles of classical narrational construction. Despite the obvious influences from European art cinema, the younger generation of American filmmakers (Robert Altman, Woody Allen, Martin Scorsese, George Lucas, Arthur Penn, Francis Ford Coppola, Brian De Palma) did not create films that could be classified within any other mode than the classical. On the contrary, in these cases Hollywood demonstrated once again its unique ability to "incorporate" and "refunctionalize" stylistic devices from other cinematic traditions through the "process of stylistic assimilation" (Bordwell 1985: 373). Therefore, films like *The Conversation*, *Taxi Driver* (1976), or *Interiors* (1978) may appear as novelties in comparison to the classical Hollywood counterparts, but a careful narrative analysis proves that their narrational idiosyncrasies, in fact, enrich the classical mode rather than subvert it.

Bordwell's argument on "stylistic assimilation" put forward as early as 1985 was a harbinger of his resistance to new terms and concepts that continues to this day. "Postmodernism" is the label that he has questioned the most, going against the current of film criticism throughout the 1990s. His objections focused mainly on two sides of the postmodern debates in the cinema. On the one hand, he questioned the argument regarding postmodernity as a new mode of perception that is reflected in contemporary cinema. His historical poetics lens would reject both the reflectionist bent and the top-down approach of the theories in question. On the other, he dismissed the postmodern repertory of terms, such as "fragmentation," "nostalgia," and "pastiche" as formal qualities that have been poorly theorized (Bordwell 1997: 146). Either way, postmodernism was considered as a "doctrine-driven conception of research" that rendered film studies a dogmatic discipline (Bordwell 2008: 801).

When faced with film narratives that did not quite fit his own modes of narration, Bordwell adopted a range of tactics. For instance, in his analysis of the Belgian film called *Toto le héros* (1991) by Jaco Van Dormael, he wondered how he could categorize the narration at hand: "Postmodernism? I would rather suggest *light modernism*, somewhere between Hollywood and Europe" (Bordwell 1994: 39 (emphasis in the original)). On another occasion, in the study of contemporary Hong Kong cinema, he opted for the term "avant-pop" to describe the mixture of Hollywood and art cinema devices that explained how the films combine mass popularity with artistic potential (Bordwell 2000a: 267). Finally, "bricolage aesthetics" is another idea that he tested in the analysis of Tom Tykwer's *Run Lola Run* as a typical example of filmmaking in the 1990s characterized by stylistic eclecticism (Bordwell 2000b).[26]

Regarding contemporary Hollywood, however, Bordwell returned with a full-blown account on the persistence of classicism in *The Way Hollywood Tells It: Story and Style in Modern Movies* (2006). After examining a wide selection of films from the period 1960-2004, his conclusion is adamant:

> Despite all the historical changes and local variants we find in contemporary film style, we are still dealing with a version of classical filmmaking. An analysis of virtually any film from the period under

> consideration will confirm the simple truth with which I started: nearly all scenes in nearly all contemporary mass-market movies (and in most "independent" films) are staged, shot, and cut according to principles that crystallised in the 1910s and 1920s.
>
> BORDWELL 2006: 180

There are some important points to be raised in regard to this particular historical poetics project. First, his sample can be largely divided into two groups: 1) the standard cases of classical narration, such as *Jerry Maguire* (1996), *Die Hard,* or *Two Weeks' Notice* (2002); and 2) examples of what he calls "offbeat storytelling" (73). The latter includes *Pulp Fiction, JFK* (1991), *Memento,* and *Eternal Sunshine of the Spotless Mind,* to name some prominent cases. These films belong to a phase of narrative experimentation, which "surged back" in the 1990s (other such phases being in the 1940s and 1960s), infusing the classical mold with a few fresh stylistic devices, such as networked plots and intensified continuity.[27] The concept of the "network narrative" allows Bordwell to acknowledge the novelty in a significant segment of contemporary American cinema, while still keeping everything within the classical mode.[28] How is that possible? Through the idea of "redundancy." Notice how this process of analysis and classification goes:

> Question: Can we trace in *Memento* a minimum number of recurring devices that hold the story together?
> Answer: Yes.
> Conclusion: Then, it is still classical.

This may sound schematic, but I am afraid it is not. In fact, it is the same line of reasoning that applies to the art cinema mode with the only difference being that in the place of "redundancy" we have the notion of "ambiguity." For all the wealth of historical knowledge, theoretical wisdom, and observational acuity that Bordwell indisputably possesses, the rather inexplicable need to cling to these two foundational modes of narration by all means puts the final nail in the coffin of historical poetics.

0.3 *A Guide to Post-classical Narration*

> We are too well trained by history itself to think that it can be avoided. When we feel that we have a theory that explains everything, a ready-made theory explaining all past and future events and therefore needing neither evolution nor anything like it then we must recognise that the formal method has come to an end, that the spirit of scientific investigation has departed from it.
>
> EICHENBAUM 1965: 139[29]

A great deal of theorising about norms remains to be done. (. . .) These are not definitive analyses; they are attempts to chart the range of constructional options open to filmmakers at various historical conjunctures, and the results are always open to revision.

BORDWELL 1989b: 381

These two positions inspired my interest in historical poetics and guided my research on post-classical narration, which crystallizes in this book. On the one hand, Eichenbaum warned of the danger of using a "ready-made" theory to explain "all past and future events." To a significant extent, the two historical modes of narration, the classical and the art cinema, became the two Tablets of Stone, containing all the poetic wisdom. Despite claims to the opposite, Bordwell did turn the norms he identified therein into "definitive analyses." Yet what we need to safeguard from his invaluable contribution is something else: it is his urge to "theorize norms" and to "chart the range of constructional options" in a way that remains "open to revision." And this is precisely the goal of this *Guide to Post-classical Narration*: to carry on the mission of historical poetics by charting the narrational norms of a new paradigm that surfaced in the 1990s and continues to gain ground in contemporary filmmaking.

In my previous study, the post-classical mode was meticulously constructed using a sample of fourteen films from different corners of the world from the years 1991–2003 (Thanouli 2009a). In this updated volume, the case studies expand to dozens of new films that appeared from 2004–22, while their geographical baseline seems to concentrate squarely on the United States and Europe. In the first phase, post-classical works were mostly independent productions with medium-sized budgets, produced in the periphery of mainstream film practices. In the current phase, the lines have increasingly blurred. Several post-classical norms entered the vocabulary of widely popular filmmakers within Hollywood, bringing post-classical storytelling closer to a larger audience. Admittedly, the classical mode still holds the reins in most Hollywood productions, while some of the most iconic American filmmakers, like Steven Spielberg or James Cameron, remain religiously classical. However, the creative options of a post-classical narration exhibit a remarkable dynamic, spreading across different genres and infiltrating the storytelling techniques of more mainstream directors.

Apart from showcasing the latest post-classical films and describing their key narrational features in a concise and systematic manner, this *Guide* also aims at placing its emphasis on the methodology of poetic research. The numerous case studies are instances of formalist analysis in action, highlighting a wide range of concepts at different levels of generality. Thus, students and scholars interested in historical poetics can acquire a certain degree of familiarity and knowingness when it comes to examining the narrational process in a film. In fact, the shifting institutional basis of post-classical works requires a subtle, but crucial, reformulation of the two key questions of historical poetics mentioned before. Specifically, I would like to recast their points of inquiry as follows:

1. What are the principles according to which films are constructed and how do these principles change in particular empirical circumstances?
2. How and why have these principles arisen?
3. How do these principles achieve particular effects?

In this version, the two fundamental queries are broken down into three separate areas: 1) the investigation of form; 2) the investigation of historical causation; and 3) the investigation of the "effects." The first domain is strictly formalist, exploring the constructional elements in any given film as well as the formal changes in larger groups of films that occur over time. The second is historical, delving into the technological, institutional, economic, and social parameters of film practice that are related to the development of the formal principles. Finally, the third domain investigates the effects of these principles in terms of cognition and reception. One could argue that this division of labor was possible before without my suggested reformulation. Besides, Bordwell, Staiger, and Thompson's aforementioned *The Classical Hollywood Cinema* largely aimed at this division. In truth, however, the two questions kept all three elements—i.e., forms, historical causes, and effects—closely interlocked. As I have repeatedly shown, Bordwell's assumptions about a film's institutional origin would delimit the options for his narrational analysis, confining the poetics elements to a preordained evaluation and classification. The proposed separation of the areas of research is not meant to signify that they are not connected, but rather that their connections are not as straightforward as previously thought. Thus, formalist analysis should remain, at least in the first instance, separated from assumptions about the historical or institutional framework of the films at hand.

A Guide to Post-classical Narration will concentrate exclusively on the first question, examining the constructional principles of post-classical narration, often in relation to the norms of other historical modes. The development of a new kind of storytelling in the 1990s occurred within a specific historical juncture wherein other modes continued to affect the filmmakers' choices. Their points of contact as well as a number of common elements will be consistently identified in order to delineate both the affinities and the boundaries of the modes in the long poetic history in the cinema.

This introduction has, thus far, elaborated on the historical and methodological stakes of this project, situating the post-classical mode of narration within the long genealogy of epochal breaks and paradigm shifts in the history of storytelling. In the coming chapters, the post-classical mode is meticulously laid out in its finest nuances through a rich array of films that share a consistent set of constructional principles. Chapter 1 introduces the post-classical narrative logic, which is distinguished for its complex and multifaceted motivations. A series of case studies, including *The Big Short* (2015), *The Grand Budapest Hotel* (2014), *Watchmen* (2009), and *Godard Mon Amour* (2017), illustrate key post-classical elements, such as modified character-centered causality, episodic plot construction, hypermediated realism, hybrid genericity, and parody. Chapter 2 continues with the dominant features of post-classical space: intensified continuity, graphic frame construction, and spatial montage. From *Europa* (1991) and *Bram Stoker's Dracula* (1992) through *The French Dispatch* (2021) and *Army of the Dead* (2021), post-classical films privilege the graphic and painterly elements of the filmic image, crafting a narrative space that can accommodate the elaborate mandates of the narrative motivations. Similarly, Chapter 3 presents the qualities of post-classical time, highlighting the notion of mediated time, complex chronology, and elastic duration through the analysis of *Trainspotting* (1996), *Fight Club*, and *Memento*. The account of the post-classical mode is completed in chapter 4 with the examination of the narrational process through the concepts of "self-consciousness," "knowledgeability," "communicativeness," and "levels of narration," all drawn from prominent narratologists, like Meir Sternberg and Edward Branigan. Case studies like *Tristram Shandy: A Cock and Bull story* (2005), *Sidewalls* (2011), and *The Laws of Thermodynamics* (2018) are typical of the post-classical transmission of story information, which strikes a unique balance between narrational complexity and accessibility. Subsequently, Chapter 5 addresses the relation between auteurism and the historical mode through Quentin Tarantino's example. As a post-classical filmmaker *par excellence*, Tarantino has repeatedly adapted post-classical norms to his personal sensibilities. *Pulp Fiction, Kill Bill: Vol. I* (2003), *Inglourious Basterds* (2009), *Once Upon a Time in Hollywood* (2019) are the case studies that illustrate how his artistic expression through post-classical options has evolved during his career. Finally, the concluding chapter returns to questions of methodology to discuss the prospects for historical poetics in future research. In the first instance, these prospects will be served through a better understanding of the role and function of the historical mode in the mapping of the poetic history of cinema. Ultimately, however, the stakes for formalist analysis and historical poetics are to prove their relevance in the vibrant, yet highly fragmented, research environment in current film studies. As cinema continues to transform through changes in technology, economics, or production and exhibition practices, the study of storytelling and its historical evolution is of utmost importance. *A Guide to Post-classical Narration* hopes to contribute to this direction.

Notes

1. Peter Munz, "The Historical Narrative" in *Companion to Historiography*, edited by Michael Bentley (© 2006). Reproduced by permission of Taylor & Francis Group.
2. My first full account of the post-classical mode appeared in the book *Post-Classical Cinema: An International Poetics of Film Narration* (Thanouli 2009a).
3. This traditional description of the birth of cinema is likely to sound ironic considering the current views on the historiography of the medium that argue for a more complex approach to the process of discovery and innovation. See Elsaesser (2016).
4. Hervé Joubert-Laurencin edited the *Écrits complets* of André Bazin comprising 2,600 articles in two volumes. See Bazin (2018).
5. Bazin's work functions more like a trove of observations on film that historians and theorists have instrumentalized in multiple ways to fit a very wide range of agendas, including the one of poetics as in the case of Bordwell's tribute. For others, see Andrew and Joubert-Laurencin (2011).
6. See Ray (1995) and Cowie (1998).
7. Given that the two books came out the same year, it would be almost impossible for them to enter into a dialogue. Yet in 1989, in his seminal piece entitled "Historical Poetics of Cinema," Bordwell dismissed Ray's account, arguing that his stylistic paradigm is merely "formalistic foreplay," while his real interest lies in "reading," i.e., the interpretation of the meaning of the films (Bordwell 1989b: 398). On the other hand, a few years later, Ray engaged in a lengthy discussion of Bordwell's *Classical Hollywood Cinema*, expressing his admiration and respect, while also questioning Bordwell's epistemological principles (Ray 1995). Although these details risk sounding like gossip, in fact they indicate the importance of personal idiosyncrasies in the way the "dialogue" has been conducted in the field.
8. For an insightful review of Ray's account of classical Hollywood, see Poague (1985).
9. For a more extended overview on postmodern cinema, see Thanouli (2009a).
10. In *Post-classical Cinema*, I was too dismissive of these postmodern debates partly because I felt the pressure to designate a new area where my theory would be situated and partly because I underestimated the importance of interpreting films in relation to wider social and historical phenomena. See Thanouli (2009a).
11. It is interesting that Elsaesser does not consider Bazin as his forefather in the way he defined classicism in Hollywood cinema. Instead, his influences include Parker Tyler, Edgar Morin, and Raymond Durgnat, as he confessed in an interview with Patrice Petro. See Petro (2014).
12. In my article "To be or not to be post-classical," I criticize Elsaesser for not holding onto his terms long enough in contrast to Bordwell who tends to hold onto his for too long. See Thanouli (2008a).

13 Among these theories is still that of postmodernism. See Cornelia Klecker's analysis of *Pulp Fiction* as "a prime example of postmodern narrative" and as "the first American mainstream film to transpose the postmodern concept of time to the screen" (Klecker 2010: 127).

14 In his book *European Cinema: Face to Face with Hollywood* (2005) Elsaesser examines the history and theory of the Hollywood-Europe relation and how it has adapted to the globalized conditions in the new millennium.

15 Henry Jenkins mentions one such opposition between Bordwell and Barry King that took place in a series of exchanges in *Screen* journal. See Jenkins (1995: 118).

16 *The Poetics of Cinema* was a collection of essays edited by the leading Formalist critic Boris Eichenbaum and published in Leningrad in 1927. It included texts by Viktor Shklovsky and Yuri Tynianov. The English edition, edited by Richard Taylor, was published in 1982.

17 What Bordwell calls "purpose" here (for the sake of having a word starting with p) is the same as what he calls "motivation" in earlier publications, which is a prominent term in my account of post-classical narration. See Chapter 1.

18 Some of Bordwell's major books include *French Impressionist Cinema: Film Culture, Film Theory and Film Style* (1980), *The Films of Carl-Theodor Dreyer* (1981), *Making Meaning: Inference and Rhetoric in the Interpretation of Cinema* (1989), *On the History of Film Style* (1997), *Ozu and the Poetics of Cinema* (1998), and *Planet Hong Kong: Popular Cinema and the Art of Entertainment* (2000).

19 The relation between Bordwell and others who work loosely with topics in poetics is a complex one and it is certainly not always amicable. Henry Jenkins aptly describes the situation (Bordwell vs. the rest) in his account of historical poetics (Jenkins 1995). Indeed, the exclusivity of the historical poetics tradition under Bordwell's guidance is reflected in the very short list of books and articles that he acknowledges as successful projects in the 2008 edition of *The Poetics of Cinema* (2008: 55).

20 For a critical presentation of Bordwell's definition of narration, see Thanouli (2013b).

21 In Chapter 5, I address the relation between the mode and the auteur, developing in greater detail Mukařovský's notion of the norm.

22 In *Narration in the Fiction Film*, Bordwell does not consider experimental cinema, while he explicitly refrains from using the term "modernism" (1985: 310).

23 For a critique of Bordwell's art cinema mode, see Thanouli (2009b).

24 Before *Narration in the Fiction Film*, Bordwell had presented his art cinema mode in an article in *Film Criticism* (Bordwell 1979). In *Poetics of Cinema*, the article is reprinted with a short addendum.

25 Elizabeth Cowie, "Storytelling" in *Contemporary Hollywood Cinema,* edited by Steve Neale and Murray Smith (© 1998). Reproduced by permission of Taylor & Francis Group.

26 For a more detailed exposition of Bordwell's arguments on contemporary cinema, see Thanouli (2009a).

27 The issue of "intensified continuity" will be discussed at length in Chapter 2.

28 Along the same lines, Kristin Thompson, the co-author of the *Classical Hollywood Cinema*, argues that storytelling in the New Hollywood remains predominantly and massively classical because the classical system is so stable that it can selectively assimilate avant-garde devices, such as fast cutting, jump-cuts, and discontinuous editing. A significant difference, however, is that Thompson acknowledges that films like *Blue Velvet* (1986) or *Pulp Fiction* are clearly non-classical, instead of stretching the classical rules to include everything in the group. Her argument regarding the classical storytelling becomes, thus, rather quantitative inasmuch as she considers these movies as "blips on the radar screen when seen within the history of Hollywood" (Thompson 1999: 340–1).

29 Reproduced from *Russian Formalist Criticism: Four Essays*, translated and with an introduction by Lee T. Lemon and Marion J. Reis, by permission of the University of Nebraska Press. Copyright 1965 by the University of Nebraska Press.

1
Post-classical Narrative Logic

1.1 Introduction

Who/What and Why, Where, and When are the key questions that we address in the analysis of any filmic narration. They allow us to break down the narrational process into three interrelated systems, i.e., the system of narrative logic, the system of narrative space, and the system of narrative time. Every scene and every shot contain narrative elements entangled in a web of causal, spatial, and temporal relations that can be unraveled with the help of analytical terms and concepts. Specifically, the system of narrative logic can be analyzed further into a series of "motivations" that determine the way that both the story and the plot evolve. According to Bordwell, "motivation is the process by which a narrative justifies its story material and the plot's presentation of that story material" (Bordwell et al. 1985: 19). Every element that appears on the screen, from an actor to a line of dialogue and from a camera angle to a lighting scheme, requires a specific justification; it serves a function within the storyworld, and its presence must make sense to the viewer according to a line of reasoning.

The four types of motivation that have been identified in the filmic narration are the following: 1) the compositional; 2) the realistic; 3) the generic; and 4) the artistic. Each mode of narration regulates the narrative logic according to a different combination of motivations, while also establishing varying degrees of equilibrium among them. In classical narration, for instance, the compositional motivation prevails, whereas in art cinema, the realistic and artistic motivations compete with one another. In the post-classical mode, on the other hand, all four types of motivation are equally significant in the construction of the narrative logic, producing a distinctly complex narrational act that differs from all other historical modes.

KEY CONCEPTS

1.2 Post-classical Compositional Motivation

The most common type of narrative motivation is the compositional, which encompasses the characters and their actions woven into in a cause-and-effect chain of events. The main building blocks of the compositional motivation include character presentation, character agency, and plot structures. Specifically, post-classical compositional motivation consists of the following: modified character-centered causality, blatant character exposition, reconfiguration of the classical mission/romance motifs, multiple protagonists, episodic structures, and multi-thread plotlines.

1.2.1 Character Presentation

The character-centered causality of the post-classical mode—even if modified, as I will explain below—requires a considerable acquaintance with the main protagonists. Unlike the classical films that embraced a gradual delineation of the characters as a means to justify their actions, post-classical narratives tend to accentuate character presentation in its own right. Instead of allowing one's personality to unfold through their speech and physical behavior, post-classical narration prioritizes a self-conscious demonstration of character traits. To condense information about the protagonists and accelerate their introduction in the plot, the films deploy powerful voice-overs, intertitles, and inserts that summarize their main chatacteristics, reveal their life experiences, and even proclaim their goals. As the case studies will attest, this type of character presentation, which relies so heavily on nondiegetic sources of information, reinforces the individuality and the consistency of each character in a way that was previously possible only through use of "recurrent" motifs, i.e., repeated habits or tags (Bordwell et al. 1985: 13–18). This classical trope is still found in post-classical films, but like all the classical devices embedded in the post-classical mode, it is imbued with an additional layer of complexity and self-consciousness.

In addition, the extended sequences dedicated to the characters' presentation often have a structural impact on the other two parameters, namely the character agency and the design of the post-classical plot. The intervention of voice-over narrators that either belong to the storyworld, as in David Fincher's *Fight Club*, or intrude from the outside, as in Lars von Trier's *Europa*, tends to challenge the protagonists' control over their lives, while it also invites the loosening of their goal-oriented trajectory. When a substantial part of screen time is dedicated to the exposition of one or, more often, multiple individuals, then the length of the diegetic segments is shortened significantly, while a more episodic construction of the plot is privileged.

ANALYSIS

CASE STUDY A: *AMÉLIE* (2001)

Jean-Pierre Jeunet's romantic comedy stormed the French box office back in 2001 and remains to this day a milestone in his career. The story portrays the life of Amélie Poulain (Audrey Tautou), a young woman who lives in Paris and devotes her time to bringing joy to the people around her. The opening scene introduces the heroine in an extraordinary fashion; a nondiegetic narrator specifies the exact moment of Amélie's conception—September 3, 1973, at 6:28 pm and 32 seconds—and chronicles a series of random events that took place that very same moment in Paris. Subsequently, the narrator says, "Nine months later Amélie Poulain was born," showing us Amélie pop out of her mother's womb. This playfully self-conscious presentation of the central protagonist soon extends to her parents, who are displayed in long frontal shots (Figures 1.1–1.2) with the camera rapidly tracking in on their faces.

FIGURE 1.1

FIGURE 1.2

When in close-up, the voice-over continues to transmit information assisted by graphic elements on the screen. For instance, in Figure 1.3, a written indication on the side of her father's face notes his pinched mouth as a sign of heartlessness, whereas in Figure 1.4 her mother's nervous spasm is interpreted as a sign of neurotic agitation.

FIGURE 1.3

FIGURE 1.4

The wealth of information contained in the first ten minutes of the film would have taken up hours had Jeunet opted for a classical exposition. Amélie's life until the point of departure for the main plotline—August 30, 1997—is compressed into a series of fragmented incidents from her childhood and early adult life, with the voice-over highlighting the life-changing moments (her fake heart condition, her mother's death) and explaining the impact they had on her personality. By the time Amélie moves to Paris and accidentally finds a secret box, we know almost everything there is to know about her, even more than she probably knows about herself.

This type of blatant character presentation is also applied to numerous secondary characters in the storyworld, especially the customers at the Café des 2 Moulins. Throughout the film, the voice-over narrator remains an openly omnipotent and omnipresent force that orchestrates the plot and presents information about the characters directly to the audience. He carefully selects important habits, likes, dislikes, or turning points in their lives to justify their behavior and anticipate some of their actions. In this typically post-classical fashion, *Amélie* explores a number of self-conscious devices (nondiegetic sources of information, graphic frames) to establish a wide and deep range of knowledge of the characters.

CASE STUDY B: *THE BIG SHORT* (2015)

Adam McKay's 2015 historical drama became a critical and commercial success, as it tackled the 2007 housing market collapse through a vibrant and dynamic storytelling attainable only through the post-classical mode. Its three concurrent storylines feature at least four main protagonists along with numerous secondary characters that populate a rather turbid financial terrain; out of that chaos, which had devastating repercussions on ordinary people's lives, McKay seeks to present and explain a complex situation in the clearest but also most entertaining fashion. For that to happen, he had to resort to a highly self-conscious diegetic narrator called Jared Vennett (Ryan Gosling) who talks us through an intricate web of actions and decisions, deploying freeze-frames, fast and slow motion as well as every other graphic trick imaginable.

The introduction of the first protagonist, however, takes place without the help of this central narrator. Instead, the name Michael Burry is typed on the left of the screen (Figure 1.5) as we watch Christian Bale for the first time explain how the housing market collapsed in the 1930s by roughly 80 per cent.

FIGURE 1.5

In the unfolding sequence that hosts Berry and his soon-to-be employee, the former's quirky character is flaunted through two devices: the subjective inserts that interrupt the diegesis; and a combination of editing and framing options in the shooting of the scene. Regarding the former, we witness an unusual disruption of Michael's recounting of the events from the 1930s as the close-up to his face is succeeded by shots that could be interpreted as two diverse kinds of memories—one from his childhood and one from his recent activities. The childhood memory is a blend of color and black-and-white images from a football incident that was traumatic, while the other is a scene in color that comes from his solo swimming routine. In his own voice, Michael explains his character: "I've always been more comfortable alone. I believe maybe it's because of my glass eye. I lost the eye in a childhood illness." The diegetic discussion comes back momentarily and then gives way again to Michael's thoughts that continue to disclose information about himself.

This explicit form of character presentation through his own words and memory trips is coupled with stylistic flourishes within the diegesis. The second mechanism that McKay regularly deploys is framing and editing parts of the human figure in a fragmented and jerky way. Instead of shooting Michael's behavior in a stable and centralized frame, the filmmaker focuses on body parts (hands, face, eyes) and highlights gestures that metonymically signify his character, whether it is his quirkiness, his insecurity, or his brilliant mind (Figures 1.6–1.8).

The framing and editing of the scene are brazenly unclassical; the classically balanced shot composition and the classical editing smoothness are replaced by a fast-paced rhythm that guides the viewer's eyes on the small but meaningful gestures and looks, making sure that we "get it." Thus, the post-classical protagonist is someone we get to know as fast as possible and—at least seemingly—in great depth.

FIGURE 1.6

FIGURE 1.7

FIGURE 1.8

CASE STUDY C: *THE GRAND BUDAPEST HOTEL* (2014)

Wes Anderson, a post-classical filmmaker *par excellence*, is not only famous for his shot composition, color palette, and art direction, but also for the idiosyncratic characters that feature in his stories. *The Grand Budapest Hotel*, which premiered in Berlin Film Festival in 2014, is no exception. The film presents a stellar ensemble of actors as characters who inhabit a mountainside resort in the fictional country of Zubrowka in the 1930s. The presentation of the hotel owner, Zero Mustafa (F. Murray Abraham), is indicative of the post-classical character exposition, which combines the element of self-consciousness and communicativeness to provide the audience with a dense yet clear acquaintance with the protagonists.

Four minutes into the film, we find ourselves inside The Grand Budapest Hotel in 1968 when the young author of the homonymous book, played by Jude Law, addresses us from the voice-over while also participating in a diegetic scene. In the voice-over, the author says that one evening he noticed a new presence in the company while the images visualize this observation with a very standard eyeline match (Figures 1.9–1.10).

FIGURE 1.9

FIGURE 1.10

The voice continues as follows:

> A small, elderly man, smartly dressed, with an exceptionally lively, intelligent face—and an immediately perceptible air of sadness. He was, like the rest of us, alone—but also, I must say, he was the first that struck one as being, deeply and truly, lonely. (A symptom of my own medical condition, as well.)

This admittedly literary description is adapted into images with the help of an unconventional synthesis of framing, cutting, and camera movement that records Mr. Mustafa's presence from different angles and distances (Figures 1.11–1.12).

FIGURE 1.11

FIGURE 1.12

The voice carries on, listing more information regarding his past, his riches, and possessions as well as his bizarre habit of occupying the servants' quarters when staying in his own hotel. The exposition of Mr. Mustafa's character is not limited to the voice-over and the diegetic space, however. Anderson provides inserts, such as newspaper headlines and paintings, that illustrate the author's verbal account. With these multiform and hypermediated representational techniques, the film becomes an ideal exemplar of the post-classical approach to character presentation.

1.2.2 Character Agency

Who is in charge of the action? What goals and motivations are pursued? Is it human initiative, luck, or fate that determines the outcome of the events? These are the questions that we pose when trying to understand the narrative agency in a story. In an average Hollywood film, we find the answers in the heroes' personal trajectory. A classical narration is built on a "character-centred causality," which means that the characters are the primal agents whose personal motives propel the chain of events. In other words, the classical hero is a "psychologically defined individual" whose behaviour is goal-oriented; he seeks to satisfy his desires through action. An art cinema protagonist, on the other hand, is someone who experiences a "boundary situation" and fails to act, drifting aimlessly from situation to situation (Bordwell 1985). European auteur films in the 1950s and 1960s, as well as their American counterparts in the 1970s, exemplified what Elsaesser named the "pathos of failure," i.e., a lack of motivation and a penchant for failure, which loosened the goal-oriented progression of the story and allowed an open ending to the characters' fate (Elsaesser 1975).

The impersonal causes, such as natural phenomena or historical facts, are other sources of agency whose impact can be varied, depending on the narrative mode. In the classical system, these causes, albeit regularly present, always play a secondary role, functioning as initiating causes or simply providing a backdrop against which the human initiative is flaunted. An earthquake, a twister, or a fire will challenge the heroes' resolve, but they will also give them the opportunity to display their power over their destiny. In the art film, impersonal agents are also kept at a distance but to the opposite effect; instead of pushing the protagonists to take action, they probe dilemmas that accentuate their helplessness even further.

Moreover, the use of unmotivated coincidences or chance encounters is another means for originating action or altering the progression of a story. The recourse to these mechanisms, however, is allowed only occasionally or in small portions when it comes to the classical film. The hero's purposeful behaviour cannot be side-lined by sheer chance. There are genres, like melodrama or comedy, that imbue the story with moments of fortuity to generate drama or laughter, yet the individuals that experience victory or defeat should ultimately appear as responsible for their actions. On the contrary, the presence of chance factors is persistent in art films to lift responsibility from individuals who are unable to act. The realism of the art mode compels us to accept lucky breaks or accidents as part of real life where humans are not always—or rather hardly ever—in charge of their lives.

Post-classical compositional motivation relies on a modified character-centered causality, which holds the individuals at the centre of the action but complicates their agency through a range of structural, stylistic, and even thematic devices. First and foremost, post-classical films have significantly increased the number of protagonists and the plotlines that those are involved in. Whereas the classical hero was a causal agent with clear goals and objectives that advanced the story and narrowed the range of alternative outcomes of the action, the post-classical hero or heroine is merely one source of agency among numerous others. Post-classical narration uses a plurality of characters and multiplies their interactions to create a diversification and fragmentation of their goals and their consequent fulfilment. The two classical plotlines—the formation of the heterosexual couple and the undertaking of a mission—remain persistently present in post-classical story construction, but they acquire other dimensions, extending and bifurcating into various parallel or intertwined subplots, as I will demonstrate in the next section.

The role of chance also plays an integral part in the complex edifice of post-classical composition. In addition to the generic imperatives—equally present in these narratives—fortuitous events or accidental encounters are practical tools for joining episodic pieces of the plot or for intertwining multiple paths. Constructional logic aside, however, post-classical films welcome the presence of good or bad luck as part of their thematic or philosophical premises. In a world of increasing complexity as well as randomness, stories cannot rely on individuals alone; human initiative is portrayed as merely one force in a web of unpredictable and unknowable factors.

The use of voice-over narrators is an additional complicating factor in terms of who is in charge of the action. Let's take *Europa*, for instance. Max von Sydow's forceful voice takes the protagonist to Germany in 1945 by counting down to ten. He then instructs him to perform specific actions before finally allowing him act on his own. Or let's look at *The Big Short* from this perspective. The voice-over narrator, despite appearing in the diegesis as Jared Vennett in flesh and blood, possesses such level of marked omniscience and omnipotence when it comes to handling the plot (flashbacks, freeze-frames etc.) that the diegetic characters often seem like puppets. The fact that post-classical narration chooses to transmit story information through what Edward Branigan calls higher "levels of narration,"[1] and particularly through nondiegetic sources (voice-over, intertitles) that are not accessible to the characters,[2] weakens the latter's agency to a considerable extent. Whereas a classical film relies on the protagonists' external behavior, using them as key conveyors of story material, the post-classical counterpart delimits their narrative powers and curtails, as a result, their positive action.

Paradoxically, the same effect stems from the lower levels of narration, i.e., the use of characters as focalizers. Post-classical films feature a form of subjective realism that surrenders the screen to the innermost thoughts and processes within the characters' mind. As we shall see in the section on the realistic motivation, the post-classical mode invites the look into the characters' brain and psyche, visualizing their mental and emotional state. This extensive exploration of the protagonists' inner lives may illuminate some of their motivations or feelings, but it does not advance their actions. The narration, thus, moves inwards but not necessarily forward; the progression of the story pauses for the characters to reflect or experience the world, but it does not encourage them to act.

Finally, the emphasis on the brain—or, more generally, on the inner life—renders the post-classical formula particularly hospitable to certain thematic concerns. Post-classical protagonists are often individuals with rare idiosyncrasies who come against problems of addiction, memory loss, and other pathologies. Their stories involve extreme conditions like chaos or exuberance, while the plot might take the shape of a puzzle, as we shall see in the discussion about plot structures. Yet it is important to underline that the relation between the post-classical narrative form and the thematic content is not absolute. Post-classical options are susceptible to the aforementioned themes, but they are not exclusive to them. For instance, many of the films listed under "complex storytelling," such as *Mulholland Drive* or the *Eternal Sunshine of a Spotless Mind* are *not* post-classical; they are either closer to the art cinema mode or they cannot be classified at all. Neither are all "mind-game films" post-classical. For example, *Interstellar* and *Arrival* are fairly classical, while *Lost Highway* features many of the norms of art cinema, especially the notion of ambiguity.

Overall, the narrative agency in the post-classical mode maintains a degree of character-centered causality but becomes conducive to more post-humanist perspectives on causality and agency. This modified character-centered causality challenges the anthropocentric approach of the classical composition and brings forward an intricate web of agents—both human and nonhuman—that determine the development and the outcome of the story.

ANALYSIS

CASE STUDY A: *500 DAYS OF SUMMER* (2009)

A huge indie success directed by Marc Webb, *500 Days of Summer* is exactly what the voice-over tells us it is: "This is a story of boy meets girl, but you should know upfront, this is not a love story." The film portrays the romantic affair between Tom Hansen (Joseph Gordon-Levitt) and Summer Finn (Zooey Deschanel), which spanned 500 days, including the time that Tom needed to get over Summer and meet another girl called Autumn (Minka Kelly). The romantic plotline dominates the entire film, even though the male character ends up making a major career change as a result of his broken heart. The compositional motivation relies on a modified character-centered causality; the two protagonists follow their feelings and impulses from the moment they first meet until their last encounter after their break-up. Yet there are three complicating factors that dominate in the progression of the story, challenging and thwarting the characters' goals.

First, the non-linear presentation of the events builds an exceptionally disjointed plot that weakens the traditional goal-oriented trajectory. Using intertitles that signal the number of the day to be depicted (Figures 1.13–1.14), the narration moves back and forth or replays certain scenes in order to dissect key moments of the romantic relationship and explain the causal parameters at play; is it Tom or Summer's emotions? Is it fate? Is it pure coincidence?

FIGURE 1.13

FIGURE 1.14

This highly self-conscious search for answers on matters of causality regarding romantic love undermines the individual will and brings center stage other impersonal agents. Second, the recurring presence of the nondiegetic narrator in the soundtrack raises once again the question of who is in command of the storytelling. The voice of God that possesses omniscience over the characters' internal and external existence confines the space of the characters as active agents who are supposed to lead their lives autonomously. Finally, the moral lesson of Tom and Summer's romance is that success in love is purely coincidental. Whereas in the opening of the film Tom believed in fate and thought that Summer "was the one," by the time the end credits roll, he has come to a keen realization expressed by the narrator thus:

> If Tom had learned anything ... it was that you can't ascribe great cosmic significance to a simple earthly event. Coincidence, that's all

anything ever is, nothing more than coincidence ... Tom had finally learned, there are no miracles. There's no such thing as fate, nothing is meant to be. He knew, he was sure of it now.

Whether fate or coincidence, however, the leeway for individuals to shape their own destiny becomes limited within this storyline. The success or failure of the affair is portrayed as contingent on impersonal causes and not on the conscious decisions or the personal determination of the characters.

CASE STUDY B: *THE TRIAL OF THE CHICAGO 7* (2020)

Written and directed by Aaron Sorkin, *The Trial of the Chicago 7* depicts the true story of a group of anti-Vietnam War protesters who are tried for inciting riots at the 1968 Democratic National Convention in Chicago. It is interesting to see how the paradigmatic options of the post-classical mode, particularly regarding the issue of agency, facilitate the representation of the historical past as a complex web of historical forces rather than as an oversimplified depiction of individual willpower. Whereas historical events have always procured themes for classical Hollywood, the classical character-centered causality dictated the treatment of history only through the personal trials and tribulations of one or two protagonists. Hence, the regular accusations leveled against those films for their lack of perspective on more systemic historical factors. Post-classical composition, however, offers the chance for a contextual approach to history, embedding the historical agents into a more complex depiction of the historical process (Thanouli 2018).

The opening of *The Trial of the Chicago 7* flaunts an impressive parallel editing sequence, which blends archival material of key historical events and figures (President Lyndon Johnson, Dr. Martin Luther King, Robert Kennedy) with the introduction of the eight main characters who are preparing to demonstrate at the Democratic Convention (Figure 1.15–1.18).

Five months after the event, they are charged with conspiracy and intent to incite a riot, thus placing the plot inside the courtroom where the numerous protagonists unravel their personalities, as they not only assert their innocence but also serve their overarching goal, i.e., to protest the Vietnam War and the Nixon administration. Politics aside, however, the narration does indeed investigate the question of "who started the riot"

POST-CLASSICAL NARRATIVE LOGIC

FIGURE 1.15

FIGURE 1.16

FIGURE 1.17

FIGURE 1.18

mainly through the defendants' chief counsel William Kunstler (Mark Rylance) but also through nondiegetic interventions that replay moments of past events, juxtapose conflicting testimonies, and adjoin non-fictional material. Was it the police? Was it the radicals that did not back off? Or was it a phrase from the most prudent voice in the group that led to that crescendo of violence? The narration seems to suggest that it was all those things coming together in ways that were both predictable but also inadvertent. Because history, viewed in this post-classical fashion, is nothing but an intricate grid of forces, interweaving the significance of each and every historical agent and diffusing individual power. Post-classical heroes are not stripped off their goals and aspirations; yet the co-existence with several other characters combined with the mediation of impersonal conditions relativize considerably the impact of personal choices. The post-classical mode does not eliminate character-centered causality but modifies it to render it overtly perplexing.

CASE STUDY C: *CITY OF GOD* (2002)

City of God, the Brazilian film co-directed by Fernando Meirelles and Kátia Lund, captures the life in the "City of God," a euphemistic name for one of Rio de Janeiro's most notorious slums. The film opens *in medias res*, showing us a young man called Buscapé (Alexandre Rodrigues) trapped between an army of menacing gangsters on one side and the police on the other. Buscapé introduces himself in the voice-over and becomes our narrator, taking us back to the 1960s when, as a kid, he began witnessing the endless string of violence in the favela. The story contains several episodes clearly marked by intertitles, such as "The story of Mane Galinha" or "The story of Ze Pequeno" (Figures 1.19–1.20), and is populated by hundreds of people usually with a very short life span.

FIGURE 1.19

FIGURE 1.20

The compositional motivation in the film relies on three main characters: Buscapé, Lil' Ze (Leandro Firmino da Hora), and Bené (Phellipe Haagensen). Unlike Buscapé, who is a pacifist and dreams of becoming a journalist, Lil' Ze and Bené are gangsters who deal drugs and run the crime scene in the slum. They are all sufficiently characterized by recurring motifs that construe them as "psychologically defined" individuals but their personal motivations are not the sole driving forces. Instead, the structural parameters that define the social life in the City of God are the real protagonists of the story: drugs, violence, and poverty.

As a typical example of post-classical narration, Meirelles' film lays out multiple plotlines that are anchored on the three characters, yet they are hardly controlled by them. The tagline of the film, also heard in the voice-over, goes as follows: "if you run, the beast will get you; if you stay, it will eat you." This brilliantly sums up the range of options that people in the favela truly have: no matter what they choose, they will end up dead in the streets. Buscapé is the only one who seems driven by his passion for photography and is lucky enough to stay around to witness Bené's death as well as the end of Lil' Ze's empire. Both events come as a result of accidental or coincidental happenings: the former is killed by mistake during his farewell party, while the latter is executed by the Runts, the gang of criminal kids who want to succeed him. No matter how optimistic Buscapé's trajectory might seem, the weight of the story falls on the futility of human existence within the dire social conditions in the slums. For the people in the City of God, including our narrator, it is only God who is in charge, and it is he who decides to turn the city from purgatory to hell.

1.2.3 Plot Structures

Post-classical compositional motivation is often a highly delicate balancing act between the need for "unity" and "fragmentation." Historically, it is fascinating to see how post-classical storytelling returns to some of the structures of early cinema that relied on the "extended incident" and the "episodic narrative" (Bordwell et al. 1985: 266). Classical Hollywood cinema moved away from its early origins already in the 1910s, developing stories with a unified cause-and-effect logic that would pass through five key stages: Exposition; Conflict; Complication; Crisis; and Denouement. Those stages would involve the two standard plotlines in any classical film, i.e., the pursuit of a goal (mission) and the formation of the heterosexual couple (romance). In the classical plot, every scene needs to build organically into the next one, leading eventually to a new equilibrium. In the art film, on the other hand, there is no such commitment. The plot may consist entirely of episodes—possibly loosely connected, if not entirely random—while the ending may come abruptly without any palpable resolution in the state of affairs.

The post-classical mode introduces a distinct logic in the plot construction that reconfigures several of the tropes found in the other modes, transforming them into a new formula. A quick look at the typical post-classical films, such as *Pulp Fiction*, *Trainspotting*, *Fight Club*, *Natural Born Killers*, *Chungking Express*, *Run Lola Run*, *Magnolia*, *The Royal Tenenbaums*, or *Watchmen*, can tell us that, despite their diverse origins, production values, or even thematic concerns, the plot structures that they share are characterized by a level of complexity that was not previously possible in mainstream cinema. The mission/romance motifs are still present most of the time, but they are plotted in a more irregular fashion as they involve numerous characters with diverging paths. The presence of multiple protagonists in these stories requires a more digressive treatment of the plot, which may take the shape of an episodic structure, a spliced plot or a "forking path narrative" (Bordwell 2002).

The variety and multiplicity of plotlines that develop at different paces within the same narration work against the tight causality, yet without eliminating it altogether. The continuity of the story slackens up considerably but the demand for unity and gap filling in the narrational process are not abandoned. Thus, a basic level of coherence and communicativeness is ensured with the aid of various narrative devices, starting with the character presentation discussed above. The clear depiction of the protagonists and their mental/emotional condition, usually performed by overwhelming and enlightening voice-overs, navigates the viewer through the bifurcating or choppy parts of the plot, gradually filling most of the basic causal gaps. In addition, the branches and diversions of the plots are signposted with unambiguous formal tactics, such as freeze-frames, intertitles, and cross-cutting, keeping the viewer constantly updated and oriented. Finally, the plot almost invariably goes through all the classical stages, from exposition to denouement, even if not in the traditional order. Sometimes, the denouement may be presented in the beginning, or the conflicts may come several times at unexpected moments. Finally, the post-classical ending will establish a sense of closure, however provisional or fragile it might appear when contrasted to the finality of the classical Hollywood finale.

ANALYSIS

CASE STUDY A: *WATCHMEN* (2009)

Watchmen is a superhero film based on the homonymous graphic novel by DC comics. Zack Snyder, who had previously exercised the post-classical formula in *300* (2007), directed *Watchmen* as a faithful adaptation of the comic. He put a great deal of effort into preserving not only the graphic style but also the complexity of the plot consisting of multiple characters and numerous lines of action.

The setting of the story is already complicated enough as it introduces us to an alternative historical and political universe: the United States wins the Vietnam War, Richard Nixon is reelected several times, while key events like the Kennedy assassination are redrafted to integrate the characters in the film. The Watchmen are a group of superheroes that are forced by law to give up their careers as costumed vigilantes and find new roles within American society. Some do so successfully, while others struggle. The Watchmen (Figure 1.21) are the following:

- Walter Kovacs/Rorschach (Jackie Earle Haley): A masked vigilante who continues his extralegal activities after being outlawed.
- Jon Osterman/Dr. Manhattan (Billy Crudup): A scientist who acquired superhuman powers after a scientific accident. He works for the US government as its formidable superweapon.
- Laurie Jupiter/Silk Spectre II (Malin Åkerman): The daughter of Silk Spectre who is in love with Dr. Manhattan.
- Adrian Veidt/Ozymandias (Matthew Goode): A former superhero turned powerful billionaire.
- Daniel Dreiberg/Nite Owl II (Patrick Wilson): A forty-year-old retired superhero with a mastery of technological tricks.
- Edward Blake/The Comedian (Jeffrey Dean Morgan): A cynical superhero who works as an independent crimefighter.

In addition to these main characters, the film incorporates several more, especially some notable members of a former superhero group, the Minutemen (Figure 1.22).

FIGURE 1.21

FIGURE 1.22

The murder of the Comedian triggers the story that causes Rorschach to contact the Watchmen. He suspects that they might be the next victims. Yet the mystery of the Comedian's violent death is not the only mission to be pursued, as this plotline is intertwined with a significantly greater one, namely Veidt's scheme to unify the US and the USSR to bring world peace.

As this broad outline of the story blatantly indicates, the compositional motivation in *Watchmen* comprises many characters, subplots, and parallel events that are handled in an efficient and communicative manner with the help of extended flashbacks and parallel editing. The structure of the plot is inevitably episodic as it is compelled to allocate parts of its screen time to each character, shedding light on their backstory and connecting their bifurcating trajectories both in the past and the current moment. The informational load of this type of narration is enormous and a sense of coherence builds gradually as the film progresses. Yet the post-classical multi-thread plot structure allows a dispersive form of unity, which is clearly distinguished from both the organic unity of the classical plot and the random fragmentation of the art film.

CASE STUDY B: *CHUNGKING EXPRESS* (1994)

Chungking Express is one of Wong Kar-Wai's most emblematic films, exploring the theme of unrequited love through the stories of four different characters living in contemporary Hong Kong. Its plot structure has been aptly described by Bordwell as follows,

> (...) *Chungking Express* focuses on boys meeting, losing, and getting, or not quite getting, girls. But Wong revivifies the formula. Instead of tightening up the plot, he slackens it beyond even Hong Kong's episodic norm, letting a fine network of parallels and recurring motifs come forward.
>
> BORDWELL 2000a: 289

Indeed, *Chungking Express* features a spliced plot, which joins together two separate stories with common themes but different protagonists. In the first plotline, we are introduced to Officer 223 (Takeshi Kaneshiro), a twenty-five-year-old cop, and an unnamed woman in a blonde wig (Brigitte Lin) who is a drug smuggler. The two characters are brought together in an impressively impressionistic opening scene and their first, chance, encounter is highlighted with slow motion and a voice-over that explains: "At our closest point, we were just 0.01cm apart from each other. Fifty-five hours later, I was in love with this woman." The spatial and temporal signaling of the key events both through the visual effects and the voice-over narration allow the spectator to follow the episodic scenes that unfold, with Officer 223 trying to cope with his breakup from a girl called May and the unnamed woman facing trouble in one of her drug deals. The loose causal chain of action gives the characters moments of introspection and existential crisis but their thoughts, confessed on the soundtrack, build connections, and make their relationship meaningful.

Romantic love is in the epicenter of the second story as well, and the passage from one splice to the next is performed in a flagrant visual and aural manner. Officer 223 goes to a food stall called Midnight Express and meets a girl named Faye (Faye Wong). As she accidentally bumps into him, the frame freezes (Figure 1.23), and his voice speaks to us for one last time: "At our closest point, we were just 0.01cm apart from each other. I knew nothing about her. Six hours later she fell in love with another man."

With these words the baton is passed on to the next couple, Faye and Officer 663 (Tony Leung), whose romantic lives sadly fail to synchronize. Officer 663 recovers from his painful breakup with an airline attendant while Faye sneaks briefly into his life, only to abandon him a little later for a career (also as an airline attendant). The accidental encounters, the mirroring events, and the missed opportunities build a very loose but enjoyable plotline that reconfigures both classical and art cinema tropes into a consistent new formula.

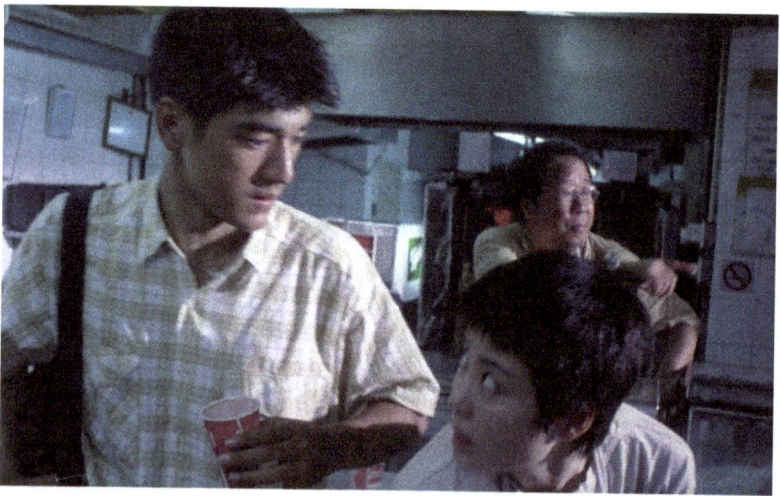

FIGURE 1.23

CASE STUDY C: *RUN LOLA RUN* (1998)

Run Lola Run caused a sensation when it premiered in 1998 and secured Tom Tykwer a place among the most celebrated European filmmakers in the recent years. It has been widely showcased as an example of complex storytelling (Buckland 2009), while Bordwell coined the term "forking-path" plot specifically to describe its unusual narrative structure (Bordwell 2002). The film begins with a very dramatic crisis situation: Lola (Franka Potente) receives a phone-call from her boyfriend Manni (Moritz Bleibtreu) asking her to come up with 100,000 marks within twenty minutes or else a murderous gangster will kill him. The mission and the extremely tight deadline put both protagonists under enormous pressure to act boldly and fast. The very classical devices of the mission and the deadline, however, are handled by Tykwer in a post-classical manner that allows the narration to explore three different possibilities. Specifically, the plot presents three consecutive drafts of the story following Manni's phone-call to Lola, each depicting a different variation of the characters' trajectory and, above all, a different finale.

All three drafts contain a series of core incidents (visit to the bank, confrontation with the police) and secondary encounters (bumping into a woman with a trolley), but small changes in their timing influence considerably the ensuing flow of events. For instance, when Lola leaves her apartment, she meets a punk kid with an unfriendly dog on her way down the stairs. The first time the dog barks but Lola continues to run down. The second time the kid trips her down causing Lola to arrive at the bank a little later. In the last draft, the dog barks at her but Lola growls back at him, determined as she is not to waste a second. Each trajectory ends quite differently; first, Lola is accidentally shot dead by the police; then, Manni is accidentally run over by a speeding ambulance, and finally, the third time Manni pays back the gangster and walks away with Lola holding a bag with 129,600 marks won in the lottery.

The overall coherence of the narration is maintained with the repetition of certain formal techniques, such as the animation sequence, while the passage from one plotline to the next is clearly indicated by replaying the shot of Lola's red phone receiver falling onto the cradle (Figure 1.24).

Ultimately, when it comes to the ending, one could argue that of the three resolutions to Lola's quest, the last one feels the least hypothetical. In other words, the last successful attempt could be interpreted as the one that happened after all. Instead of understanding the three parallel plots as mutually exclusive, we could deploy the film's video-game logic to approach the characters as players who can start over until they get it right. Tykwer seems to advocate this position when he explains,

FIGURE 1.24

> At the end, the viewer must have the impression that Lola has done everything that we've just seen (and not just one part, a third of it). She has lived it all—she has died for this man, he has died, and everything that was destined to happen has happened. She has all that behind her, and at the end, she's rewarded.
>
> Quoted in BORDWELL 2002: 100

Admittedly, Tykwer's explanation is not binding. *Run Lola Run* is, in fact, an exemplary case for the post-classical compositional motivation; it embraces complexity both at the level of plot structure and narrative agency to elucidate the multiple forces at work in every particular circumstance. As motivated as Lola may be to save her boyfriend, it may only take the bark of a dog to throw her off course. This is a possibility that the film lays out for us to consider, even if we choose to hold the happy ending closer to our hearts in the end.

1.3 Post-classical Realistic Motivation

The realistic motivation is the second type of motivation that we may trace in the narrative logic of a film. This kind of motivation justifies the representation of story and plot material in terms of verisimilitude and plausibility. Put plainly, something is justified realistically if it resembles the real world or, at least, our perception of it. Post-classical realistic motivation consists of two dominant forms of realism: 1) hypermediated realism; and 2) subjective realism.

1.3.1 Hypermediated Realism

Film's relation to reality is the oldest and most persistent problem not only in the writings of film theorists and critics, but also in the most mundane discussions of ordinary filmgoers. Is this real? Could it be real? Does it *feel* real? These are the key questions that we ask when judging the realistic aspect of everything that appears on the screen, from the characters and their actions to a camera angle or a visual effect. The answers are never definitive; they vary depending on the notion of realism at play within each particular context. At its most fundamental level, realism is defined as a set of conventions that aspire to approximate reality, to show "things as they really are" (Hill 1986: 55). These conventions, however, are prone to change depending on the aesthetic, the technological, the institutional, and even the social developments that affect *both* worlds, the world of the cinema and our own.

Historically, the two major modes of narration, the classical Hollywood and the European art cinema, formed two distinct approaches to realistic representation, molding the narrational elements and our expectations accordingly. On the one hand, the Hollywood industry gradually shaped the *mise-en-scène* and the editing of the films in ways that served all those principles that André Bazin cherished in filmmakers like Orson Welles and William Wyler, i.e., stability, continuity, unity, and balance. European auteurs, on the other hand, questioned Hollywood's realism and explored "objectivity" and "subjectivity," inspired by modernist art movements. According to art cinema narration, as Bordwell observes, "the world's laws may not be knowable, personal psychology may be indeterminate" (Bordwell 1985: 206). Hence, the two strands of realism that we encounter in the art film: the objective (real locations, natural lighting, episodic plots) and the subjective (mental states, dreams, and emotions).

The post-classical mode of narration introduces its own kind of realism, the "hypermediated realism," as I chose to name it (Thanouli 2009a). Hypermediated realism is a form of realism that seeks to capture "things as they really are" through the multiplication of the signs of representation. To understand this approach, we need to look closer into the concept of "hypermediacy" put forward by Jay David Bolter and Robert Grusin in their seminal book *Remediation: Understanding New Media* (1999). Bolter and Grusin described hypermediacy as a "representational logic" that has appeared side by side the logic of "immediacy" in the history of Western representation. As they explain,

> If the logic of immediacy leads one either to erase or to render automatic the act of representation, the logic of hypermediacy acknowledges multiple acts of representation and makes them visible. Where immediacy suggests a unified visual space, contemporary hypermediacy offers a

heterogeneous space, in which representation is conceived of not as a window on to the world, but as a rather "windowed" self—with windows that open on to other representations or other media. The logic of hypermediacy multiplies the signs of representation and in this way tries to reproduce the rich sensorium of human experience.

BOLTER and GRUSIN 1999: 33–4

Post-classical films are indeed characterized by a strong realistic motivation, yet they no longer seek to represent reality by means of transparent and seamless images, like the classical counterparts. Instead, they privilege a fragmented construction of the film frame, invite heterogeneous images and stocks, and foreground the materiality of the medium with a wide array of formal devices,[3] which will be elaborated further in the discussion of narrative space and time.

The strategy of hypermediacy has a long lineage in other art/media forms and has traditionally functioned as immediacy's alter ego, usually diminished to a secondary status. From painting to digital technology, the two tactics have shaped contrasting approaches to visual representation, with Virtual Reality and the World Wide Web as two emblematic cases of immediacy and hypermediacy respectively. Specifically, in the history of cinema the logic of hypermediacy has been partly embraced by modernist movements seeking to openly oppose the immediacy of Hollywood realism. The battle was, first and foremost, of an ideological nature. For instance, Soviet filmmaking in the 1920s attacked the transparency and unity of the classical image, opting for a form of hypermediacy that would lay bare the device and dismantle the ideological mechanisms of classical realism. In other words, the function of hypermediacy in those cinematic works was to break the illusion of the classical image and create a feeling of estrangement.

Post-classical hypermediacy, on the other hand, attempts to achieve the reverse: namely, to offer an immersive experience that captures the real through all the senses. Hypermediated realism is, therefore, a set of narrative and stylistic conventions that abandon the notion of "transparent realism" of the classical mode for the sake of a "heightened realism," or what Raymond Durgnat has dubbed "energy realism." As he notes, in this kind of realism "what matters, above all, is the headlong, tense, unbroken, 'you are there' movement of cameras and cast, the confused imbroglio of bodies gestures, shouted accusations, the sense of mounting spectacle" (quoted in Martin 1992: 89). The pursuit of the real is thus performed through highly excessive mediation aiming for "a feeling of fullness, a satiety of experience, which can be taken as reality" (Bolter and Grusin 1999: 53).

The hypermediated realism as a governing principle of the post-classical narrative logic is one of the most substantial differentiating factors that set the post-classical mode definitively apart from the other historical modes. Against the transparency of the classical image that treats the filmic frame as a window to the world, post-classical narration counter-suggests foregrounding the act of representation and using the frame as a windowed world like the one we currently live in. The hypermediated images are self-conscious images that, nonetheless, do not seek to generate a feeling of estrangement; rather their purpose is to approximate our mediated experience of the world in the digital age. Given that technology has become a second nature in our everyday lives, the presence of mediation no longer contradicts the authenticity of the experience and no longer needs to be hidden (Huhtamo 1995: 171). The post-classical mode puts hypermediacy to the service of a realistic depiction because the audience relates to media forms and materials in a much more organic way than before. As a result, hypermediated realism introduces a new logic for realistically motivating the elements on the screen and updates once again the ever-evolving definition of realism.

ANALYSIS

CASE STUDY A: *SUICIDE SQUAD* (2016)

Based on the homonymous DC comic, *Suicide Squad* is a superhero film directed by David Ayer. Its story focuses on an exceptionally hazardous operation: in order to combat a rising surge of metahuman threats, a top intelligence officer, Amanda Waller (Viola Davis), gets the US government to form a highly unconventional task force consisting of criminals and supervillains. In fact, the stellar ensemble of characters is so extensive that the plot dedicates the first hour to the exposition of their key traits and backstories. This typically post-classical compositional element is coupled with a hypermediated presentation of story material that combines the cinematic frame with the logic of video games and graphic novels.

Starting with the character presentation, Ayer chooses to accompany Waller's description of the potential members of the Task Force X with inserts that blend diegetic scenes with nondiegetic images. For instance, Floyd Lawton—aka Deadshot (Will Smith)—is presented as follows:

1 a close-up on his file with Deadshot's mugshot (Figure 1.25)
2 the mugshot transforms into a CGI image (Figure 1.26)
3 a CGI sequence emulates the video-game player format (Figure 1.27)
4 a diegetic scene shows Deadshot in action (Figure 1.28)
5 a scene with Waller talking about Deadshot's daughter (Figure 1.29)
6 a flashback showing Deadshot and his daughter (Figure 1.30)
7 a scene with Waller explaining how she got him arrested (Figure 1.31)
8 a flashback where Deadshot is arrested by Batman (Figure 1.32)

FIGURE 1.25

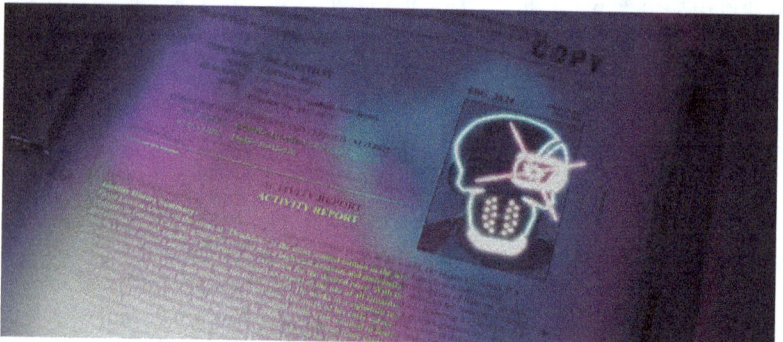

FIGURE 1.26

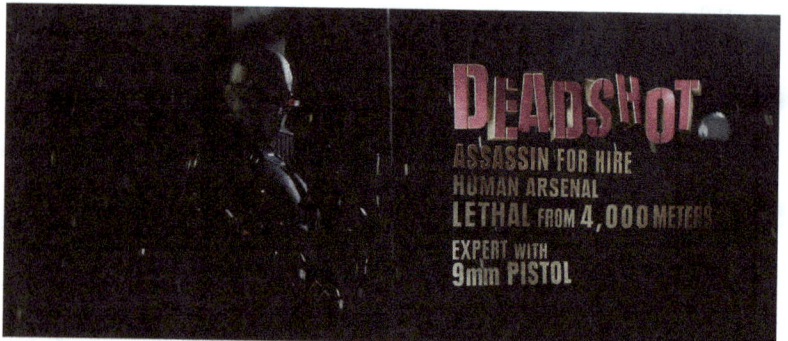

FIGURE 1.27

FIGURE 1.28

FIGURE 1.29

FIGURE 1.30

FIGURE 1.31

FIGURE 1.32

The film returns to Waller, who continues with another inmate from Belle Reve Penitentiary called Harley Quinn (Margot Robbie), a former psychiatrist who became Joker's (Jared Leto) partner in crime. Her exposition is similar to Deadshot's, containing CGI images and revelatory flashbacks (Figures 1.33–1.34).

FIGURE 1.33

FIGURE 1.34

These narrational devices seek to transmit story information through a constant hypermediated play that treats the filmic elements as malleable entities for emulating different media formats. Both in terms of space and time, the narration relishes creative freedom. It goes to impossible places, offers impossible views and moves back and forth between different moments in the story, hoping to serve the compositional needs of the plot. It is important to underline that the post-classical mode has these two motivations working in tandem; hypermediated realism remains in thrall to the post-classical story.

The element of hypermediacy is also quite prominent in the combat scenes where the visual effects, the slow motion, and the lighting schemes mix the cinematic with the graphic novel and the video game aesthetics. The end result is an energetic realism that depicts faithfully the paradox entailed in the adaptation of a superhero comic, namely to breathe plausibility into characters and situations that are supernatural. As Ayer confesses, "The trick for me is how do you take the tropes and set pieces of a comic book movie and ground them in incredibly believable ways? I want a movie where you feel like you could pass that shot on the street and not know that's fake" (quoted in Chitwood 2016). *Suicide Squad* portrays the story in realistic terms without betraying the intermedial nature of the superhero genre.

CASE STUDY B: *SCOTT PILGRIM VS. THE WORLD* (2010)

Listed among the 100 Greatest Cult Films, *Scott Pilgrim vs. the World* is a romantic comedy that stands out for the hypermediated logic of not only its visual style, but also of its plot structure. Despite flopping at the box office during its first run in 2010, Edgar Wright's film garnered favorable reviews—as well as an enthusiastic cult—in subsequent years (Olson 2018: 210). The film features the story of Scott Pilgrim (Michael Cera), who falls in love with Ramona Flowers (Mary Elizabeth Winstead), and tries to win her over by battling her seven evil ex-partners. The classical formula of "boy meets girl" is brilliantly transformed through the post-classical norms into a highly enjoyable visual experience that merges the cinematic aspects with those of the graphic novel and the video game.

From the opening moments we are struck by the "visual onomatopoeia," i.e., the appearance of words that match the sounds in the storyworld. For example, when the doorbell rings, "DING DONG" flashes on the screen in complete synchronization with the actual sound, generating a form of hypermediated redundancy (Figure 1.35).

Moreover, various words like "Blam," "Krow," or "Pow" appear in moments of action in a highly stylized fashion in terms of font, speed, and other transition effects. These choices can be motivated in multiple ways: compositionally (the sound of action), realistically (intensifying the feeling of the moment), generically (convention of the graphic novel/video game) and artistically (allusion to other cultural products) (Figures 1.36–1.37).

FIGURE 1.35

FIGURE 1.36

FIGURE 1.37

Apart from the sounds, other elements of the story are conveyed through the logic of hypermediacy. For instance, when we enter Scott's shared apartment, the narration gives us an "ownership diagram," which specifies the items that belong to him and his roommate Wallace (Kieran Culkin) (Figure 1.38). The camera pans to reveal the photographic parts of the *mise-en-scène* (the décor, lighting, staging) while the frame becomes gradually overlaid by text identifying the characters' possessions. Later on, Scott goes to the bathroom and, while peeing in the urinal, a "peebar" on the right informs us of the diminishing levels of urine in his body (Figure 1.39). Although narrational redundancy has always been a staple of classical Hollywood cinema as part of its realism, the post-classical mode opts for a self-conscious play with redundancy via the treatment of the screen as a graphic surface.

FIGURE 1.38

FIGURE 1.39

Another recurrent device is the use of split screens that emulate the look of the graphic novel, dividing the screen horizontally or vertically in several pieces that either contain faces or fragments of the action (Figures 1.40–1.42). This visual effect combined with the energy of the depicted events give the audience the chance to experience the story in a hypermediated environment. The connection to the original sources becomes even more direct when Wright inserts animated sequences as episodic flashbacks that give away backstory information (Figure 1.43).

FIGURE 1.40

FIGURE 1.41

FIGURE 1.42

FIGURE 1.43

Admittedly, however, the most impressive feature is the depiction of Scott's fights with the seven exes. In those scenes, the hypermediated nature of the film reaches an apex, as the narration embeds the styles and the conventions of numerous media, both new and old. Johannes Fehrle insightfully describes the first fight as follows:

> In the fighting sequence we do not only have the remediation of arcade fighting and beat 'em up video games (...) but also a TV aesthetic, the film's foregrounding of its own mediality as well as a play with some iconic film genres, a remediation of the comics medium, and finally a strong link to the theater as a fifth medium thrown into the mix when we see Ramona on a Shakespearean balcony placed at the center of an extremely conspicuous spotlight.
>
> FEHRLE 2015: 9–10

The presence of a long media history as well as an eclectic selection of fighting styles in the depiction of the battles does not diminish the excitement of the audience as they watch the protagonist trying to win his girl. The self-conscious traces of other media in the filmic representation do not aim at creating a feeling of estrangement. In fact, they achieve quite the opposite. As Lida Zeitlin Wu aptly notes, "despite the impossibility of the events that ensue, both viewers and characters suspend their disbelief," adding that Wright's expressed intention was to "embrace the magical realism of comic books" (Wu 2016: 421).

Overall, the role of hypermediacy within the post-classical narrative logic inaugurates a new kind of realism that profits from the expressive potential of transmediality and invests in our experience and familiarity with diverse media forms. As a result, *Scott Pilgrim vs. the World* can flaunt its ties to the graphic novel and the video game without diminishing the audience's ability to engage with the characters and their adventures.

1.3.2 Subjective Realism

The second type of realism identified in post-classical narration is subjective realism, i.e., a tendency to represent mental processes or emotional conditions. The plot is often taken over by the characters' dreams, thoughts, hallucinations, and feelings. Subjective realism is not anything new in the poetic history of cinema, but it has been utilized for different artistic purposes within various creative contexts. For instance, French impressionist film in the 1920s deployed techniques like superimposition for rendering subjective images, while art cinema in the 1950s and 1960s embraced subjective realism as part of its exploration of the human condition. According to Branigan, a filmic narration—at its most basic level—performs what he calls "internal focalization" in depth, penetrating the characters' brain and allowing us a glimpse into their innermost places (Branigan 1992). In post-classical storytelling, the internal focalization is often combined with the highest levels of narration, i.e., the nondiegetic narrators, to complicate the narrational act, on the one hand, and to render it communicative and accessible to the audience, on the other.[4]

The widespread presence of subjective realism in post-classical narratives is derivative of and interwoven with two aforementioned post-classical norms, namely modified character-centered causality and hypermediated realism. Regarding the former, we discussed how post-classical protagonists are partly driven by personal goals, while narration dedicates significant plot time to the exploration of their personalities as a means for justifying their external behavior. Both subconscious drives and inner motives are often addressed, compelling the narration to enter their minds in search for answers. In many cases, these characters suffer from extreme conditions that transform the cinematic frame into a portal into their soul. In *Fight Club*, for instance, the schizophrenic personality of the unnamed protagonist provides a thematic pretext for the visualization of his brain processes, stretching the boundaries of what can be represented and what not. The frame becomes a vehicle of his stream of consciousness to the extent that, for a considerable part of the plot, we are hardly aware of the distinction between the internal and the external world.

The post-classical mode broadens the palette of cinematic representation developing a form of subjective realism that exceeds the limits of previous historical instances focused mostly on memories, dreams, and hallucinations. A wide range of feelings, such as anger, sadness, disappointment, fear, confusion, and happiness, are visualized through highly inventive techniques that transmit the characters' experience in a staggering fashion. In *Amélie*, for instance, the feeling of elation and gratitude is conveyed through a yellow glow surrounding the body of the character, whereas the feeling of despair is emulated through the transformation of the heroine into falling water. And these moments reveal the close collaboration between subjective and hypermediated realism within the post-classical paradigm. Specifically, the logic of hypermediacy reinforces the use of new technological tools for dramatizing the mental processes and other highly subjective and emotional experiences in a mannerist but, nonetheless, realistic way. In sharp contrast with the logic of art cinema, the subjective realism of post-classical films does not aim at ambiguity or introversion; it expresses the need for a heightening of reality and for duplicating the energy and the intensity of real-life experiences. The representation of the psychological states and feelings of the characters is thus significantly hypermediated and excessive, while remaining engaging and accessible to the audience.

ANALYSIS

CASE STUDY: *REQUIEM FOR A DREAM* (2000)

In *Requiem for a Dream*, Darren Aronofsky depicts the struggle of four people with drug addiction. The trajectories of these individuals converge and diverge several times before finally reaching separate but equally horrific destinations. A lonely older woman called Sara Goldfarb (Ellen Burstyn) becomes addicted to a TV show and starts taking diet pills in the hope of fitting into a beautiful red dress and appearing on the show. Her son Harry (Jared Leto), along with his girlfriend Marion (Jennifer Connelly) and their friend Tyrone (Marlon Wayans), are heroin addicts who try a series of get-rich-quick schemes that involve selling drugs.

The dominant theme of addiction inspires numerous sequences of subjective realism in the plot, illustrating how the compositional motivation collaborates with the realistic to build a very intense and multi-layered representation of the characters' dependence on drugs. The subjective experience of external reality becomes Aronofsky's focus throughout the entire narration, with the device of the split screen used as one of his creative tools. From the very first sequence, the argument between Harry and his mother over a TV set is shot with the two protagonists in two different screens (Figure 1.44) to show how they "were having two completely different subjective experiences of the same event," as he explains (quoted in Pizzello 2000: 57).

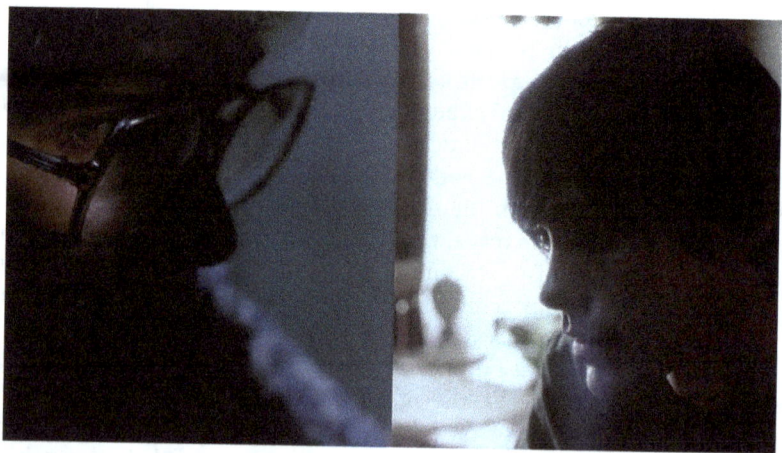

FIGURE 1.44

The depiction of subjective experience is further accentuated in the moments of drug use, this time via graphic and rhythmic editing.

Specifically, an accelerating series of extreme close-ups of white powder, a lighter, a mixture of substances boiling, the syringe, their arms, the injection, the reaction in their blood, and the dilation of their pupils flash on the screen momentarily, seeking to emulate the energy that the drugs induce in their bodies (Figures 1.45–1.47). The cutting pace then slows down and their euphoric state is indicated with a white dissolve (Figure 1.48).

A similar strategy to transmit the inner energy is found in the party scene, where the fish-eye distortion of the lens and the speeded-up action convey the intensity of the characters' feelings under the influence of drugs (Figure 1.49).

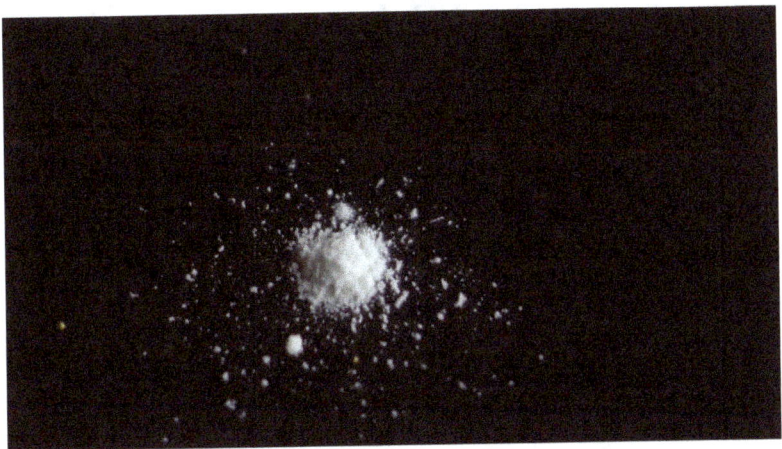

FIGURE 1.45

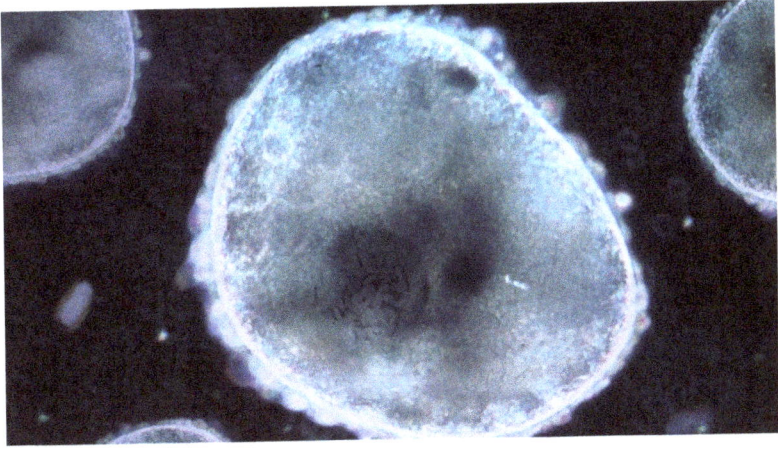

FIGURE 1.46

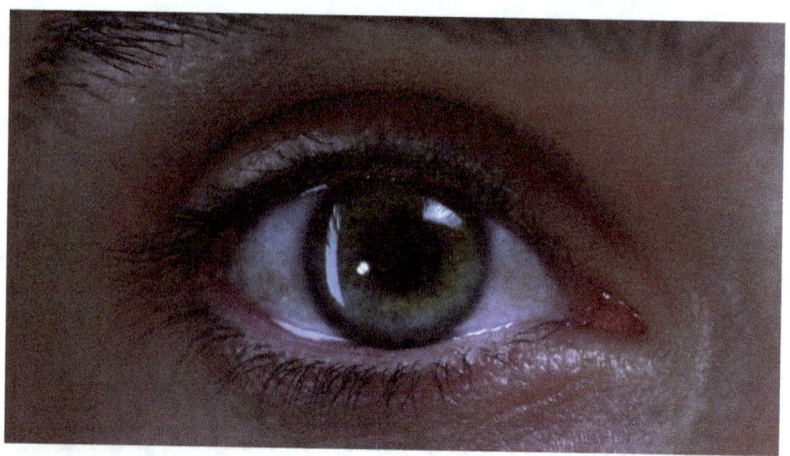

FIGURE 1.47

FIGURE 1.48

FIGURE 1.49

On the other hand, Sara's addiction to the TV show and the diet pills is often portrayed through a series of hallucinations. For instance, a five-minute-long hallucination begins with Sara watching TV and imagining herself on the show with her red dress. Suddenly, however, the host steps out of the screen, and her apartment is transformed into a TV stage. The audience and the crew revolve around her frantically, yelling "feed me, Sara" while she sits in her armchair looking horrified (Figure 1.50). Finally, when the refrigerator bursts open, trying to devour her, she runs to the street in a state of shock. Sara's deteriorating mental condition is rendered through extended subjective sequences that transform the frame into a hypermediated world of chaos and suffering.

FIGURE 1.50

CASE STUDY B: *SLUMDOG MILLIONAIRE* (2008)

The story of Jamal Malik, an eighteen-year-old from the slums of Mumbai who hits the jackpot on *Who Wants to Be a Millionaire*, is narrated through the standard post-classical norms, with subjective realism standing out as one of the key tropes. In fact, the entire plot is drafted in a way that invites Jamal's recollections, revealing piece by piece the secret of his success.

The film opens in 2006 with a torture scene: Jamal is held captive and abused by the Mumbai police, disputing his ability to answer the questions on the quiz show without cheating (Figure 1.51).

FIGURE 1.51

At that point, Jamal had unexpectedly won 10 million rupees and would be taking part in the next episode, one question away from the Grand Prize. The purpose of the interrogation is to discover an incidence of fraud and disqualify him from the game. The ingenuity of the narration in *Slumdog Millionaire* consists in the complex interweaving of the diegetic level with the internal focalization on the protagonist's mind where all the answers of the puzzle lie. For example, the first question—"Who was the star in the 1973 hit film *Zanjeer*?"—stirs his childhood memory of the day he had to jump into a cesspit in order to get an autograph from Bollywood star Amitabh Bachchan. That memorable experience provides him with the right answer. The next question probes an even more painful memory. When the host asks "In depictions of the god Rama, he is famously holding what in his right hand?," the words instantly trigger a flashback on the day he lost his mother in a religious riot. As the incident comes to a close, the memory appears next to Jamal's face (Figure 1.52). To indicate the traumatic effect of that experience and the recurring presence of those images in his mind, Jamal confesses, "I wake up every morning wishing I didn't know the answer to that question."

FIGURE 1.52

As the film goes on, the process of confession to the two police officers, intertwined with other moments of introspection, causes sustained and often abrupt changes in the narrative levels, moving in and out of the protagonist's thoughts in a way that fragments the exposition of the story to a considerable extent. Flashbacks motivated by police interrogations have been regular in classical films, yet the frequency, the depth, and the stylization of the personal reminisces in *Slumdog Millionaire* are exemplary of the role of subjective realism in the post-classical narrative logic. On the one hand, it serves the compositional commitments (the mystery, the romance), while, on the other, it collaborates with hypermediated realism to craft a very dense and highly subjective rendering of a story that paradoxically unfolds in front of the eyes of millions of TV viewers.

1.4 Post-classical Generic Motivation

The third possible type of motivation in a fiction film may be called generic[5] and it justifies the presence of filmic material by means of its relation to the established cinematic genres. Something is justified generically if it pertains to particular generic conventions, as those have been formed by the industry and the audience alike. Post-classical films are genre films that display two distinct tendencies, namely the hybridity and the archaeological celebration of the generic past.

1.4.1 Hybridity

The role of genres in the narrative logic of post-classical storytelling is just as significant as it has been in the classical version for over a century. In Hollywood cinema, genre has always been the locus where industrial concerns meet with the spectatorial pleasure. Generic formulas and conventions regulate the flow of production on one end, while shaping audience expectations on the other. In contrast, art cinema never relied on genres. They were considered as restrictions to the personal expression of the auteurs, diminishing the value of film as a unique artistic creation. In post-classical narration, the generic elements become once again an integral part of the narrative logic, regardless of the production values of the film. Whether we take an independent film like *Requiem for a Dream*, a major studio production like *Natural Born Killers*, or an art film like *Chungking Express*, we find the traces of Hollywood genres (iconography, plot elements, style, structures etc.) as key constructional elements.

Specifically, we discover a playful mixture or juxtaposition of diverse and often incongruent generic codes; in *Chungking Express*, for instance, the romantic comedy meets film noir and melodrama without generating much conflict in the audience's so-called "horizon of expectations" (Neale 1995). One could argue that film noir had also intersected with melodrama in the classical years, as in the example of *Mildred Pierce* (1945). Indeed, generic hybridity was by no means "a rarity," according to Steve Neale, who reminds us that all genres—even the purest ones—sprang out of combinations of disparate elements across separate categories (Neale 1995: 171). What seems to distinguish the post-classical from the classical generic motivation, however, is the extent of selectivity and eclecticism that the former openly parades. Post-classical hybridity becomes not only the norm, but also a knowing juxtaposition of formerly incompatible generic tropes. In this sense, the tendency towards blatant hybridity in post-classical narration derives much less from the need to keep the industrial and spectatorial imperatives in "a ritual/ideological fit," as Rick Altman would call it, but rather from the intention to question and unsettle previous generic regimes (Altman 1995). And this sort of provocation becomes feasible within the post-classical narrative logic thanks to two further changes in this narrative mode, namely the role of parody and the degree of self-consciousness indulged in this framework.

ANALYSIS

CASE STUDY: *THE MILLION DOLLAR HOTEL* (2000)

Wim Wenders' *The Million Dollar Hotel* opens with the protagonist, a young man called Tom Tom (Jeremy Davies) on the roof of an LA hotel, ready to plunge to his death. Before crushing to the ground, he looks inside the rooms of the hotel and catches glimpses of everyday life that make him realize that "life is the best." Using a match-cut and a communicative voice-over, Wenders rewinds the clock to fourteen days earlier, giving the opportunity to the character to recount what led to his tragic fall. Like most post-classical films, the story flaunts an episodic plot populated with many characters, while the voice-over helps maintain a sense of coherence. The compositional elements (characters, goals, events) as well as the stylistic options, are also generically motivated drawing forms and conventions from the murder mystery, the film noir, the romantic comedy, and the satirical film.

On the one hand, the murder mystery and the noir atmosphere contribute to the film's dark melancholic side. The leading character speaks to us from another world, reminding us of *Sunset Boulevard* (1950) and evoking the feeling of hopelessness that pervaded the classical film noir

(Schrader 1995). The investigation of the death of an eccentric junkie called Izzy (Tim Roth) at the Million Dollar Hotel triggers all the familiar semantic elements; Special Agent Skinner (Mel Gibson) arrives at the crime scene as a hard-boiled detective, working for a rich patron (Izzy's multi-millionaire father), lining up the hotel's residents as suspects and gradually revealing the secrets behind Izzy's death. The deadly fall that brackets the plot echoes the tragic fate of most noir heroes, while the lighting style throughout the film, despite the presence of color, reminds us of how the noir characters are trapped in their surroundings (Figures 1.53–1.56).

What differentiates, on the other hand, this post-classical generic mix from its classical antecedents, is the discordant juxtaposition of the dramatic elements with comic situations and satirical tropes overridden by a romantic thread connecting Tom Tom and the female protagonist Eloise (Milla Jovovich). A fallen angel herself—and, rather inadvertently, a femme fatale—Eloise becomes the object of Tom Tom's affection, initiating a relationship that displays the power of unconditional love. In the hotel's derelict setting and among the freaks that reside therein, Tom Tom maintains a lighthearted tone in his voice and brings out the comic side of his troubles. The gatherings of the hotel residents are rife with humorous moments, while the media and the art world are regularly attacked with biting satire.

FIGURE 1.53

FIGURE 1.54

FIGURE 1.55

FIGURE 1.56

Overall, Wenders' complex relation to Hollywood filmmaking is illustrated in the rich generic texture that coats the compositional elements in his story. The characters, their lines, the surroundings, and even the *mise-en-scène* may stem from different generic universes but their blatantly eclectic mixture epitomizes the new possibilities within the post-classical mode and reinvigorates the power of genericity as a means of artistic creation.

1.4.2 Archaeology

Apart from the tendency to reshuffle the generic rules, forms, and conventions of the classical Hollywood tradition, there is also the option of selecting one or two genres—celebrated and obscure ones, alike—and reviving their tropes. In this case, the filmmakers make an archaeological investigation into the cinematic history of a certain genre and bring together a series of distinctive elements as if performing a peculiar form of historical mapping. I have chosen to call this approach "archaeological" for two reasons: one is more literal, while the other is more philosophical in line with a rather Foucauldian spirit.[6] Specifically, we could argue that the generic motivation in these post-classical films can be deemed archaeological because they dig out a series of elements from the history of a genre, along with the material culture that surrounded it. This is, for instance, how Lars von Trier shapes the compositional elements of his story in *Europa*, when he molds his characters and stylizes their actions in a way that revisits all the norms of the classical film noir. On the other hand, it could be considered as "archaeological" in Foucault's sense, because it foregrounds the rules that regulate the generic discourse and lays out all those elements on the filmic surface for us to see. The end result of this creative effort is not merely another film noir; instead, it is a complex piece of storytelling whose generic identity is both comprehensive and fragmented. Such similar attempts we find in Damien Chazelle's *La La Land* (2016) and Marc Webb's *500 Days of Summer* (2009), where the conventions of the classical musicals and the romantic comedies respectively, are carefully excavated and showcased. As with generic hybridity, however, the archaeological approach to classical genres would not be permitted in the post-classical structure if the forces of parody and narrative self-consciousness did not invite the foregrounding of the narrational act. Post-classical generic motivation invests in the audience's knowledge of the classical Hollywood genres and creates a highly engaging viewing experience that plays with the viewers' expectations without disappointing or estranging them.

ANALYSIS

CASE STUDY: *MOULIN ROUGE!* (2001)

Baz Luhrmann's *Moulin Rouge!* was released in 2001 and immediately made its mark for its idiosyncratic approach to the Hollywood musical. Set in Paris, 1900, it depicts the story of Christian (Ewan McGregor), a young British poet who arrives at the famous French cabaret in Montmartre and immediately falls in love with a courtesan called Satine (Nicole Kidman). Their dramatic love affair is tangled with the staging of Christian's play at the Moulin Rouge where Harold Zidler (Jim Broadbent), the club's owner, is determined to stand in the couple's way.

Moulin Rouge! is an ambitious attempt to revisit the musical formula decades after its heyday. As Luhrmann explains, "we did an archaeological dig through the history of the musical. What we found is that the stories don't change but the way you tell them does" (quoted in Fuller 2001: 16). Although his storytelling differs remarkably from the classical way—mostly thanks to the hypermediated realism—the generic motivation draws from the rich musical tradition and inventories some of its most celebrated traits.

Inspired by the "backstage musicals" in the 1930s, *Moulin Rouge!* sets up the plot around the staging of a show and intertwines it with the "offstage" conflicts of the performers. Among the latter, we find a series of staple characters (the theater director, the talented courtesan, the writer, the patron), while the events unfold in familiar steps; the ideal couple in musicals is not usually together in the beginning but gradually works its way out of a complex romantic tangle and celebrates its union in the final show (Schatz 1981: 197). Also from the 1930s, Luhrmann borrows the romantic duets from the operetta tradition, reminding us of Ernst Lubitsch and Rouben Mamoulian's golden moments, while he choreographs some of his musical numbers in the style of Busby Berkeley (Figures 1.57–1.58). Finally, *Moulin Rouge!* also incorporates the norms of the "integrated musical" from the 1940s, deploying songs and dance sequences that advance the plot.

FIGURE 1.57

FIGURE 1.58

Aside from the musical formula, however, the film's generic motivation revisits the key codes of the classical Hollywood melodrama of the 1950s. The star-crossed lovers, the Manichean conflicts between good and evil, and the moral dilemmas of the protagonists take us back to the Sirkian world where adult love always comes with a price. Stylistically, *Moulin Rouge!* also brings to life one of melodrama's most memorable aspects, namely its excessive stylization, which sublimates "dramatic conflict into décor, gesture and composition of frame" (Elsaesser 1991: 76). In addition, the use of coincidences and the uneven distribution of knowledge among the characters are two standard melodramatic devices that contribute to the genre's poignant nature, reaching a climax in the closing scene and fueling the feeling of despair, the feeling of "too late" that leaves us in tears.

Overall, Luhrmann's conscious attempt to dig into the two major Hollywood genres, the musical and the melodrama, produced a film that is not simply another "musical melodrama." Instead, *Moulin Rouge!* knowingly foregrounds the generic conventions of the past, as if offering a "stratigraphic" view of the generic elements in their complex relations and sequences.

1.5 Post-classical Artistic Motivation

The last type of motivation in the narrative logic of a fiction film is called artistic; it consists of all those elements that call attention to the narrational process and expose the means of its construction. In the poetic history of cinema, particularly as it has been documented in the work of David Bordwell, the role of artistic motivation within each historical mode is easily differentiated from the other three kinds (compositional, realistic, generic). In classical narration, artistic motivation is limited because it undermines the workings of the others; in art cinema, it serves the artistic expression of the auteur and counterbalances the principles of objective/subjective realism, whereas in the historical-materialist cinema, it reinforces the ideological purpose of the films within the Communist regime (Bordwell 1985).

Yet to evaluate the role of artistic motivation in the post-classical mode, we need to unravel the notion of "laying bare the device," which was the core objective of this motivation according to the Russian formalists (Shklovsky 1965). Specifically, we cannot explain as "artistic" *everything* that raises our awareness of the means of representation. As I have previously argued, post-classical films contain a high level of self-consciousness that does not always distance us from the storyworld; instead, a fair amount of self-reflexive stylistic and narrative techniques achieve precisely the opposite. They constitute an integral part of the hypermediated realism that seeks to immerse us into a powerful diegesis. These devices, which have become normalized mainstream conventions, create a discontinuous and self-conscious act of representation as a strategy for capturing the real through hypermediacy. Therefore, the majority of hypermediated images in a post-classical film are motivated realistically and not artistically. There is, however, a very strong artistic motivation in post-classical narration in the form of parody. In fact, the widespread use of parody within the post-classical narrative logic constitutes another major differentiating factor between the classical and the post-classical. Whereas classical storytelling avoided parody for fear of laying bare the device, the post-classical mode consistently embraces it without jeopardizing the functions of other motivations. On the contrary, parody layers the compositional elements with an additional historical/artistic significance and reinforces the generic elements with a sense of playful historicity.

1.5.1 Parody

Parody is a significant form of contemporary self-reflexivity that establishes a relation between two different pieces of art, or even more broadly, between two different cultural works. It is an "inter-art discourse," as Linda Hutcheon calls it, defining parody as "repetition with critical distance, which marks difference rather than similarity" (Hutcheon 2000: 6). In the case of cinema, we could describe parody as the strategy of revisiting, recalling, and re-writing forms and conventions from the long media and art tradition aiming to establish a meaningful artistic dialogue. This parodic dialogue between the old and the new elements—this "repetition with a difference"—results in a critical re-evaluation of both and encourages us to reflect on the historicity of form.

Approaching parody through Hutcheon's neutral and spacious definition, we can account for several formal and structural characteristics found in post-classical films whose purpose is to create an involvement with and a distance from other works with ironic or estrangement effects. As she explains, "parody paradoxically enacts both change and cultural continuity: the Greek prefix para can mean both 'counter' or 'against' and 'near' or 'beside'" (Hutcheon 1988: 26). Therefore, parody should not be viewed through a restrictive lens either as an American genre or a sub-genre of comedy. Neither should it always be expected to generate laughter. As Gary Saul Morson explains, "parody recontextualizes its object so as to make it serve tasks contrary to its original tasks, but this functional shift need not be in the direction of humor" (Morson 1989: 69).

Aside from parody, there is a series of other terms that describe similar processes, such as "reference," "quotation," "homage," "allusion," or "pastiche." The line separating these intertextual relations is never definitive because the distinctions depend on degrees of intertextuality, authorial intentions, or ideological implications that are never easily substantiated or quantified. I have opted for the term "parody" as a form of artistic motivation, because it encompasses a wide variety of intertextual relations detected in post-classical works and it foregrounds the element of "ironic distance" that I consider to be of essence. Whether they refer to past genres, auteurs, specific scenes, stylistic choices, or even dialogues from other works, post-classical narratives imbue their compositional and generic elements with an additional layer of meaning that disrupts the diegetic world, at least for those who are aware, aiming to establish a critical dialogue between the diegetic and the extra-diegetic material.

ANALYSIS

CASE STUDY A: *DEADPOOL* (2016)

Tim Miller's *Deadpool* is an American superhero film and one of the few post-classical cases in the Marvel Cinematic Universe, which otherwise remains predominantly classical. The plot presents the adventures of Wade Wilson (Ryan Reynolds), a former special forces officer who is diagnosed with cancer. An experimental treatment leaves his entire body brutally scarred but endows him with a superhuman healing ability. Wade adopts the name Deadpool and takes on the mission to track down the man who performed the treatment, hoping to find the cure. This deceptively classical premise is represented on the screen in a most outspoken post-classical manner with the element of parody unequivocally noticeable.

As early as the opening credits, *Deadpool* ironically nods to the superhero comic tradition by listing the actors and actresses not by name but as stereotypes, such as "a hot chick," "a British villain," "the comic relief," "a CGI character," and "a gratuitous cameo" (Figures 1.59–1.60).

FIGURE 1.59

FIGURE 1.60

Similarly, Wade openly acknowledges his fictional status by regularly breaking the fourth wall and commenting on textual and extratextual issues involving other Marvel films, particularly those from the *X-Men* franchise. Throughout the film, the characters, the *mise-en-scène*, and even the cinematography are constantly double-coded; on the one hand, they perform their compositional function, i.e., they progress the story, while, on the other, they instigate a parodic dialogue with notable works from the long history of cinema and television.

On IMDB we find a list of over seventy films and TV shows that are openly referenced either through iconography, dialogue, or story action. For instance, Wade's first mask after the accident is inspired by James Whale's classic *The Invisible Man* (1933) (Figure 1.61), while later his opponent comments on his disfigurement with the line "hello, gorgeous!," echoing Barbara Streisand in *Funny Girl* (1968). On other occasions scenes from well-known films motivate the protagonist or foreshadow the action. Before cutting his hand off, for example, Deadpool turns to the audience asking if they have seen *127 Hours* (2010) and declares "a spoiler alert." This constant awareness of the filmic construction and the flagrant reference to other artworks generates a level of artistic motivation that cannot go unnoticed. Even after the end credits, Deadpool returns to parody the post-credit scene of *Ferris Bueller's Day Off* (1986), where Ferris (Matthew Broderick) in a bathrobe tells the audience to go home (Figure 1.62). In his take, Deadpool wears a similar garment (Figure 1.63) and rehashes some of the lines while also giving away information about the sequel.

Overall, the creators of *Deadpool* meticulously crafted a diegetic world that tirelessly reaches out to extratextual elements and never ceases to remind the audience of the film's constructed nature. In *Deadpool* we find a typical example of post-classical artistic motivation, a type of motivation that significantly differentiates this new mode from the preceding ones.

FIGURE 1.61

FIGURE 1.62

FIGURE 1.63

CASE STUDY B: *GODARD MON AMOUR* (2017)

Michel Hazanavicius' biopic about Jean-Luc Godard and his marriage to Anne Wiazemsky in the late 1960s becomes another opportunity for the French director to celebrate the history of cinema through parody. Focusing on the life of one of the most emblematic figures of European cinema, and particularly his struggle to transform cinema through radical politics, *Godard Mon Amour* is a playful exercise in film language that seeks to reflect the philosophical and personal dilemmas of its protagonist.

In the opening scene we hear Anne's voice reciting a description of Godard as a pioneering filmmaker while he appears to shoot a scene from *La Chinoise* (1967) (Figure 1.64). The film presents the main character through her eyes and the reference to the story's literary source, namely Wiazemsky's memoir *Un an après*, is demonstrated not only via the stylized voice-over but also the initial framing of her character (Figure 1.65).

FIGURE 1.64

FIGURE 1.65

Yet, as expectedly, it is cinema that permeates the entire narration of *Godard Mon Amour*. At the level of the story, the film begins with *La Chinoise* and ends with *Vent d'Est* (1970) in order to highlight Godard's creative crisis and his transition to a new phase in his career; one that required the rejection of his popular work and the experimentation with collaborative filmmaking. Whereas Jean-Luc argues about the bourgeois superfluousness of films like *A bout de souffle* (1960) and *Le Mépris* (1963), Hazanavicius pays tribute to those memorable cinematic moments by emulating their aesthetics. For instance, one of the recurring devices is the stylized presentation of the female body, which reminds the viewers of Godard's famous female characters and their iconic moments (Figures 1.66–1.68).

FIGURE 1.66

FIGURE 1.67

FIGURE 1.68

At the same time, the film plays tricks on the leading character by deploying the expressive means he desperately seeks to leave behind: long-tracking shots, close-ups, intertitles (Figure 1.69), negative images (Figure 1.70), looks to camera (Figure 1.71–1.72) and a color palette that is uniquely tied to Godard's filmography. In Figure 1.73 for instance, the décor consists of the three key colors (blue, white, red) that instantly bring to mind *Pierrot le Fou* (1965).

FIGURE 1.69

FIGURE 1.70

FIGURE 1.71

FIGURE 1.72

FIGURE 1.73

Even if the parodic connections evade those who are unfamiliar with the content of Godard's work, Hazanavicius makes sure that some intertextual references become intelligible anyway. For example, the plot is sliced into chapters that bear titles such as "Pierrot le Mépris" or "Sauve qui peut (les meubles)," making sure that the parodic dialogue with the filmic past cannot go unheeded. Finally, Jean-Luc and Anne are regularly seen at the movies, watching films that reflect the mood of their relationship. The most notable of those moments comes during the screening of *The Passion of Joan of Arc* (1928) where the film builds a brilliant *mise-en-abyme* structure of art imitating art, as we watch Jeanne d'Arc's tears sync with Anne's (Figures 1.74–1.75).

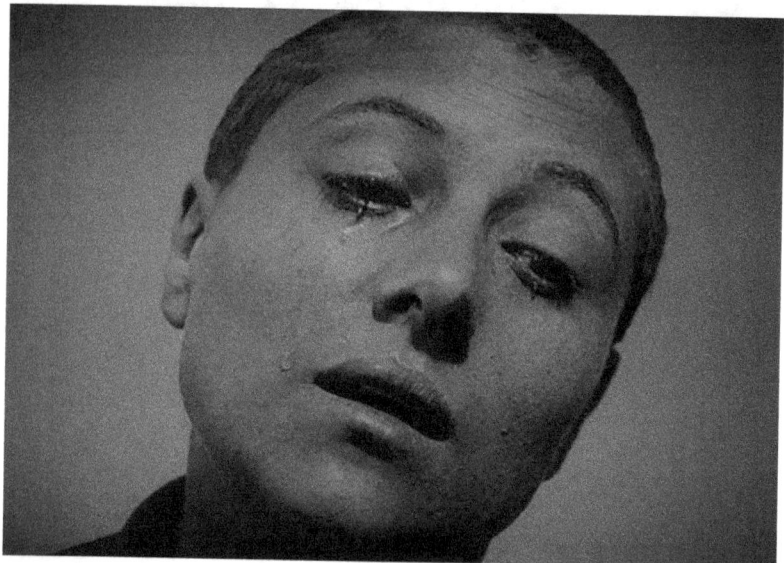

FIGURE 1.74

FIGURE 1.75

> Overall, *Godard Mon Amour* features a post-classical narration on many counts, one of which is the parodic motivation that complements the story's compositional elements. Every frame and every scene constantly strive to serve a double purpose—namely, to depict a period in Godard's life while imbuing the story events and their formal representation with Godard's own artistic work as well as with other milestones in the history of cinema.

1.6 Conclusion

The post-classical narrative logic is an exceptionally intricate edifice that accommodates complex and fascinating stories such as those analyzed above. Regardless of the enormous variety of the case studies, the consistency of the creative norms of post-classical storytelling is still impressive. The system of narrative logic in this new mode activates all four types of motivation, extending and enriching their devices. The compositional motivation dwells on a self-conscious character presentation and a modified character-centered causality that acknowledges a complex web of forces, both human and nonhuman, while the plot is presented in various forms of episodic structures. The realistic motivation, on the other hand, introduces an entirely new philosophy for approximating reality through hypermediated images. The screen becomes a fragmented surface that represents the rich sensorium of human experience while often infiltrating the most subjective and internal processes. Moreover, post-classical narrative logic embraces the generic conventions of the past, either by mixing formerly incompatible formulas or by commemorating the rich generic history in an archaeological spirit. Finally, the artistic motivation adds yet another layer of signification to the filmic material by establishing an ironic dialogue with other cultural works, particularly from the long cinematic past. This elaborate narrative agenda, however, could never materialize without the full support of the other two narrative systems: space and time.

Notes

1 Branigan's theory of narration will be discussed in detail in Chapter 4.
2 There are various definitions of the term "diegesis," drawing a different line each time between what is contained and what not therein. The only unequivocal point is that everything nondiegetic is accessible only to the viewer and not to those within the storyworld. See Thanouli (2013a).
3 The logic of hypermediacy also foregrounds the inherently intermedial nature of every medium, openly confirming Bolter and Grusin's following statement: "a

medium is that which remediates. It is that which appropriates the techniques, forms, and social significance of other media and attempts to rival or refashion them in the name of the real" (Bolter and Grusin 1999: 98). Thus, post-classical works emphasize their intermedial characteristics, emulating an extensive array of other media, both old and new (painting, literature, video games, animation, and comic books), as several of the case studies attest.

4   The concepts of the "levels of narration," "self-consciousness," "knowledgeability," and "communicativeness" will be analyzed in Chapter 4.

5   In Bordwell's account of classical narration, the third type of motivation is called "intertextual" with generic motivation as its most common subcategory (Bordwell et al. 1985: 18). In my account of the post-classical mode, the generic motivation is a type of motivation in its own right, whereas the more complex issue of intertextuality becomes part of the artistic motivation for reasons that I explain in the respective section.

6   For Foucault's concept of "archaeology" and its application to historical research in the cinema, see Thanouli (2018).

2

Post-classical Space

2.1 Introduction

The system of narrative space is the second major axis that we identify in every filmic narration, alongside the narrative logic and the narrative time. A fiction film portrays the characters and their actions within a specific setting, deploying a wide range of stylistic techniques for the representation of the spatial features of the story. Traditionally, the cinematic space is distinguished into two major dimensions: 1) the space "in frame," i.e., the space held and organized within each frame; and 2) the space "out of frame," i.e., the space created by the editing of the shots or the camera movements (Heath 1986: 390). In most films, the two kinds of filmic space are combined in order to serve the process of narrativization, which turns the two-dimensional filmic image into a three-dimensional storyworld that can host the actions of the characters.

Every historical mode of narration handles the role of cinematic space differently. In classical narration, for example, the system of narrative logic holds the reins. As a result, the frame composition and the editing collaborate consistently in the effort to subordinate space to the compositional and realistic motivations. Specifically, the former requires the prominence of the story information, the character development and the centrality of the action, while the latter regards the filmic frame as a transparent window onto the fictional world. Thus, the classical space is a photographic space that favours staging in depth, linear perspective, central positioning, and continuity editing. In art cinema, on the other hand, the drive for a different sort of objective and subjective realism, as well as the creative freedom of the authorial commentary, allow the cinematic space to come to prominence and develop a range of forms. Art films may feature real locations, highly subjective places or, occasionally, graphic spaces that point to the authorial presence.

In the post-classical mode, the graphic qualities of the filmic frame come centre stage. Although classical elements can also be traced,[1] the dominant logic for generating images in post-classical narration lies on the notion of cinematic space as graphic space. This transition from the photographic to the graphic derives from the passage to a hypermediated realism that invites the fragmentation of the representation and brings the medium materiality to the fore. The new system of cinematic space replaces the classical continuity with intensified continuity and the classical editing with spatial montage. The post-classical space is a layered space that openly deploys special effects, such as back projections, CGI, split screens, miniatures, and other tricks, both analogue and digital. Yet the post-classical space remains a *story space*. The flaunted constructedness of the spatial features does not relinquish their narrative strength. The post-classical system of space obeys the mandates of the post-classical narrative logic, sustaining all four types of motivation, from the compositional to the artistic. The three key strategies for fulfilling the narrative purposes of the post-classical film through the construction of cinematic space are intensified continuity, the graphic frame, and spatial montage.

KEY CONCEPTS

2.2 Intensified Continuity

The term "intensified continuity" was coined by Bordwell to describe a set of new stylistic techniques in contemporary American cinema. Having analyzed closely an extensive body of works from the 1960s to the 2000s, he concluded that "far from rejecting traditional continuity in the name of fragmentation and incoherence, the new style amounts to an intensification of established techniques. Intensified continuity is traditional continuity amped up, raised to a higher pitch of emphasis" (Bordwell 2006: 120). Specifically, this higher pitch of emphasis is achieved through an increasing cutting rate, the use of bipolar extremes of lens lengths, a reliance on tight singles instead of master shots, and, finally, the fluidity of a free-ranging camera.

Before looking more closely into these four stylistic innovations, it is important to stress that Bordwell considers the emergence of intensified continuity as proof of the persistence of classicism rather than a passage to a post-classical phase. Indeed, most of the film examples in his analysis do fit the classical formula, while cases that I consider to be typically post-classical like *Requiem for a Dream* or *Moulin Rouge!* are mentioned only in passing without any in-depth consideration of their overall narrative structure. In fact, intensified continuity viewed as four stylistic devices is too limited a criterion to prove the classification of a film in any narrative mode.

And this is a point that Bordwell inadvertently corroborates when writing that intensified continuity "has become the baseline style for both international mass-market cinema and a sizable fraction of exportable 'art cinema'" (Bordwell 2006: 141). In other words, the technical devices that intensify the representation of the plot can be incorporated in different cinematic traditions, ranging from Hollywood blockbusters to international art films, without determining in a definitive manner the narrative "identity" of a film. In each case the function of intensified continuity differs, depending on the other narrative elements at work. In the post-classical system of narrative space, the style of intensified continuity is fully embraced for the purposes of hypermediated realism, i.e., the desire to capture the energy of the action and heighten our experience of the storyworld. The expressive qualities of the new stylistic devices are deployed persistently, compelling our attention and augmenting the emotional impact of every scene. Let us briefly review the four key devices that constitute this new type of continuity before proceeding to the case studies, which will showcase them in greater detail.

First and foremost, the intensity of this new style results from the rapid editing pace reflected in the drastic diminution of the average shot length (ASL).[2] While the average ASL of a Hollywood film from the period 1930–60 ranged from eight to eleven seconds, the typical feature today is likely to have an ASL of between three to six seconds. Such a fast cutting rate has led to an elliptical type of editing that eliminates many of the redundancies of classical continuity, such as the many establishing shots and the long two-shots. Second, a higher visual impact is achieved through the extensive use of extreme lens lengths, namely wide-angle and telephoto lenses. They are both deployed in unusual circumstances to produce distorting effects. For instance, a wide-angle lens filming the close-up of a face warps the edges and amplifies the distances between the front and back planes. Telephoto lenses, on the other hand, are transformed into an "all-purpose tool, available to frame close-ups, medium shots, over-the-shoulder shots, and even establishing shots" (126–7). Third, intensified continuity dictates the closer framing of the action, especially in dialogue scenes, as well as the abandonment of the *plans américains* and the group framings. Finally, the exploration of the story space becomes possible with the free-ranging camera movements facilitated by lighter filming equipment and flexible cameras. In the place of establishing shots or stable group gatherings, the new style introduces an "omnipotent" camera that can move in all directions; it can follow the characters wherever they go and penetrate even the most impossible spaces, both real and imaginary. All in all, the result of all four techniques is a more dynamic cinematic space that becomes malleable to the complex demands of the post-classical narrative logic.

ANALYSIS

CASE STUDY A: *THE WOLF OF WALL STREET* (2013)

With several post-classical films under his belt, such as *Goodfellas* (1990), *Casino* (1995), and *Gangs of New York* (2002), Martin Scorsese chose to depict the life of Jordan Belfort (Leonardo DiCaprio), a New York stockbroker, with the help of the post-classical norms. For the visual style, he collaborated with cinematographer Rodrigo Prieto, who viewed the film as a challenge in terms of the technical devices required "to capture the energy Scorsese wanted" (quoted in Goldman 2013). Selecting a wide array of film stocks, combining analogue and digital technologies, and exploring the powers of intensified continuity, Scorsese and Preto crafted a complex filmic space that sought to match Belfort's exuberant life.

Starting with the cutting rate, *The Wolf of Wall Street* exhibits an ASL of 4.7 seconds, maintaining a brisk tempo from start to finish. The rapid editing is coupled with other techniques, such as whiplash pans and swift reframings, ideal for transmitting the bustling energy of the stock trading business. Moreover, the blatant use of rack focus, as demonstrated in Figures 2.1–2.2, creates a very palpable cinematic frame that epitomizes the post-classical paradox, namely the ability to combine narrative self-consciousness with story progression.

In relation to the extreme lens lengths, Prieto consistently used wide-angle lenses for interior shots in the offices. In Figure 2.3 we see Mark Hanna (Matthew McConaughey) in a wide composition where the distorting effect is exaggerated to emulate "the sense of instability," as Prieto explains (quoted in Goldman 2013). The wide lens is also used in tight spaces, as in Figure 2.4, with the curved edges of the frame matching Belfort's playful tone.

FIGURE 2.1

FIGURE 2.2

FIGURE 2.3

FIGURE 2.4

At the same time, the telephoto lens is a recurrent option in the film, especially in scenes that seek to single out the main protagonist from his crowded surroundings. Belfort's performance is often accentuated with the flattening effect of the telephoto lens that allows him to stand out from his colleagues, whether positioned in the background (Figure 2.5) or in the foreground (Figure 2.6).

In terms of framing, *The Wolf of Wall Street* complies with the logic of intensified continuity that opts for close views, particularly of faces and objects. In Figure 2.7 we see a typical shot of Belfort addressing the camera, as he does throughout the film, with half his forehead remaining off-screen. Similarly, Figure 2.8 shows the conversation between him and his wife in a significantly tighter framing than the classical shot/reverse-shot. The intimacy of the camera with the characters and the storyworld is also a regular feature, as illustrated in the extreme close-up of the nostril (Figure 2.9) and the piece of paper (Figure 2.10).

FIGURE 2.5

FIGURE 2.6

FIGURE 2.7

FIGURE 2.8

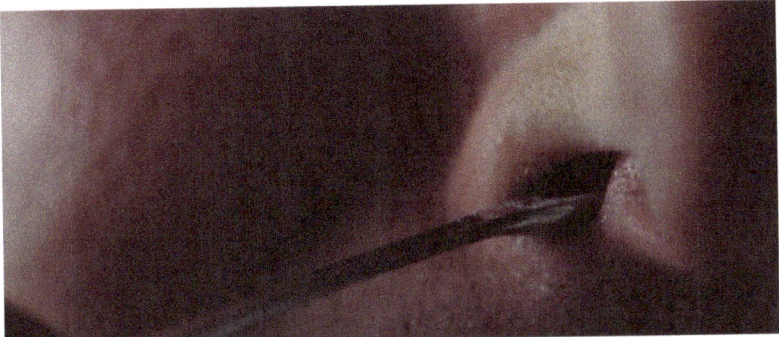

FIGURE 2.9

FIGURE 2.10

Finally, the filmic space seeks to transmit the dynamics of the characters and the plot with powerful camera movements. In fact, the scenes in the crammed office spaces with dozens of brokers talking on the phone, exchanging information, and fighting for profit, are shot with a combination of swift cuts and fluid tracking shots among desks and chairs, following the frantic gestures of the bodies and keeping us "in the moment." A series of push-ins and pull-outs on the feverish faces blend motion and speed in the effort to constantly place the audience right at the heart of the action. Throughout the film, the camera follows the protagonists, moves in all directions, and penetrates possible and impossible spaces alike, contributing to the post-classical construction of space and its key objectives.

CASE STUDY B: *OLDBOY* (2003)

Park Chan-wook's *Oldboy* was released in 2003 as the second installment of a trilogy on the theme of revenge. Its complex plot relies heavily on a convoluted compositional motivation that twists the characters' goals and delays the exposition of their dark secrets. The temporal and the spatial axes in the film follow suit, emulating the density and the layered nature of its key narrative premise. Particularly on the matter of cinematic space, Park's choices seek to mirror the perplexed nature of the story, enriching the classical options with a long list of new stylistic devices.

Regarding its cutting rate, *Oldboy* holds an ASL of 8.6 seconds, which is slightly longer than the typical range of intensified continuity. However, the pace feels a lot faster thanks to other devices, such as occasional jump-cuts or the persistent and emphatic use of the rack focus (Figures 2.11–2.12).

Another element that intensifies the effect of the editing is the recurrent juxtaposition of extreme close-ups with extreme long shots. For example, in Figure 2.13 the overhead view of Oh Dae-Su's (Choi Min-sik) release on the rooftop is immediately followed by the extreme close-up of his eye reacting to the daylight (Figure 2.14). This type of editing in some cases becomes particularly demanding, as the viewer is required to swiftly adjust to the extreme changes in distance and perspective.

FIGURE 2.11

FIGURE 2.12

FIGURE 2.13

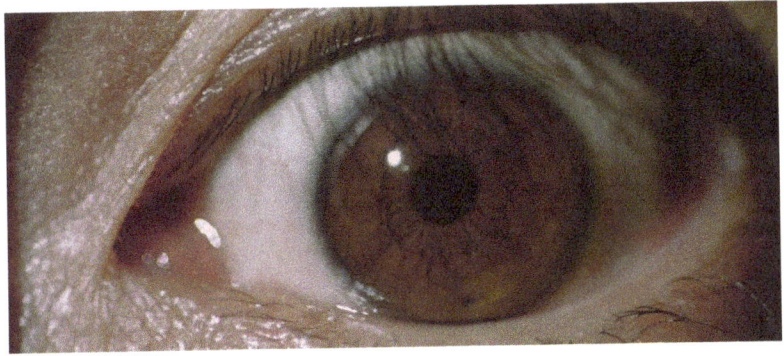

FIGURE 2.14

Framing is also crucial in *Oldboy*. Apart from the standard trait of intensified continuity, namely the tight framing of the faces (Figures 2.15–2.16), the film regularly resorts to extreme close-ups on objects or body parts (Figures 2.17–2.18).

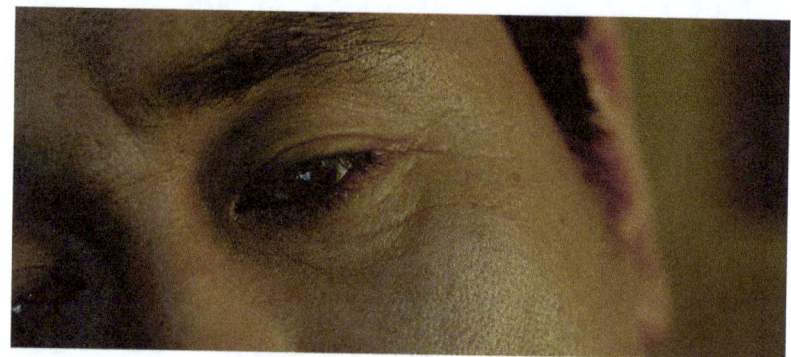

FIGURE 2.15

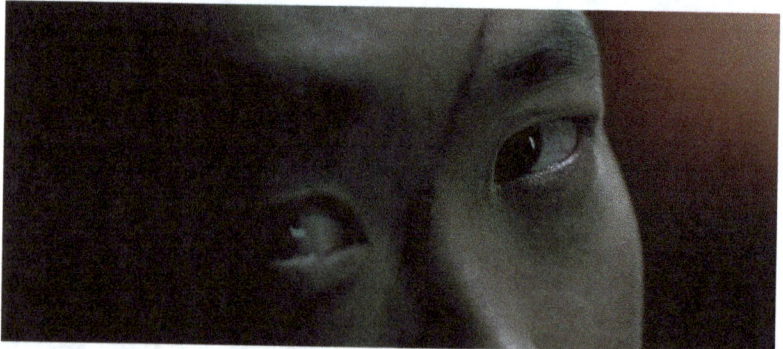

FIGURE 2.16

FIGURE 2.17

Another consistent deviation from the classical image composition is the filming of the action from up above. The characters are positioned in ways that invite the overhead exposition of the storyworld, probing questions regarding the narrative levels (Figures 2.19–2.20). In other words, the planting of the camera in impossible places raises the issue of narrative agency, making manifest the presence of a nondiegetic force.

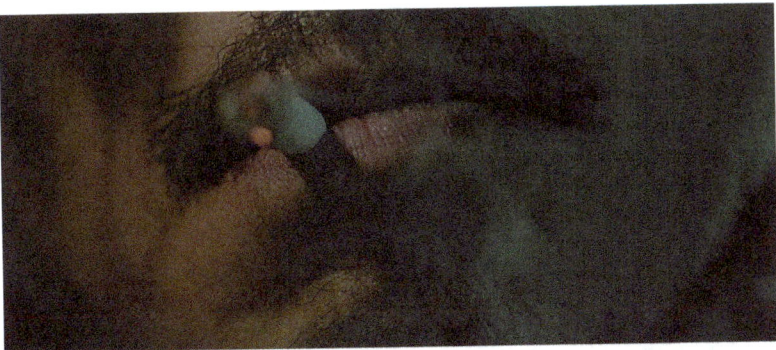

FIGURE 2.18

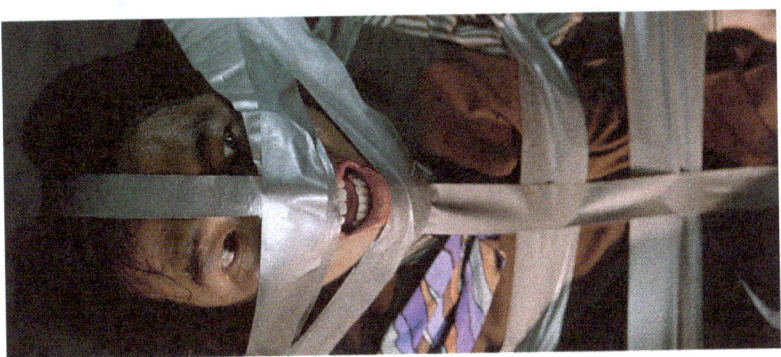

FIGURE 2.19

FIGURE 2.20

In addition, the graphic elements of the filmic frame are accentuated not so much from the extreme lens lengths, but rather from the expressive lighting and color palette as well as the constant use of shallow focus (Figures 2.21–2.22). At the other end of the spectrum, Park resorts to the use of the split-diopter to maintain an extreme depth of field that captures the complexity of the characters' history (Figure 2.23). The penchant for extreme stylistic options feels entirely appropriate for capturing the violence, cruelty, and perversity of the story.

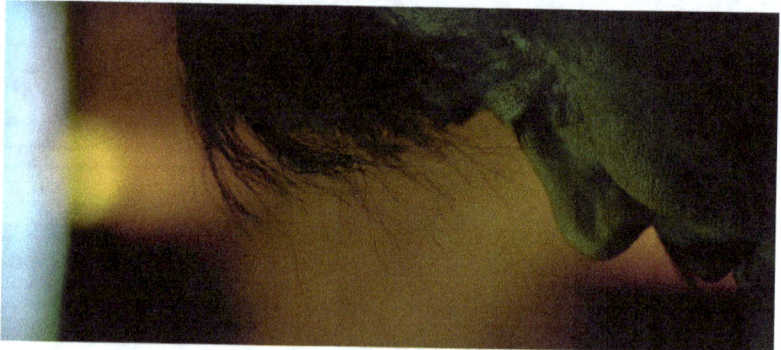

FIGURE 2.21

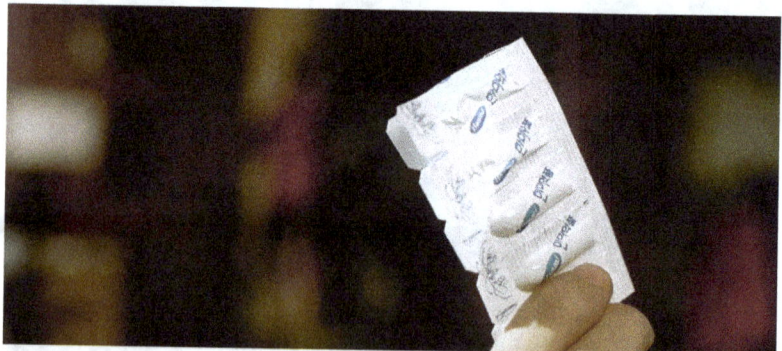

FIGURE 2.22

Finally, in longer scenes, the camera tends to make its presence felt through fluid movements that seek to transmit the energy of the moment, whether it is suspense, fear or even hypnosis. The first arresting maneuver comes four minutes into the film to stage Oh Dae-Su's kidnapping after he makes the last phone call to his daughter and wife. The camera arcs around the telephone booth allowing enough time for the character to disappear, while the ensuing hovering crane shot over the street in the dark heightens the enigmatic nature of the incident. Throughout the film,

FIGURE 2.23

there are slow tracking movements of the camera, in and out of the action, adding dramatic value to the characters' emotional state and the tragic events that they find themselves caught up in.

CASE STUDY C: *SNATCH* (2000)

Guy Ritchie's *Snatch* was widely received as a follow-up to *Lock, Stock and Two Smoking Barrels* (1999), and rightly so, as Ritchie applied the post-classical formula in both films down to the last detail. Roger Ebert's following comment is telling: "Ritchie is a zany, high-energy director. He isn't interested in crime, he's interested in voltage" (Ebert 2001). Stylistically, the energy and the high voltage partly derive from the techniques of intensified continuity pushed to the extremes.

In terms of the cutting rate, *Snatch* holds an ASL of 3.6 seconds, which feels even faster thanks to a series of additional tricks that accelerate the tempo. For instance, there are many jump-cuts, particularly in the first half, that imbue the scenes with added intensity. In other cases, there is a rhythmic and graphic type of editing that cuts regular shots with freeze-frames while the sound effects magnify the visual impact of this technique. Another regular device is the flashing of shots, usually close-ups, that are focalized moments, i.e., either things that the characters observe or that pass through their minds.[3] Finally, even when there is no cutting, rack focus splits the image into two, accentuating its graphic composition (Figures 2.24–2.25).

The framing in the film is varied, containing mostly medium shots, close-ups, and extreme close-ups, while many conversations are filmed with the standard tight composition (Figures 2.26–2.27).

The use of slanted angles is also a recurrent trait, as in Figures 2.28 and 2.29, where Ritchie creates an irregular frame with very strong diagonal

FIGURE 2.24

FIGURE 2.25

lines that vie for our attention. In addition, he often resorts to framing the characters from below as in Figure 2.30, especially when there is a person, alive or dead, on the ground. And in *Snatch* there is no shortage of people lying dead or wounded on the floor.

Admittedly, however, the most stunning effect in Ritchie's toolkit is his dizzying camera movement. There is a constant sense of motion, rising from all the possible ways that a camera (or a lens) can follow the action or the characters; from typical tracking shots and whip pans to frantic push-ins/pull-outs and arc shots. Among his most eccentric moves is the camera roll, which spins uncontrollably in the storyworld, as well as the crash zoom, which rapidly zooms in on the faces to instantly capture their reactions (Figures 2.31–2.32).

FIGURE 2.26

FIGURE 2.27

FIGURE 2.28

FIGURE 2.29

FIGURE 2.30

FIGURE 2.31

FIGURE 2.32

Finally, what makes *Snatch* feel so aggressively visceral is that Ritchie tends to combine all the aforementioned techniques within the same sequence. In two climactic moments, namely the confrontation between the four gangsters in the pub and the final boxing match, we witness a masterful synthesis of framing, editing, and camera mobility that creates a very intricate cinematic space designed to engage the viewer while serving the demands of the story with laser-guided precision. For all its stylistic idiosyncrasies, *Snatch* remains a highly pleasurable and accessible piece of storytelling, where formal experimentation reinforces the power of the narrative logic and allows it to reach a level of complexity that was not previously possible.

2.3 Graphic Frame

The role of intensified continuity is only the first step towards the construction of a hypermediated space that obeys the narrative logic of post-classical realism. In fact, the spatial system in this new mode proceeds to a more radical transformation by shifting the emphasis from the photographic to the graphic qualities of the cinematic image. This shift has profound implications for the theory and history of cinema that I would like to address briefly.

One of the prominent features of the filmic frame has been its photographic realism. The mechanical reproduction of reality through moving images has been discussed for almost a century as cinema's essential characteristic. In Siegfried Kracauer's words, film is "uniquely equipped to record and reveal physical reality and, hence, gravitates toward it" (Kracauer 1960: 28).

According to this line of thought, celluloid possesses a unique capacity to record physical elements, transforming the filmic screen into a window onto real life. In terms of narration and style, this tendency of the cinema to frame reality was historically translated into the creation of the classical frame distinguished for its transparency, linear perspective, and staging in depth, as well as the centrality of the human figure. With the coming of digital technology, cinema's natural ties with external reality had to be reconsidered. According to Lev Manovich, the advent of digitality imposed a distinct logic to the moving images, subordinating the photographic and cinematic qualities to a painterly and graphic spirit. Whereas analogue cinema emphasized its recording capacity by using live-action footage and representing space realistically through the logic of immediacy, digital techniques brought back into the limelight the features of a rather marginal filmic practice, that of animation. As he notes:

> The opposition between the styles of animation and cinema defined the culture of the moving image in the twentieth century. Animation foregrounds its artificial character, openly admitting that its images are mere representations. Its visual language is more aligned to the graphic than to the photographic.
>
> MANOVICH 2001: 298

All the technical devices and special effects that were central in animations remained peripheral to mainstream cinematic practices for several decades for fear of revealing the constructed nature of filmic representation. This tendency would be reversed in the 1990s, according to Manovich, thanks to the emergence of "digital cinema," defined as "a particular case of animation that uses live-action footage as one of its many elements" (302). Historically, however, animation was not the only form of cinema that foregrounded the materiality of the image and its graphic dimension. Avant-garde artists throughout the twentieth century had also experimented with celluloid as a material object that could be scratched, pasted, or painted over. These revolutionary processes, as Manovich argues, have been "appropriated" by the digital software and have become "the normal, intended techniques of digital filmmaking, embedded in technology design itself" (307).

Yet the fact that the digital tools facilitate these stylistic options does not necessarily mean that contemporary filmmakers are going to deploy them. In fact, most digital effects are still striving for a greater sense of classical realism that replicates a sense of transparency and photographic verisimilitude. Given that computer software has the capacity to emulate both photographic and graphic spaces, the reasons why one opts for a classical transparent spatial construction or a post-classical hypermediated one are not to be grounded on technology alone. Other cultural, institutional, and social practices need to be examined in order to comprehend why the option of a graphic frame became part of mainstream filmmaking from the 1990s onwards and, perhaps most importantly, why it still remains a secondary option.[4]

Overall, whether composed with digital or analogue means, the post-classical mode approaches the filmic frame as a graphic frame, i.e., as a representational surface that does not hide the signs of its materiality. The latter may come forward through a series of techniques, such as the deployment of diverse film stocks, the incorporation of other media formats (animation, comics, video games, television), the emphasis on painterly elements (color, *mise-en-scène*), the playing with angles and lens focus, and the blatant use of special effects (back projections, CGI, miniatures, matte shots). All those characteristics of the graphic frame are not gratuitous, nor do they stand autonomously from the other two narrative systems—narrative logic and time. On the contrary, the graphic construction of space in the post-classical mode obeys the compositional motivation and facilitates the progression of the story, while also satisfying the demand for hypermediacy and subjective realism. The paradoxical balance between foregrounding the materiality of the image and pursuing its narrative mission will become demonstrably clear in the analyses that follow.

ANALYSIS

CASE STUDY A: *NATURAL BORN KILLERS* (1994)

Natural Born Killers is Oliver Stone's anthropological study into the schizophrenic madness of twentieth-century America, encapsulated in the killing spree of two psychopaths. Trying to match the visual style to the theme, Stone crafted a polystylistic film that caused a sensation among reviewers and audiences alike. In fact, it even compelled Thierry Jousse, the famous French critic, to declare the death of the image and to describe the filmic frame as "a space where everything is on the surface, like in a baroque sphere" (Jousse 1994: 50). Indeed, what he acutely observed was the passage from a photographic to a graphic space that initiates its own distinct logic.

Natural Born Killers literally contains more than 2,000 shots, the graphic elements of which are accentuated by the particularities of the film stock, the media format (e.g., entire sequences shot as TV sitcom), the exuberant colors, the slanted angles, the expressionistic lighting, and a series of special effects like superimpositions and back projections.

A shot-by-shot analysis of a key scene, the marriage between the two protagonists, is illustrative of the properties as well as the narrative function of the graphic space in the film.

The sequence in question opens with the following shots:

Shot 1 (Figures 2.33–2.34): close-up of a hand dropping a red puppet into a gorge. The puppet falls until it becomes a red dot (color, 35mm).

Shot 2 (Figure 2.35): cut to an extreme long shot of the bridge over the gorge from an entirely opposite angle (black-and-white, 16mm, digitally enhanced).

Shot 3 (Figure 2.36): medium shot of Mickey and Mallory on the bridge. The camera hovers over their heads, moving freely in a 360° space (color, 35mm).

Shot 4 (Figure 2.37): jump-cut to high-angle shot while the camera keeps floating (color, 35mm).

Shot 5 (Figure 2.38): cut to an establishing shot of the bridge from a slanted angle (color, 35mm).

Shot 6 (Figure 2.39): cut to a medium close-up on Mallory's profile (color, 35mm).

Shot 7 (Figure 2.40): cut to a reverse-shot of Mickey (color, 35mm).

Shot 8 (Figure 2.41): cut to a medium shot of Mallory putting a wedding headband from a slanted angle (color, Super 8).

Shot 9 (Figure 2.42): cut to a medium close-up on Mickey slashing his hand (color, 35mm).

Shot 10 (Figure 2.43): cut to a medium shot of Mickey, the camera pans to include Mallory in the shot (color, Super 8).

Shot 11 (Figure 2.44): cut to Mallory again (color, 35mm).

Shot 12 (Figure 2.45): cut to a high-angle double shot of the characters (color, 35mm).

Shot 13 (Figure 2.46): cut to Mallory again (color, 35mm).

Shot 14 (Figure 2.47): cut to a medium shot of the characters. The camera is hand-held and tilts up to show Mickey's face (color, Super 8).

Shot 15 (Figure 2.48): jump-cut, similar camera movement as in shot 14 (color, Super 8).

Shot 16 (Figure 2.49): cut to a medium close-up on Mickey (color, 35mm).

Shot 17 (Figure 2.50): overhead-shot of the characters (color, 35mm).

Shot 18 (Figure 2.51): cut to a close-up of their clasped hands (color, 35mm).

Shot 19 (Figure 2.52): dissolve into a sequence showing their blood transforming into snakes (color, animation).

FIGURE 2.33

FIGURE 2.34

FIGURE 2.35

FIGURE 2.36

FIGURE 2.37

FIGURE 2.38

FIGURE 2.39

FIGURE 2.40

FIGURE 2.41

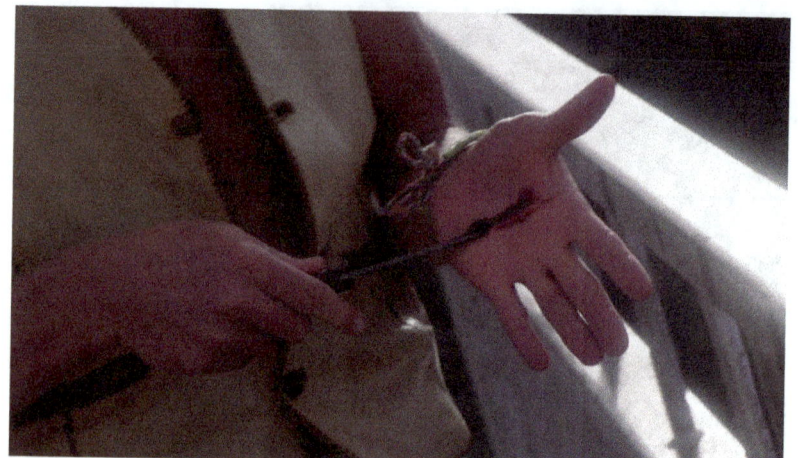

FIGURE 2.42

FIGURE 2.43

FIGURE 2.44

FIGURE 2.45

FIGURE 2.46

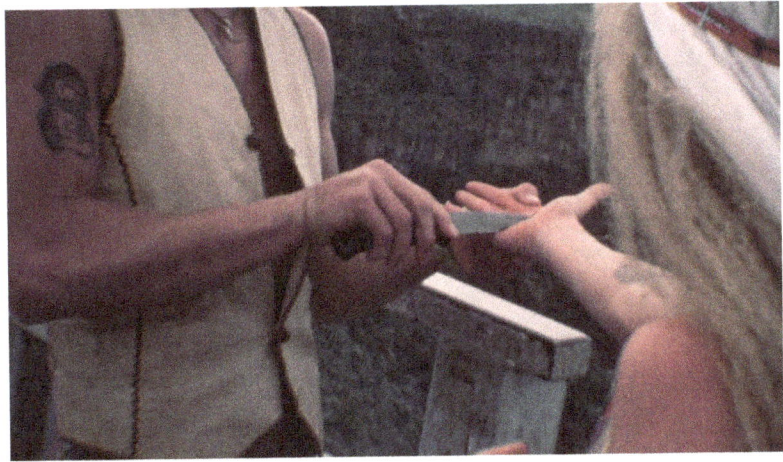

FIGURE 2.47

FIGURE 2.48

FIGURE 2.49

FIGURE 2.50

FIGURE 2.51

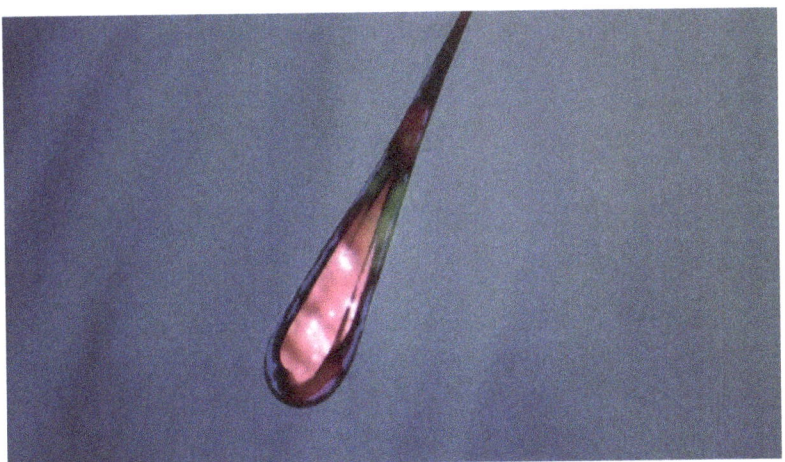

FIGURE 2.52

Experimenting with a series of flaunted editing techniques, camera movements, film stocks, and digital effects, Stone and his cinematographer, Robert Richardson, intended to break the classical rules of immediacy to discover a new mode of storytelling that could narrate a powerful story through a different logic, that of hypermediacy. As a result, the film's remarkable stylistic freedom is not gratuitous; rather, it is paired with the deliberate attempt to maintain narrative coherence and intelligibility. Overall, the graphic frame in the context of the post-classical mode is not an abstract frame; it is a form of representation amenable to a significantly more complex and layered narrative logic than in any other historical mode.

CASE STUDY B: *THE FRENCH DISPATCH* (2021)

Released in 2021, *The French Dispatch* is (at the time of writing) the most recent work of Wes Anderson, a post-classical filmmaker *par excellence*. The film brings to life a series of articles published in the last issue of a fictional newspaper called *The French Dispatch of the Liberty, Kansas Evening Sun*, after the sudden demise of its editor. Its episodic plot consists of five segments and an ensemble cast sprinkled into a densely woven fictional world. Yet the most prominent element in the film is its flauntingly graphic frame.

One of the principles of the graphic space construction is the foregrounding of its materiality. In *The French Dispatch*, this not simply a recurring characteristic but rather a constant one. For instance, the source medium of the story, namely the magazine, is directly evoked in the beginning of each episode as in Figures 2.53 and 2.54.

Moreover, the regular switch from color stock to black-and-white (Figures 2.55–2.56) is a constant reminder of the filmmaker's conscious selection of the filmic materiality.

FIGURE 2.53

POST-CLASSICAL SPACE

FIGURE 2.54

FIGURE 2.55

FIGURE 2.56

Similarly, the presence of animation is strongly felt, particularly in the third story, where a significant chunk of the action progresses through animated sequences instead of live action (Figure 2.57). Finally, the screen often becomes a graphic surface where the diegetic images blend with letters that either contain dialogues or other story information (Figures 2.58–2.59).

FIGURE 2.57

FIGURE 2.58

FIGURE 2.59

The painterly approach to the cinematic frame is also dominant, as Anderson takes the notion of "painterly" quite literally. One option is to craft images that resemble paintings, whether in traditional style as in Figure 2.60, or with more geometric shapes as in Figure 2.61.

FIGURE 2.60

FIGURE 2.61

Another impressive device is to narrate parts of the story, using a moving tableau vivant. This reveals the actors standing stationary and silent, striking impressive poses in a highly elaborate setting (Figures 2.62–2.63).

POST-CLASSICAL SPACE   129

FIGURE 2.62

FIGURE 2.63

Sometimes, the frame can be painted over, transforming the screen itself into a canvas (Figures 2.64–2.65).

FIGURE 2.64

FIGURE 2.65

The painterly feeling, however, is persistent even in more ordinary frames, thanks to the stylized *mise-en-scène*. Anderson not only opts for staging in depth but also for an unusually long depth of field. In

Figure 2.66 there is a standard composition that divides the space into distinct planes, layering the characters into the office space in a way that highlights their unique individuality. It is impressive how the writing on the notebook in the extreme foreground remains legible as much as some of the writings on the board at the far end. The same logic applies in Figure 2.67 combined with the technique of *mise-en-abyme* to create a mirroring effect. Several of these images would qualify for Bordwell's term "planimetric," a style of framing that involves the frontal presentation of the action (Bordwell 2014). It is important that he characterizes this kind of shot construction as blatantly unclassical, tracing it only to some relatively rare cases of European or Asian cinema. He aptly observes that the planimetric shot "is well-suited to a 'painterly' or strongly pictorial approach to cinema," while Anderson employs it to gain "a somewhat awkward formality, a sense that we are looking from a distance into an enclosed world that sometimes looks back at us" (Bordwell 2007; 2014).

FIGURE 2.66

Finally, *The French Dispatch* is noteworthy for its special effects, both analogue and digital, that construct a layered image consisting of different materials. In one of the most iconic moments, the lecture at the art gallery, the screen is divided into smaller sections, each filmed with a different format (color film, black/white film, black/white video), while the décor (stage, cameras), the lighting (spotlight), and the staging (speaker, screens in the front and at the back) build a cinematic frame that plays with its own self-referentiality (Figure 2.68).

FIGURE 2.67

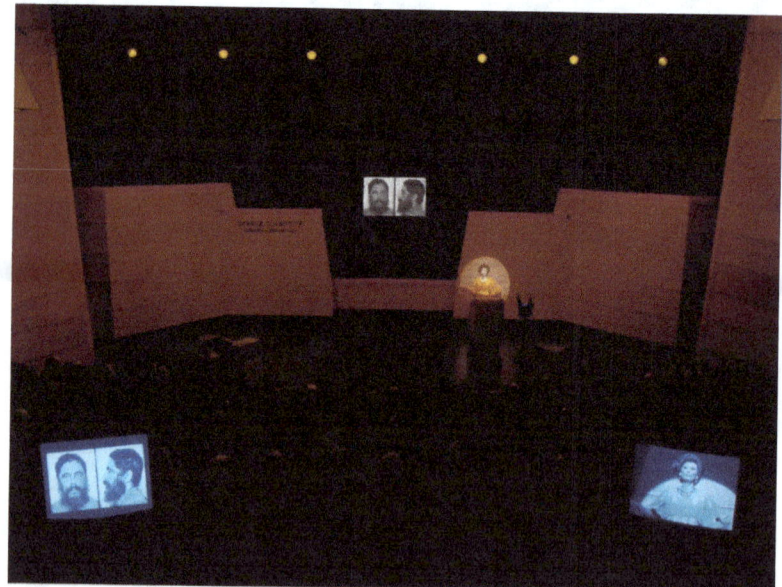

FIGURE 2.68

Throughout the film, Anderson and his creative collaborators relied extensively on visual effects in order to produce an image that would stand out not for its photorealism but for its intriguing graphic design.

CASE STUDY C: *ARMY OF THE DEAD* (2021)

After directing several comic book adaptations, some of which are exemplars of post-classical storytelling, Zack Snyder returned to the zombie genre, carrying along his penchant for graphic imagery. In this case, he devised a very idiosyncratic filming style, which combined a vintage lens from the 1960s with the latest digital cameras to create a look that would set *Army of the Dead* apart from the bulk of the blockbusters. The main feature of this old lens, also known as "dream lens," is its capacity to maintain only a very small area of the frame in focus, resulting in extremely blurry images that bear a dream-like quality.

One of the effects of this shooting style is the constant foregrounding of the filmic materiality. At no point can the audience escape the fact that the camera is emphatically present, offering us only a partial view of the action. Given that this technique was deployed in the entire film, it is interesting to examine the graphic compositions that ensue in the different framing distances and to analyze Snyder's *mise-en-scène* constraints, which he explored for their artistic merit.

The long shots in the film tend to be impressionistic tableaus that are striking for the way they merge the human figures with their surroundings. In Figures 2.69–2.70, the staging in depth is beautifully balanced but the lack of deep focus urges us to experience the scenes mostly intuitively. Similarly, in Figures 2.71–2.73, the graphic qualities of the setting, such as the helicopter, the sun, and the statue of Liberty, dominate the frame, overshadowing its narrative components.

FIGURE 2.69

FIGURE 2.70

FIGURE 2.71

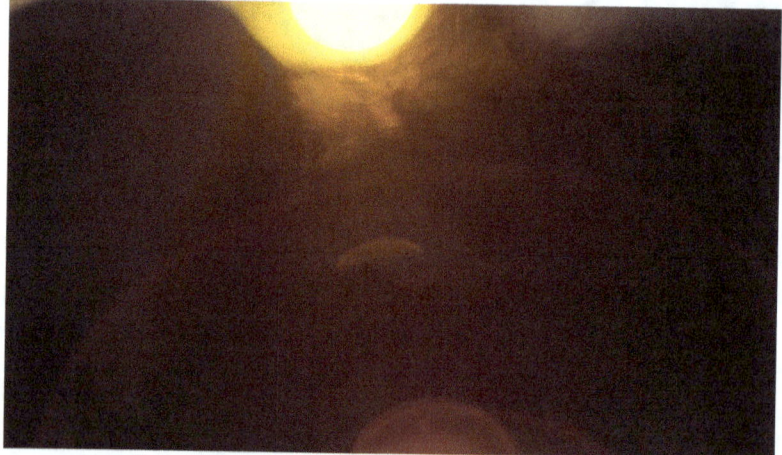

FIGURE 2.72

FIGURE 2.73

In the numerous middle shots that carry the larger part of the action, the blurry element becomes an intrinsic rule that the viewer grows promptly accustomed to. The large number of protagonists requires several group shots, but the lens can only keep some of them in focus each time, turning the rest into blurred phantasms. In Figures 2.74–2.76 we see the blur appearing on all possible parts of the frame, i.e., the background, the foreground, and the sidelines respectively.

In Figure 2.77 the low angle builds an even more graphic frame, while in Figure 2.78 the characters appear only as silhouettes.

FIGURE 2.74

FIGURE 2.75

FIGURE 2.76

FIGURE 2.77

When it comes to close-ups, the "dream lens" tends to produce a visually disturbing effect. Apart from cases that are comparingly normal as in Figure 2.79, other close ups on faces (Figure 2.80) or body parts (Figure 2.81) seem to lose their photographic elements and transform into graphic surfaces.

FIGURE 2.78

FIGURE 2.79

In fact, in many cases the graphic aspect is so dominant that the frame becomes an abstract composition as in Figures 2.82–2.83. In other cases, the photographic trace is present but there is such a complex layering of details in the *mise-en-scène* that it feels like a form of collage that, nonetheless, maintains its realistic sway. In Figure 2.84, for instance, the pilot, the blooded windshield, and the reflection of the missile are all laid out on a flat plane, illustrating an ingenious frame construction that stays true to the story while approaching the filmic screen as a painted surface.

FIGURE 2.80

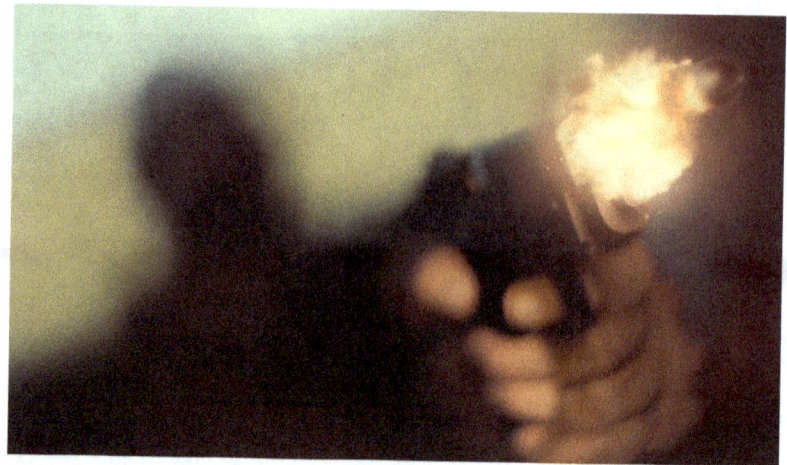

FIGURE 2.81

Overall, the space construction in *Army of the Dead* is a brilliant example of the post-classical logic that privileges the painterly character of the cinematic frame over the photographic. In addition to the techniques mentioned above, Snyder deploys a rapid cutting rate, hand-held camera, and slow motion—especially in the fight sequences—to fabricate a visually stunning film that rivals *300* (2006) and *Watchmen* (2009) for the graphic depiction of the plot.

FIGURE 2.82

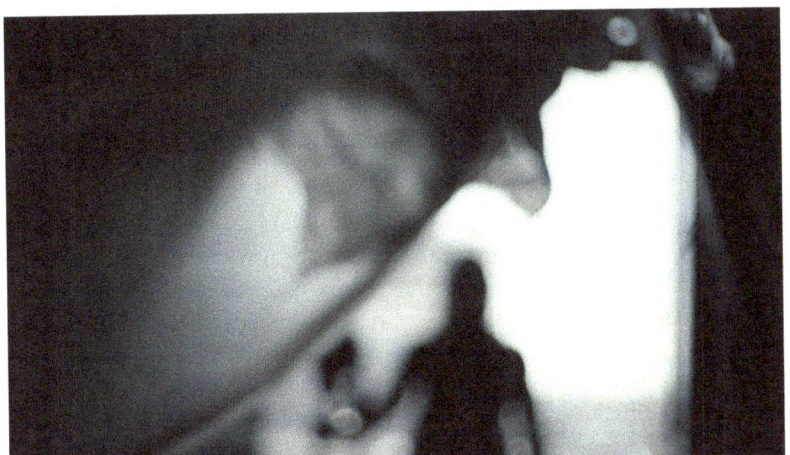

FIGURE 2.83

FIGURE 2.84

2.4 Spatial Montage

Spatial montage is a form of editing that has become increasingly popular in contemporary cinema and is included in the paradigmatic options of the post-classical system of narrative space. Montage as an editing technique has traditionally involved the sequencing of images that either have temporal/spatial proximity or are juxtaposed for the purposes of visual conflict, as in the case of Eisenstein's montage. In both cases, the sequencing is temporal and requires that the images appear one *after* the other. The spatial montage, on the other hand, relies on the joining of images in the same space. According to Manovich,

> In general, spatial montage could involve a number of images, potentially of different sizes and proportions, appearing on the screen at the same time. The juxtaposition by itself of course does not result in montage; it is up to the filmmaker to construct a logic that determines which images appear together, when they appear, and what kind of relationships they enter into with one another.
>
> MANOVICH 2001: 322

Spatial montage breaks the logic of one image/one screen and introduces the logic of addition and coexistence, allowing a number of "texts" to appear simultaneously on the surface of the screen and compete for prominence. Manovich further distinguishes two types of spatial montage based on compositing: the "ontological" and the "stylistic." The former allows incompatible elements to coexist within the same time and space, while the latter facilitates the merging of different media formats, such as 35mm and 8mm film, within the same shot or more generally within the same film. Both these forms of frame construction entail a large degree of informational density that outshines the capacities of the classical device of "depth of field" (328).

Historically, spatial montage is not a new technique, as the process of compositing can be traced in several analogue media, such as painting, photography, television, and video art, all of which predate the advent of digitality. Yet it is undeniable that digital tools increase its applicability to an exponential degree. Computer technology at the phase of post-production facilitates the creation of spatial montage and invites the widespread use of compositing for designing spatial images and clusters with more complex narrative and stylistic functions. The end result is a form of graphic frame construction that enriches the photographic elements of the live-action footage and challenges the traditional distinction between the space in and out of frame.

Spatial montage transfers the logic of temporal montage into the space of a single frame. All the types of relations (spatial, temporal, causal, conceptual) that were possible in the joining of two images in a linear order can be equally articulated within the same composite image. For instance, the analytical editing that builds a transition from an establishing shot to a closer view of the action can be performed with a spatial montage that relates the two views through a visual effect, like a superimposition or a split screen. The same principle applies to all the devices of continuity editing, such as eyeline matches, shot/reverse-shots, cross-cutting, and point-of-view shots. Moreover, the graphic and rhythmic relations that were previously constructed in a linear fashion can now co-exist in the same frame, intensifying even further their visual and emotional impact.

Overall, spatial montage produces layered graphic images that are suitable for carrying complex story information. Thus, it is an ideal device for serving the narrative logic of the post-classical mode, which relies on four powerful motivations, each with its own creative purposes.

ANALYSIS

CASE STUDY A: *EUROPA* (1991)

Europa remains Lars von Trier's most visually stunning film to date. One of its powerful elements is the extensive use of spatial montage to portray the complex trajectory of the characters, their ambiguous moral allegiances, and their tormented personal moments. Using only analogue means, von Trier constructs a layered cinematic frame that combines multiple back projections, superimpositions, and the mixture of black-and-white images with color.

Among the classical devices that are reworked through the process of spatial montage, staging in depth admittedly stands out. An intriguing example is found in the scene where Leo (Jean-Marc Barr) meets Kate (Barbara Sukowa) for the first time in the train compartment. The following shots are indicative of von Trier's spatial montage.

1. Medium black-and-white shot of the interior of Kate's compartment from a low angle. In the foreground on the left, Leo is on his knees making the bed. In the background on the right, Kate is looking at Leo; she gradually slips out of focus. Leo pulls up the sheets covering the whole frame (Figures 2.85–2.86).

2. Cut to a medium close-up. Leo is now in the foreground in color and Kate in the background in a black-and-white back projection. Kate slowly walks behind his back and leaves the frame for a moment. She then re-enters the frame in the foreground and in color next to Leo. At this point the two protagonists are both in color against a black-and-white back projection. Kate starts making the bed herself and Leo leaves the frame. He re-enters the frame in the black-and-white back projection in the background (Figures 2.87–2.89).

FIGURE 2.85

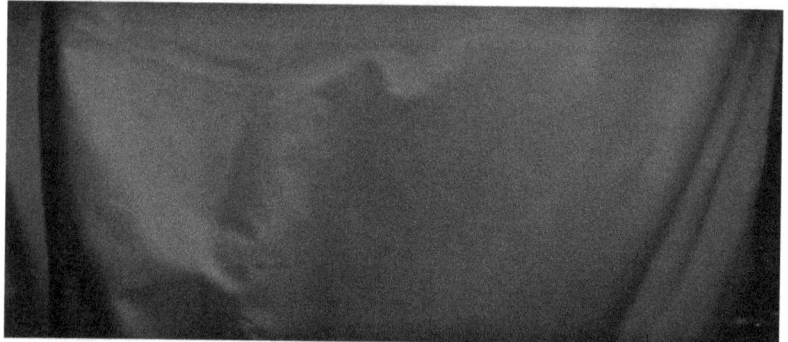

FIGURE 2.86

FIGURE 2.87

FIGURE 2.88

FIGURE 2.89

This is a typical example of the intricate staging of the action in separate planes, projections, and colors throughout *Europa*. What is remarkable, however, is that the shifting of planes among the two protagonists is not gratuitous; in fact, it foreshadows the progression of their relationship and the distance between them. When Katarina utters "What you say seems to come from a place far away" in the final moment, Leo's position in the separate projection becomes an ironic play on her words.

Moreover, the continuity editing that ensures a realistic and smooth transition from place to place is replaced by a spatial montage that relies on changes in the back projections. For instance, in Figure 2.90 we see Leo and Kate framed in close-up in color against the black-and-white projection of a river. Kate says, "Marry me, please" and Leo says "yes" and kisses her. When the kiss is over, the back projection dissolves into the figure of a priest in a church and the two characters turn to face him (Figure 2.91). A cut to the other side of the axis shows the priest in the foreground and the couple in the back projection in their wedding clothes (Figure 2.92). In these three shots, the story progresses without an obstacle, despite the ontologically impossible spatial movement of its participants.

FIGURE 2.90

FIGURE 2.91

FIGURE 2.92

Another recurring use of spatial montage aims at creating subjective spaces that express the characters' emotional state. Leo, in particular, experiences several moments of insomnia, or high anxiety, until he finally sinks in the bottom of the sea, leaving the nightmare behind him (Figures 2.93–2.95).

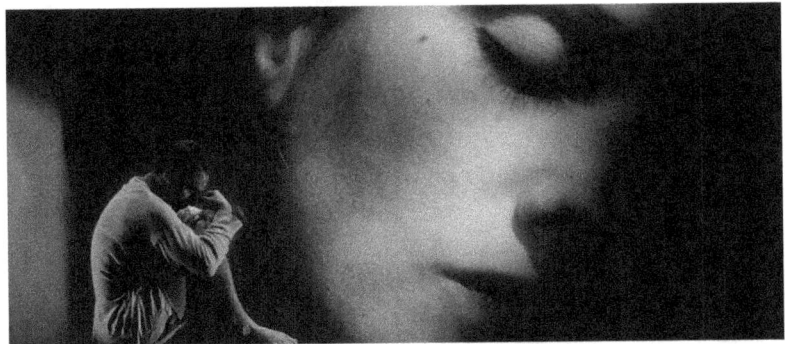

FIGURE 2.93

FIGURE 2.94

FIGURE 2.95

Finally, I would like to highlight an intricate visual cluster that only becomes intelligible with the help of the voice-over. In Figure 2.96 we see Max (Jørgen Reenberg) on the left, looking towards a piece of paper in color on the right. His look is misleading, though. The voice-over addresses another character, Leo, with the following words: "You have left the house

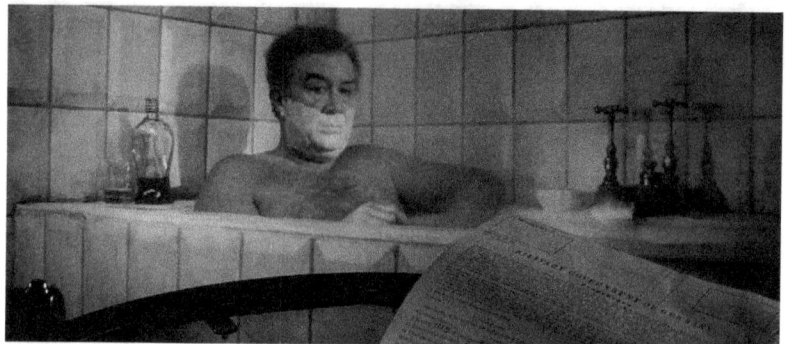

FIGURE 2.96

... Before you, is the questionnaire." Only then do we realize that the paper in the colored foreground is not located in the bathroom where Max is seen in black-and-white. The connection between the two "images," however, could be interpreted differently. We could assume that Max, haunted as he is by the questionnaire, cannot stop thinking about it. In this case, the front layer becomes an internal focalization that represents his inner thoughts.

On the whole, the visual clusters that von Trier ingeniously crafts throughout *Europa* demonstrate the creative power of spatial montage and its potential for narrative complexity within the overall structure of post-classical storytelling.

CASE STUDY B: *BRAM STOKER'S DRACULA* (1992)

Described as "one long, uninterrupted special effect" by the *New York Times* (Canby 1992), Coppola's film is a rather odd post-classical example within an oeuvre that largely falls within the boundaries of classicism. In this adaptation of Stoker's titular novel, Coppola crafts a very graphic portrayal of Count Dracula's story, deploying the powers of intensified continuity and spatial montage. For the latter, he remains stubbornly faithful to traditional analogue techniques for the creation of hypermediated images that not only pay tribute to the history of cinema but also evoke their literary sources.

One of the recurring elements is the use of composite frames to indicate changes in the location of the characters. Given that the plot contains several journeys between Transylvania and London, Coppola transforms the screen into a surface that bears the traces of these geographical movements. In Figure 2.97, for instance, a map is superimposed over the ship that sails towards the port of Varna while another trail by land shows the route followed by Dracula's hunters. In Figure 2.98, on the other hand, the map is printed on the face of the character to indicate his destination. Finally, on another occasion, the map of London and a magnified view of an address label position the action to a specific setting, namely Carfax Abbey (Figure 2.99).

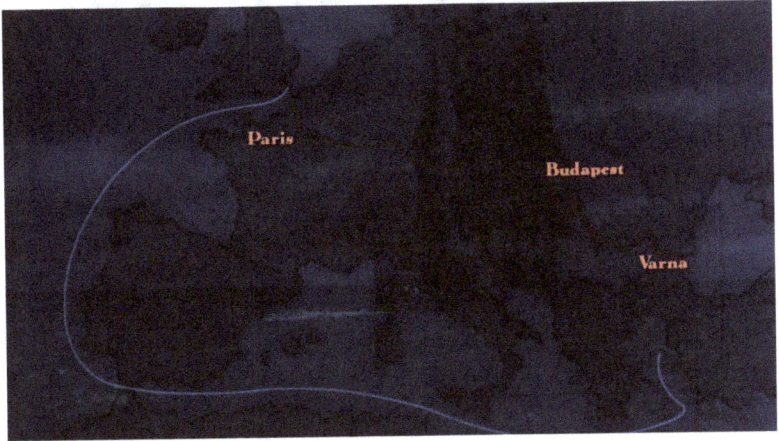

FIGURE 2.97

FIGURE 2.98

FIGURE 2.99

Another function of the visual layering is the construction of graphic images that trigger strong associations. In Figure 2.100 there is an impressive graphic collage of the eyespot of a peacock feather and the end of a railroad tunnel. Shortly after, there is another highly expressionistic composition that unites the slanted image of Jonathan Harker (Keanu Reeves) with an eye against a red background (Figure 2.101). This figurative space can invite various interpretations relating the color red (danger, evil) with the character's gaze, as well as the eyes of the other two protagonists, Count Dracula (Gary Oldman) and Mina (Winona Ryder), who are mentally present in the scene. Similarly, the color green, a bottle of Absinthe, and images of liquids being poured into glasses blend together to evoke the feeling of intoxication caused by the "Green Fairy" (Figures 2.102–2.103).

FIGURE 2.100

FIGURE 2.101

FIGURE 2.102

FIGURE 2.103

Moreover, the epistolary form of the film's source novel is regularly foregrounded with the characters' writings merging with the diegetic world (Figure 2.104). In Figure 2.105, for instance, there is an intriguing shot of Jonathan looking at a mirror while his entry into his journal appears on the right. With the help of the voice-over, the connections in the spatial montage are elucidated and the scene becomes intelligible.

FIGURE 2.104

FIGURE 2.105

Finally, Coppola deploys image compositing for focalized shots that transform the screen into a mental space. In the prologue of the film, soon after his victorious battle, Dracula has a premonition that his beloved Elisabeta is in danger and her concerned face is superimposed on the upper left of the screen (Figure 2.106). Similarly, in a pivotal scene between

Mina and Count Dracula, the latter confirms that Mina is a reincarnation of Elisabeta, when she begins to experience a series of visions about the past. First, she begins to describe the "majestic beauty" of the countryside in Transylvania, while she gradually sees Elisabeta and her tragic fate (Figures 2.107–2.108).

Those metaphysical moments are portrayed on the screen with superimpositions, back projections, or matte shots that allow the two planes of reality to coexist in the same space. Overall, Coppola does, indeed, approach the cinematic frame as a prolonged visual effect suitable for narrating a mighty story about love and death. His return to cinema's graphic origins allows us to get a glimpse of how the post-classical mode thrives on cinema's painterly spirit and transforms into a powerful vehicle for contemporary storytelling.

FIGURE 2.106

FIGURE 2.107

FIGURE 2.108

CASE STUDY C: *REQUIEM FOR A DREAM* (2000)

Requiem for a Dream was previously showcased for its highly subjective realism, which consists of an emphatic depiction of the characters' inner psychological state. The hypermediated approach to the representation of the subjective experience required a graphic construction of the frame based on both the techniques of intensified continuity and the use of the split screen. Instead of back projections and superimpositions, Aronofsky opts for the digital technologies that enable him to construct a narrative space suitable for telling this painful story of addition and mental breakdown. As he explains, "all of the special techniques we applied had to advance the story, because we didn't want the film to turn into this self-indulgent, MTV type of thing" (quoted in Pizzello 2000: 51).

In the opening moments, the spatial montage becomes one of the film's distinctive features, producing images that are graphically disturbing. A careful look, however, reveals that the purpose of the composite frames is to reconfigure the logic of continuity editing within the space of one shot. In Figure 2.109, for instance, there is a play with the device of the point-of view shot. We see Sara (Ellen Burstyn) on the left looking through the keyhole while the image on the left shows what her son Harry (Jared Leto) sees. In Figure 2.110 we see her point-of-view through the keyhole while Harry looks at the door. Another attempt to show point-of view without cutting in a linear fashion is found in Figure 2.111, where a horizontal split screen shows us the character above and the object of her look below.

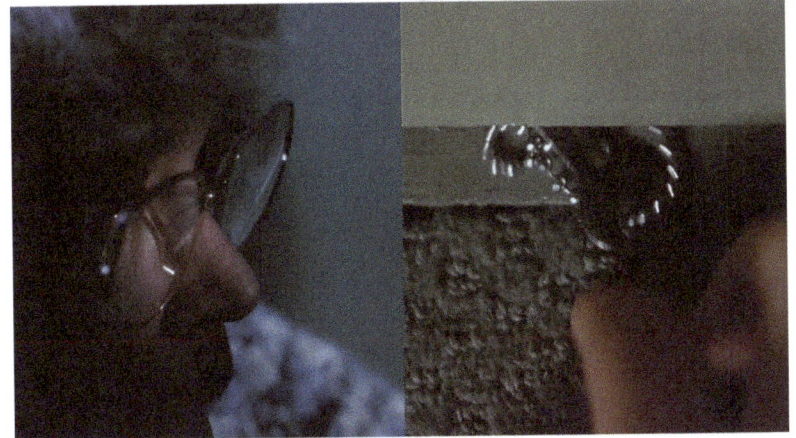

FIGURE 2.109

FIGURE 2.110

FIGURE 2.111

Moreover, the spatial montage is also deployed for the fragmentation of a romantic scene between Harry and his girlfriend Marion (Jennifer Connelly). The first shot (Figure 2.112) shows them in close-up next to each other against a black background, creating a misleading impression that they both occupy the same screen space. The next shot, however, reveals that they are contained in separate split screens, which feature shifting close-ups of their faces and bodies for the entire minute-and-a-half scene (Figures 2.113–2.115). The graphic frames that result from the juxtaposition of different body parts increases the feeling of intimacy and heightens the haptic quality of the images, engaging the spectators' other senses.

FIGURE 2.112

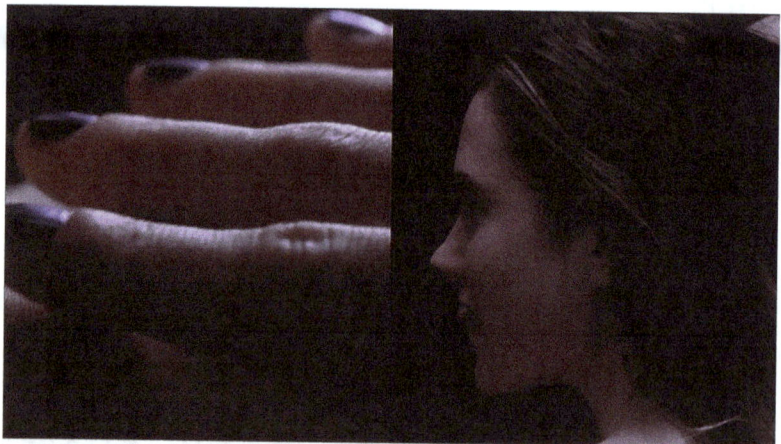

FIGURE 2.113

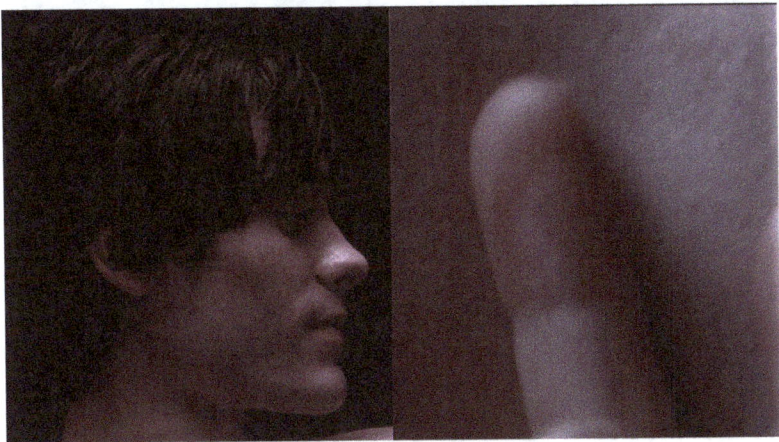

FIGURE 2.114

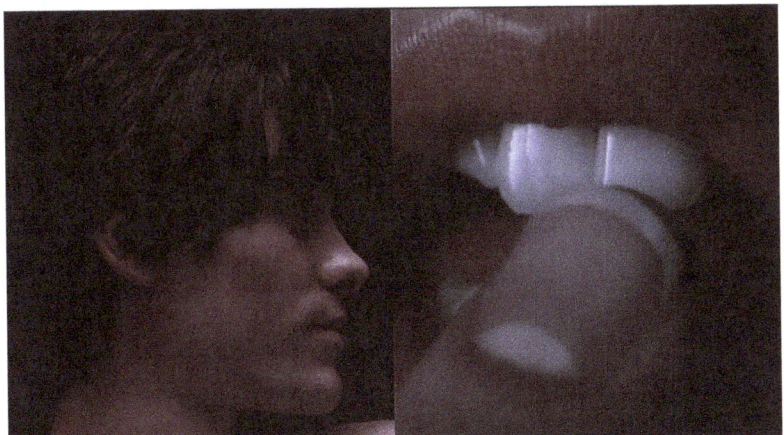

FIGURE 2.115

Finally, the emotional effect of the split screens is further intensified when there is camera movement or changes of focal length in one or both frame sections. For example, as Sara tries to refrain from eating, we see a medium shot of her on the left and the object of her thought, the fridge, on the right of the screen (Figure 2.116). A slow zoom-in begins in both sections and ends in extreme close-ups (Figures 2.117–2.118).

FIGURE 2.116

FIGURE 2.117

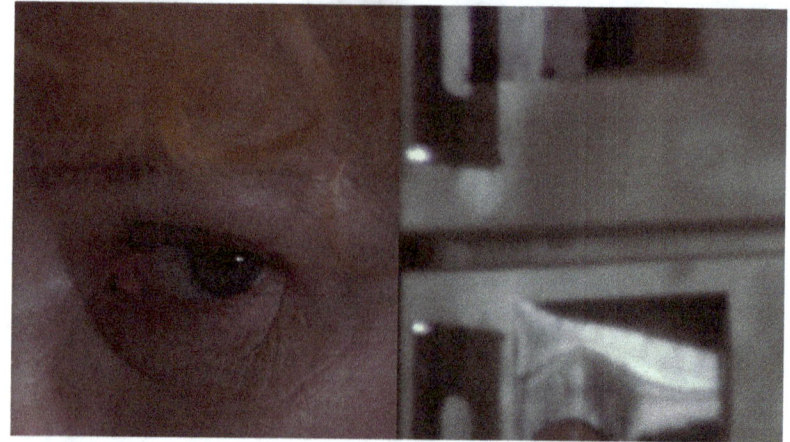

FIGURE 2.118

> The synchronized zoom on Sara's face and the fridge builds a highly focalized image that seeks to represent not only her mental image but also the increasing sense of deprivation that she experiences. In this spatial montage, as in all the previous cases, Aronofsky experiments with new devices in order to convey narrative information. These fragmented frames may require from the viewer an adjustment to this idiosyncratic mode of representation, but it soon becomes clear that the purpose of this hypermediated space is to provide room for a complex and multi-dimensional approach to the characters and their predicaments.

2.5 Conclusion

Despite the different personal styles of their directors and the diversity in production values or countries of origin, the films that were showcased in this chapter illustrate that the system of post-classical space consists of distinct constructional principles. These principles privilege the graphic and painterly qualities of the filmic space, deploying the techniques of intensified continuity, the graphic frame, and the spatial montage. Though stylistically more creative and experimental, the paradigmatic options of the post-classical space continue to serve the mandates of the narrative logic. Specifically, the post-classical space is designed to meet the requirements of a complex agenda that includes new compositional norms (multiple protagonists, modified character agency, new plot structures), new types of realism (hypermediated and subjective realism), self-conscious generic motivations, and parodic intertextuality. Hence, the need for the screen to metamorphose into such diverse shapes and forms, as is evident in the variety and richness of the images analyzed in this chapter.

Notes

1 See the discussion on the concept of the "dominant" in Chapter 6.
2 For the concept of ASL and the way to calculate it, see Salt (1992).
3 For the concept of focalization and the levels of narration, see Chapter 4.
4 For a discussion of the institutional parameters of post-classical narration, see Thanouli (2009a: 187–207). For a discussion about the relation between the classical and the post-classical mode in contemporary cinema, see Chapter 6.

3

Post-classical Time

3.1 Introduction

The system of narrative time is the third axis of the narrational act, which works in tandem with the narrative logic and narrative space. Every frame holds elements that may possess temporal qualities but, unlike space, the cinematic temporality has proven significantly more difficult to measure. For years, cinema's direct comparison to literature troubled film scholars regarding the temporal nature of the filmic image, debating whether its key feature is its "presentness" or its "tenselessness" (Cardwell 2003). Brian Henderson's following statement is indicative of the theoretical conundrum: "Cinema has no built-in tense system as language does. One cannot write a sentence without indicating tense but one can apparently make a shot, and therefore perhaps a film, without indicating tense" (Henderson 1983: 6). On the other hand, every fiction film narrates a story that has temporal coordinates just as much as it has spatial or causal ones. In fact, cinema can express temporal relations through a wide range of techniques, whether visual, aural, and even textual, endowing the filmic narration with the subtlest nuances of time (Sesonske 1980; Cardwell 2003). The description of narrative time in the cinema has been cogently laid out in Bordwell's *Narration in the Fiction Film*, where he adapts Gérard Genette's work on time-relations in literary narratives to the cinematic ones (Bordwell 1985). The features of narrative time can be classified along three broad categories: 1) order; 2) duration; and 3) frequency. Each category contains different options for organizing and presenting the narrative information, allowing a wide range of temporal relations between the story and the plot to unfold.

In the poetic history of cinema, there have been different approaches to cinematic temporality. In the Hollywood tradition, the dominance of the classical narrative logic dictates an unmediated representation of time. The tight cause-and-effect chain of events and the adherence to an immediate type of realism call for a construction of time that feels natural, coherent, and unproblematic. Hence, the penchant for a linear chronology in the ordering of the events and a depiction of duration that comes across as equivalent to the actual duration of the action. Unlike the classical narration, art cinema, on the other hand, may highlight the workings of the temporal system for various purposes. For instance, ambiguous flashbacks and flashforwards may be instigated by personal memory or insight, temps mort may reinforce objective realism, whereas a freeze-frame may be a sign of authorial presence. In all these cases, time does not function autonomously. The temporal devices in an art film may occasionally call attention to themselves, but they are still justified by the overarching norms of the art mode, namely objective/subjective realism and authorial commentary.

In the same vein, the post-classical mode requires a temporal construction that serves the complex post-classical motivations, as we have described them so far. The dominant principle of post-classical time is that of mediated time, i.e., of time that has been manipulated and is contingent upon a series of creative or narrative decisions. To that end, it develops and experiments with an extensive array of paradigmatic options for shaping the order, the duration, and the frequency of the story components, rendering filmic time more palpable than ever before. In terms of temporal order, post-classical films opt for a non-linear presentation of the story, favouring self-conscious and blatant movements in time, while also underscoring the relation of simultaneity embedded in the spatial montage. Similarly, the parameter of duration is widely explored through varying degrees of fast and slow motion to intensify the action and heighten its emotional impact. And in addition to moving back and forth or going quickly and slowly, narrative time in the post-classical system may also pause. Freeze-frames have become common tropes deployed either to indicate closure or grant the audience time to register key information. Finally, the quality of frequency, although less malleable than the order and the duration, is often challenged as well, allowing the plot to repeat shots or even entire scenes. Overall, this new system of time consists of techniques that construct an overtly convoluted and mediated temporality. The governing notion of mediated time is primarily served through complex chronology and elastic duration, as explained in detail below.

KEY CONCEPTS

3.2 Mediated Time

The post-classical mode establishes as dominant the logic of mediated time as opposed to natural time, which characterized the classical and the art cinema, even if for different reasons. The impact of computer technology, as well as the ever-evolving perception of time in our media-saturated world, have facilitated a conceptual transformation in the construction of temporality that supports the overt manipulation of time. Like the transition from the graphic to the photographic space, the passage from natural to mediated time brings to the surface the marginal practices of animation and the avant-garde, impregnating them with powerful narrative possibilities.

The role of digitality is felt as palpably in the articulation of filmic time as in the composition of filmic space. Digital tools are capable of producing not only spatial montages but also temporal effects that reinforce a sophisticated approach to cinematic temporality. The two transformations, namely the spatial and the temporal, tend to cooperate closely, sustaining a clear distinction between the post-classical mode and the others, particularly the classical. Whereas the photographic images of classical cinema depict natural time as a sign of their ties to external reality, the graphic images of the post-classical mode are freed from such constraints; in fact, their representation of time can still pursue its realistic purposes liberated from the Bazinian illusion of linear temporal movement. Timothy Murray points up the irony in this lengthy quote:

> You might recall, in this context, how cinema was praised by its influential French theoretician, André Bazin, for freeing time from its "embalmment" in photography. In contrast to cinema, he writes, "photography liberates its object from temporal contingency in a way that 'embalms time' in the click of the instant and thus heightens the photograph's ontological value or 'presence.'" It's hard not to be amused by how this logic has come full circle, in that digitality, the medium of virtuality, could be said to free time from the hallucination of analogue movement, from the hallucination of cinema's temporal movement from point A to point B to point C.
>
> MURRAY 1999: 6

The main feature of the digital moving images is the representation of reality through pure simulation. Digital technology can affirm the characteristics of its analogue predecessor, or it can choose to transgress them (Spielmann 1999: 146). Thus, by embracing the full potential of digitality, post-classical time meticulously crafts an intricate temporal system that maintains both options, i.e., the combination of natural time with multiple variations of mediated time.

In terms of technology, the construction of narrative time in the post-classical works relies entirely on the digital post-production process. Although films may still be shot on film and spatial effects can still be performed in an analogue fashion, temporal editing and its tricks are no longer created through analogue means. Admittedly, all temporal manipulations, whether at the level of order, duration, or frequency, had been possible before; yet the digital software renders them effortless and accessible, providing contemporary filmmakers with exceptional creative freedom. Once again, however, technology should not be confused with technique. The emphasis of the post-classical mode on mediated time—and its consequent application in the form of complex chronology and elastic duration—is primarily a narrative choice, one that falls in line with the principles of the wider narrative structure.

It is essential to underline that the systems of time, space, and narrative logic are inextricably linked in every cinematic image, but they are not always of equal importance. In post-classical storytelling the system of narrative logic prevails, subordinating space and time to its mandates. As a result, the mediated construction of time should be considered as derivative of the pivotal changes at the level of the narrative motivations, particularly the compositional and the realistic. Regarding the former, the presence of multiple characters and the diversification of the plot structures necessitate a temporal fragmentation of the chronology and invite a non-linear presentation of the story material. This in turn inaugurates innovative devices for establishing the successivity and simultaneity of the events. At the same time, the hypermediated realism compels the representation of time as a mediated experience, which can be accelerated or prolonged, paused or replayed at will. Post-classical time contains a varied set of paradigmatic options that seek to transmit the complexity and the variation of mediated temporalities in the digital age.[1]

3.3 Complex Chronology

The discussion about temporal order in the narration of a fiction film involves the events of the story and the order in which they are presented in the plot.[2] Bordwell's account of narrative time introduces two ways of analyzing order; one raises the issue of simultaneity and successivity, while the other that of chronology. The matter of simultaneity is rarely discussed, as most films are bound by the sequential projection and the linear editing of the images. However, the filmic frame can present different events simultaneously, deploying deep space compositions, split screens, or other effects (Bordwell 1985: 77). In terms of chronology, the plot can stage the events of the story in chronological order or move backward and forward in their timeline. The shift to a moment in the past, known as a "flashback," or—more infrequently—to the future, known as a "flashforward," disrupts the linear order and the illusion of the natural progression of time.

The post-classical system of time invites a systematic, and often ingeniously plotted, break in the linear chronology to emphasize the mediated nature of cinematic temporality. The device of the flashback is a recurrent trait of the post-classical works, which handle this unnatural reversal of time in a self-conscious manner. Specifically, apart from the traditional justification of the flashback through a character's recollection, the post-classical mode allows the backward movement to occur through nondiegetic sources that may function autonomously from the protagonists' goals. Thus, the disruption of the temporal flow no longer requires a solid compositional motivation, as was the case for classical narration. The "flashforward," on the other hand, remains a less common option, though not a prohibited one. Post-classical time may incorporate such challenges that offer the audience the opportunity to catch glimpses of future events. In both movements, whether in the past or the future, the constraints of linearity are considerably loosened, granting the filmmakers the freedom to transfuse their films with the flexibility and the omni-directionality embodied in the digital technology. It is important to stress, however, that the play with the temporal order does not aim a creating a permanent sense of ambiguity, as was the case in famous examples from the art cinema tradition like *Hiroshima mon amour* (1959) or *Otto e Mezzo*[3] (1963). Post-classical flashbacks are signposted through the voice-over, the use of intertitles, or other techniques that help the audience navigate the timeline.

Aside from temporal movement, post-classical time also encourages the relation of simultaneity. The extensive role of spatial montage facilitates the simultaneous presentation of story events within a single frame, reinforcing the logic of addition and coexistence. The visual clusters that develop in this new mode can be distinguished into four categories: 1) depictions of simultaneous events in the same shot; 2) depictions of successive events in the same shot; 3) depictions of a single event from different angles in the same shot; and 4) presentations of a single event with elements belonging to a different diegetic level (graphics, titles, or other nondiegetic elements). The graphic construction of the cinematic space and its liberation from the photographic imperatives has allowed the post-classical mode to develop a significantly more complex presentation of the story material.

Finally, complex chronology opens up the option of non-linearity or, in Allan Cameron's terms, that of "modularity." According to Cameron, a "database or modular narrative goes beyond the classical deployment of flashback, offering a series of disarticulated narrative pieces, often arranged in radically achronological ways via flashforwards, overt repetition, or a destabilization of the relationship between present and past" (Cameron 2008: 1). Although modular narratives are not necessarily post-classical, modularity can be an option within the system of post-classical time. *Run Lola Run* and *Pulp Fiction* are two prominent cases that display how the plot may take the form of a loop, problematizing the traditional relation between the past, present, and future. The episodic structure of the post-classical plot is highly germane to the organization of the story events into achronological segments whose temporal interconnection ranges from problematic to impossible.

Overall, one key feature of post-classical time is the ordering of the story events into a complex chronology that defies certain key principles of classical storytelling, namely linearity and successivity. The emphasis on simultaneity and the manipulation of temporal order either through constant jumps in the timeline or through a modular construction of the plot result in a new configuration of the cinematic system of time that is uniquely post-classical.

3.4 Elastic Duration

The second major quality of narrative time is duration, which is distinguished into three categories: 1) story duration; 2) plot duration; and 3) screen duration or "projection time" (Bordwell 1985: 81). For example, the action of the story might extend over a period of years, while the plot will focus on only a few months or even days that are portrayed in screen time that lasts just a few hours. The three variables are closely connected through the relations of equivalence, reduction, and expansion. Equivalence takes place when a film presents an event in its entirety; no part is missing. This kind of relation can be maintained only very briefly, as the plot is expected to present events that temporally exceed far beyond the limit of projection time. Instead, the most dominant strategy is that of reduction, which is achieved through ellipsis or compression. The former omits segments of the story from the duration of the plot, while the latter condenses the story and plot duration in the screen time. Finally, there is the option of expansion, which extends the story duration either through insertion or dilation. Insertion entails the interruption of the action with nondiegetic material, whereas dilation stretches out the depicted action with slow motion. In addition to these options, post-classical duration includes the possibility of the pause. Although, in technical terms, the moving image itself never stops moving, the use of a freeze-frame can indeed stop the story time. During the pause the narration may continue to add information about the story through voice-overs, music, or even text.

Post-classical time is characterized by its elastic duration, i.e., for the manipulation of the story and plot duration in ways that challenge the impression of equivalence and demonstrate the expressive power of reduction and expansion. The duration becomes elastic in this mode in order to accommodate the compositional needs of the story as well as the hypermediated realism that motivates its construction. For instance, fast-paced editing techniques often create blatant ellipses that are necessary for the presentation of complex causal relations and multi-thread plotlines. Whereas the classical film maintained the illusion of equivalence through continuity editing, the post-classical film strives to contain multiple characters and actions within its limited projection time. Apart from the ellipsis, however, the device of compression becomes a recurring preference that adds to the hypermediated energy of this new representational mode.

The use of fast motion serves multiple expressive needs, helping the filmmakers visualize the emotional resonance of key scenes in the plot.

On the other hand, durational expansion has become popular, too. The post-classical plot is regularly interrupted by nondiegetic inserts that can comment on the action or even refer to extratextual parameters. The interruption may last but a few seconds if the insert is merely an intertitle. Likewise, it can expand to several minutes if the insert is an entire scene. Similarly, the duration of an event may be dilated through varying degrees of slow motion for a number of reasons, including the following: 1) to render action sequences more spectacular; 2) to give the audience time to observe key details in the frame during intricately staged scenes; or 3) to depict the subjective experiences of characters in moments of inner tension.

Finally, it is important to highlight the increasing use of the temporal pause in the works of post-classical filmmakers who have transformed the freeze-frame into an ordinary device. The frozen image was never part of the classical repertory, as it contradicted what was considered to be cinema's most inherent capacity, namely movement.[4] Acknowledging now that this movement is optional, the post-classical mode welcomes the freeze-frame as one of its paradigmatic choices. One of its main purposes is to function as a form of punctuation, signaling the beginning or ending of an episode. In some cases, the freeze-frame becomes a still tableau that graphically displays story information. In others, it is explored for its rhythmic potential as its stillness counterpoises the motion of the regular frames and contributes to an expressive and stylized tempo.

ANALYSIS

CASE STUDY A: *TRAINSPOTTING* (1996)

Danny Boyle's *Trainspotting*, an adaptation of Irvine Welsh's novel, caused a sensation upon its release for its provocative depiction of drug addiction. Mark Renton (Ewan McGregor) is the key protagonist in a group of young addicts who struggle with drugs and crime in an underdeveloped area of Scotland. His playful and blatantly self-conscious voice-over holds together a string of episodes that feature the adventures of the following characters: Spud (Ewen Bremner), Sick Boy (Jonny Lee Miller), Tommy (Kevin McKidd), and Begbie (Robert Carlyle). Their intertwining paths, as well as their occasional conflicts, require a complex construction of the chronology, while the emphasis on drug dependency from a subjective point-of-view also demands a level of elasticity in relation to the duration.

Chronology

The pre-credit opening lasts for almost six minutes and could be regarded as a long montage sequence that introduces the characters and weaves together several incidents, some of which will be replayed again at a different section of the plot. The position of these incidents in the timeline of the story can only be vaguely determined. Instead, they constitute disarticulated segments, parts of a modular mini-narrative, that seek to condense the purpose (or the lack thereof) in the characters' lives. Indeed, the loose character motivation results in a series of episodes that exult at what Thomas Elsaesser would call the "pathos of failure."[5] Instead of the typical wanderings of the art mode, however, *Trainspotting* adopts the post-classical hypermediacy to inject the characters' trajectory with the energy that heroin strips them of.

After the credits, the story focuses on Mark's attempt to get clean, while remaining in close contact with his friends who either suffer from addiction or violent impulses. Both influences make his goal almost unattainable, condemning him to recurrent relapses. The key events of the story, such as Mark's relationship with Diane, the death of the baby, the shoplifting arrest, Mark's move to London, the heroin scheme and, finally, Mark's betrayal, follow a largely linear order, which is regularly interrupted by brief or even longer breaks. An impressive treatment of the chronology comes early in the plot when Mark, as the film's forceful narrator, flaunts his omniscience by openly manipulating the temporal coordinates of the narration.

Specifically, during an evening at the pub, the gang is sitting around Begbie, listening to his account of a pool game he played with Tommy a few days before (Figure 3.1). His verbal account shown in the scene is interrupted by a brief shot of that day that visualizes his flashback (Figure 3.2).

FIGURE 3.1

FIGURE 3.2

Then, the plot returns to the present and allows us to hear Begbie's version while cutting to the listeners' faces to register their reactions (Figures 3.3–3.4).

As soon as his story concludes, Mark freezes the frame and explains in the voice-over: "And that was it. That was Begbie's story. Or at least that was Begbie's version of the story. Two days later I got the truth from Tommy." The freeze-frame on Begbie's face changes to a freeze-frame on Tommy's (Figure 3.5) to initiate a flashforward. The segment from the future moment takes place in Tommy's room and includes a scene between Tommy and Mark that will prove pivotal in many respects besides the truth about the pool game (Figure 3.6–3.7).

FIGURE 3.3

FIGURE 3.4

FIGURE 3.5

FIGURE 3.6

FIGURE 3.7

FIGURE 3.8

Tommy's account of that incident is visualized with intermittent shots that establish a different perspective on what happened that day (Figures 3.8–3.9). Tommy's flashback within the flashforward eventually ends, allowing the plot to return to Begbie's freeze-frame and pick up the story linearly from there (Figure 3.10).

The freedom to break the linear chronology is illustrated several more times during the second hour of the film, but these interruptions concern movements backwards in time rather than forward. The highly self-conscious voice-over, which sets the tone from the opening moment, familiarizes the viewer with the formal manipulation of its narration and justifies every jump on the timeline. *Trainspotting* opts for a complex chronology in the presentation of the events in the effort to accommodate its multiple characters and their never-ending predicaments.

FIGURE 3.9

FIGURE 3.10

Duration

The concept of mediated time is also evident in the treatment of the story duration. One of the recurring elements in *Trainspotting* is the creation of the impression of speed (or slowness) in order to match the emotional state of the characters. For example, the feeling of excitement during the football game is built through a combination of jump cuts and freeze-frames. On another occasion, Spud's interview is edited with a rhythmic alternation of a medium and a long frontal shot, seeking to transmit his inner energy under the influence of speed. These are cases of ellipsis that are stylistically flaunted to illustrate the elastic duration of the plot. In addition, there is an interesting instance of compression that results from the partial use of fast motion. In Figure 3.11, we see Mark sitting at a table with family and friends.

FIGURE 3.11

While he remains thoughtful and motionless, the people around him move in fast motion. This combination of stillness and motion within the same frame strives to visualize the feeling of estrangement he experiences and the lack of contact with his surroundings. On the other hand, the scenes that depict the heroin use tend to have a slower pace overall, emulating the relaxation and the euphoria that the characters enjoy, albeit fleetingly.

Frequency

The quality of frequency in *Trainspotting* presents some aberrations from the standard norm of representing each action only once. As noted above, the pre-credit sequence consists of shots that will reappear at other parts of the plot without any additional narrative purpose. For instance, the sequence showing Mark and his friends being chased by the police is repeated later on with a different voice-over. Unlike other films that repeat shots or sequences to elucidate key story information, *Trainspotting* replays those scenes merely for the purpose of playfulness. In other moments, however, such as the recounting of the pool game analyzed above, the repetition of certain freeze-frames functions as punctuation that helps the viewer navigate the timeline. Overall, the repetitive form in the post-classical mode does not contradict the realistic depiction of the story. The general conception of mediated time that governs the post-classical system of time incorporates the repetitions in the temporal scheme, rendering them normal and anticipated.

CASE STUDY B: *FIGHT CLUB* (1999)

Fight Club is a widely acclaimed film and remains to this day one of David Fincher's most influential works. The story depicts the plight of an unnamed protagonist (Edward Norton) who suffers from chronic insomnia and loses all his possessions when his condo explodes. He seeks help from Tyler Durden (Brad Pitt), an enigmatic character he met on a business trip, and together they start a Fight Club, at which people regularly engage in violent fights. Gradually, the members of the Fight Club develop an anti-corporate scheme called Project Mayhem, which aims to tear down Western consumerism. The twist of the story, revealed only in the last part, is that Tyler Durden is an imaginary character projected mentally by the protagonist throughout the plot. His psychiatric condition and Tyler's fictional status are two fundamental compositional elements that need to be suppressed until the very end. As a result, the plot explores the post-classical temporal possibilities that uphold the mystery and serve the complex narrative logic.

Chronology

Fight Club opens at a climactic point in the action. The credit sequence is located at a diegetic threshold, as it depicts the fear centre of the narrator's brain. When the camera emerges in the outer world, we see him in close-up with a gun barrel in his mouth, saying in the voice-over: "People are always asking me if I know Tyler Durden" (Figure 3.12).

As soon as the gun is removed, he carries on describing the critical moment of the story. To tell us more, he needs to take us back in time. Thus, he initiates a flashback showing him in the arms of a man named Bob (Meat Loaf) during a therapy session for men with testicular cancer.

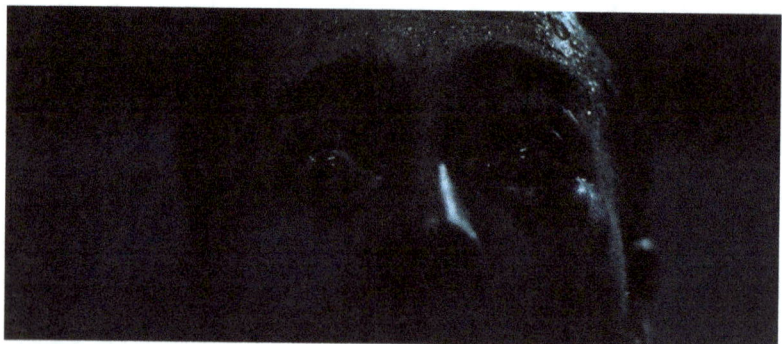

FIGURE 3.12

A few seconds later, he stops the flashback saying, "No wait! Back up! Let me start over." The plot moves further back in time to the moment when his chronic insomnia first appears. The self-conscious narrator's playful liberty to manipulate the chronology of the events is a constant feature of the film and a paradigmatic demonstration of the notion of mediated time—the trademark of the post-classical temporality.

The second flashback takes us, indeed, to the source of the protagonist's problem and continues the portrayal of the events in a largely linear order with multiple shorter flashbacks regularly providing additional story information. For example, his frequent encounters with Marla Singer (Helena Bonham Carter) at the support groups are presented as a flashback, while the explosion of his condo is shown through a cross-cutting between the current moment (Figure 3.13) and the past (Figure 3.14). Although these breaks in chronology are aided by the voice-over narration, they do not constitute traditional flashbacks. The latter tend to consist of entire sequences that are sufficiently separated from the present moment. In *Fight Club*, however, Fincher fuses the past with the present

FIGURE 3.13

FIGURE 3.14

in a more integral fashion, while signposting the transitions through the voice-over.

After all the twists are revealed, we reach the opening scene with the protagonist having the gun in his mouth. At that point, the loop is fully formed, and the voice-over openly remarks, "I think this is about where we came in." His alter ego, Tyler Durden, talks about "flashback humour," raising yet higher the level of self-consciousness of the narrational act. From this moment onwards, only a few minutes remain until the closing scene shows the protagonist and his girlfriend Marla witnessing the explosions of the buildings around them. The complex chronological order in *Fight Club* serves an equally complex narrative logic that meticulously plots the characters and their trajectories to withhold the secret of the split personality disorder. Could the same story have been told in a linear fashion? Undoubtedly so. Yet the form of the loop combined with a free movement on the timeline of the events forges an intriguing narration and a fine example of post-classical storytelling.

Duration

The parameter of duration in *Fight Club* manifests a wide range of variations, illustrating the significance of mediated time in the post-classical mode. One of the key devices is the expansion of the story duration through the insertion of nondiegetic segments. For instance, in the opening scene—and right before the flashback—the protagonist offers the viewer a brief nondiegetic tour of the premises. As we watch him and Tyler look outside the window of the skyscraper (Figure 3.15), the camera drops vertiginously down thirty stories, goes through the sidewalk into the underground garage, passes through the bullet-hole in the van with the explosives, and then moves out to the side.

FIGURE 3.15

Those images are accompanied with his voice explaining:

> We have front row seats for this theatre of mass destruction. The demolitions committee of Project Mayhem wrapped the foundation columns of a dozen buildings with blasting gelatine. In two minutes, primary charges will blow base charges and a few square blocks will be reduced to smouldering rubble. I know this because Tyler knows this.

This can be viewed as a nondiegetic insert because the camera offers a view of the storyworld that is accessible only to the audience and nobody else within it. In this sense, it interrupts the regular flow of the story and expands the duration of the plot. Similarly, and even more spectacularly, the presentation of Tyler's personality is conducted through an extensive two-minute insert that appears after a freeze-frame. Thus, the story literally freezes, and the protagonist tells us "Let me tell you a little bit about Tyler Durden." In the scenes that follow, Tyler's character and his activities are introduced in a highly self-conscious manner with both characters recurrently looking at the camera (Figures 3.16–3.17).

FIGURE 3.16

FIGURE 3.17

On other occasions, the expansion of the duration is carried out through dilation, i.e., the use of slow motion. For example, Marla is regularly filmed in slow motion, particularly when she lights up a cigarette. Moreover, the tendency to manipulate the speed of the image is manifested in scenes with increased physicality, such as the fight scenes, the sex scenes, or the intense running scene in the finale where the protagonist rushes to avert the disaster of his own making. The elastic duration renders those moments more sensational and contributes to the hypermediated nature of the post-classical realism.

Frequency

Temporal frequency is a quality that draws attention in *Fight Club* for the way it represents, among other things, the regularity of certain actions. The protagonist's life is full of routines; first, it was his sleepless nights; then, it was the attendance of group therapy sessions; then the fights at the Fight Club, and, finally, the preparation of Project Mayhem. A significant number of scenes portray only once activities that took place several times, while the recurrence is openly indicated in the voice-over that contains the necessary expressions, such as "every time," to articulate the proper tense.

On the other end, there are several unique moments that are replayed at least twice. The repetitions become frequent in the last part of the film, when the protagonist discovers that he is Tyler Durden. The secret of the story is emphatically revealed as the narrator visits the places that Tyler had visited, gradually realizing that they are the same person. Several moments of the past now reappear without Tyler's presence, revealing the action from an objective point of view instead of the character's focalized perspective that we have been witnessing all along. When we return to the present moment, the opening is replayed with a subtle change in the dialogue. Instead of "I can't think of anything," the protagonist says, "I *still* can't think of anything," with Tyler adding the line "flashback humor," which did not exist in the beginning. These playful repetitions benefit the work's compositional and generic motivations and testify to Fincher's freedom to explore the temporal possibilities of the filmic narration without the constraints of the classical representation of time as a natural current.

CASE STUDY C: *MEMENTO* (2000)

Memento is a landmark film in the history of complex storytelling, one that prompted reviewers and scholars alike to reconsider their conceptual schemata. Yet, unlike other similar examples, such as *Lost Highway* and *Donnie Darko*, Christopher Nolan's work combines enough elements to qualify as post-classical, particularly in relation to its narrative logic and the system of narrative time. Its story features Leonard Shelby

(Guy Pearce), a former insurance investigator, who suffers from short-term memory loss as the result of an assault that killed his wife and left him permanently injured. His goal is to avenge her death by killing the perpetrator. This deceptively classical premise, however, is challenged through an intricate play on causality and time. The presentation of the story in the plot is carried through a series of episodes that belong to different temporal planes and give away little by little the key compositional ingredients: the characters, the events, the goals, and the motives. Each episode is a piece of a puzzle, which requires considerable effort and multiple viewings in order to be fully comprehended.[6] To tell a twisted story, Nolan chose to meddle with the parameters of order and frequency.

Chronology

Memento's plot consists of twenty-one segments shot in black-and-white and twenty-three shot in color. The arrangement of these segments is quite unique in many respects: the film opens with color, and then alternates between color and black-and-white in a stable pattern. In addition, there is a second pattern in the ordering of the story events in the plot; the black-and-white parts follow a linear chronology, while the color segments move from the past to the present. The notion of time reversal is highlighted in the opening scene which plays backwards: a Polaroid photograph begins to fade to white (Figure 3.18) and soon returns to the camera (Figure 3.19).

FIGURE 3.18

FIGURE 3.19

Then, a killing is played back to front, and the retrogression of time becomes overtly exposed. This color passage is followed by one in black-and-white that shows the protagonist in a motel room wondering about his condition and his surroundings. This sequence runs in a linear fashion and continues as such for the rest of the film. Yet the temporal connection between the two scenes can become intelligible only after the end of the film and for some viewers—especially those without a DVD player—not even then. The first black-and-white scene in the motel is the beginning of the story, while the first color scene is the very last. Thus, *Memento*'s plot starts from the very end and moves back in time through the color sequences while interweaving black-and-white moments from the beginning of the story. As the black-and-white scenes progress in a linear fashion and the color ones progress in reverse, there will be a time in the film when the two story moments will meet and the plot will visualize the connection through the passage from black-and-white to color within the same frame, using once more a Polaroid photograph (Figures 3.20–3.21).

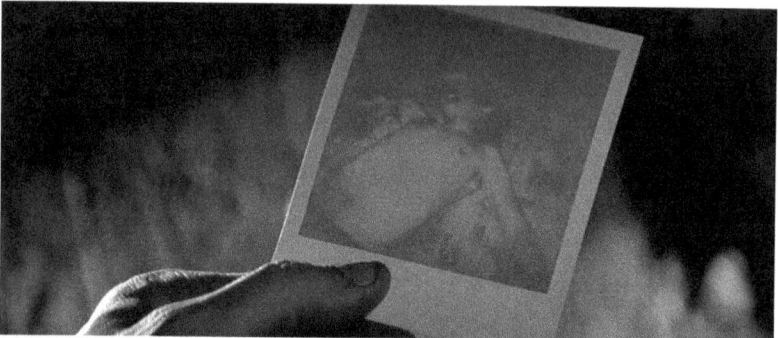

FIGURE 3.20

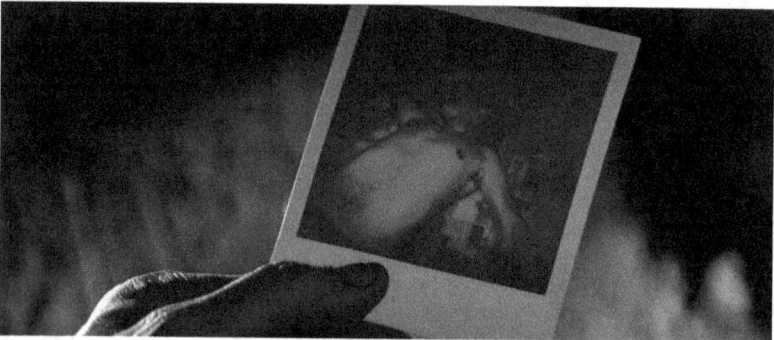

FIGURE 3.21

In this highly elaborate temporal structure, a key compositional element—namely Leonard's memory problem—becomes an ingenious device for manipulating the order of the events, and above all, their causal connections. For the most part, we are misled regarding the main story events, particularly those around his wife's death as well as the pursuit of the killer. The protagonist's condition also triggers a series of flashbacks and memories that complicate even further the already puzzling exposition. Apart from the temporal construction described above, there are regular breaks in chronology that occur in both types of sequences (color and black-and-white). Most prominent is the story of Sammy Jankis, contained in the black-and-white sequences, which supposedly takes us back to the time before Leonard's memory loss. The color segments, on the other hand, are interspersed with flashbacks to the night of the assault and other moments that feature his wife. In both cases, however, these are false flashbacks. The images contained therein do not represent the actual events; instead, they project the distorted images of a mentally disturbed character. With this unorthodox type of flashback, reminiscent of Alfred Hitchcock's *Stage Fright* (1950), Nolan raises the level of complexity even higher and crafts an exceptionally challenging viewing experience.

Duration

The representation of the story duration is the least experimental aspect in *Memento*. Unlike the order and the frequency, the duration of the events is portrayed through a series of conventional techniques that reinforce the illusion of equivalence, i.e., the impression that the action within each scene appears in its entirety. In fact, the reduction through ellipsis is the dominant option in most scenes in a concerted effort to accommodate the story within the plot duration. The forty-four short episodes that comprise the body of the film contain a series of dialogues, encounters, phone calls, and car rides that require the use of intensified continuity to transmit a significant amount of story information within a limited time frame. For instance, the use of eyeline matches and point-of-view shots is essential throughout. In Figures 3.22–3.25, we find two typical cases of focalized editing that shows the character and the object of his gaze, emphasizing his struggle to put together the pieces of the puzzle.

The low ASL of the film, which is measured to 3.5 seconds, indicates the enormous amount of cutting that is required to maintain the impression of continuity in the action while performing all the necessary ellipses. All in all, the parameter of duration is the one that stands out the least in *Memento*. Given the degree of complexity in the chronology and the marked significance of frequency, I believe that the moderate treatment of duration in the temporal system grants the narrational act a vital sense of balance.

FIGURE 3.22

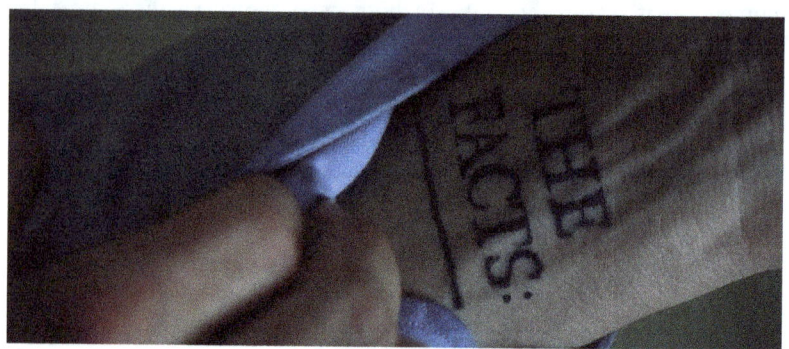

FIGURE 3.23

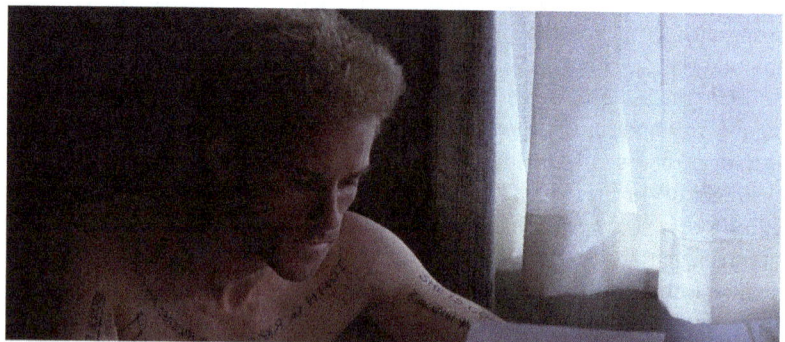

FIGURE 3.24

FIGURE 3.25

Frequency

The highly complicated construction of the plot and the convoluted chronology of the events maintain a level of intelligibility thanks to the workings of frequency in the system of narrative time. Specifically, the color sequences seek to signpost the actual order of the events by repeating shots in the beginning and ending of each segment. Thus, Nolan shows the viewer brief parts of the action twice with consistent regularity, encouraging them to "make the operation of mental rotation, which consists in putting the events of the two sequences in the right chronological order, to verify the temporal and causal relationships" (Guislotti, 2009: 96). Thus, the repetition of several adjoining sections becomes an essential mental tool for putting together the pieces of the puzzle, despite the thwarting force of the retrograde order.

On other occasions, however, a number of shots are repeated either exactly as they are or with slight alterations aiming to illustrate the unreliability of the protagonist as a narrator. As a result, the flashbacks on the night of the assault are replayed with variations and so are the memories of his wife. For instance, in Figure 3.26 we see Leonard pinching her, while in Figure 3.27 he gives her an insulin injection.

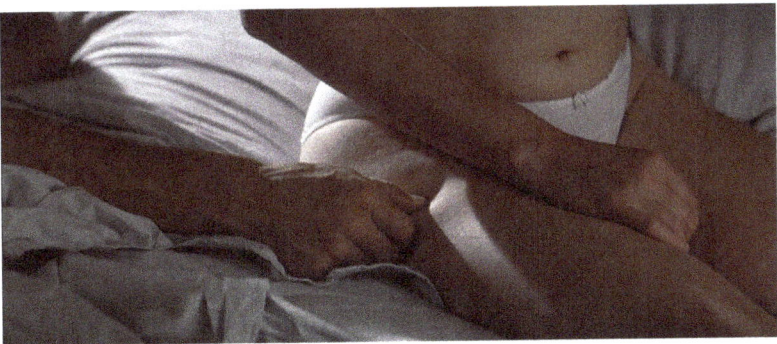

FIGURE 3.26

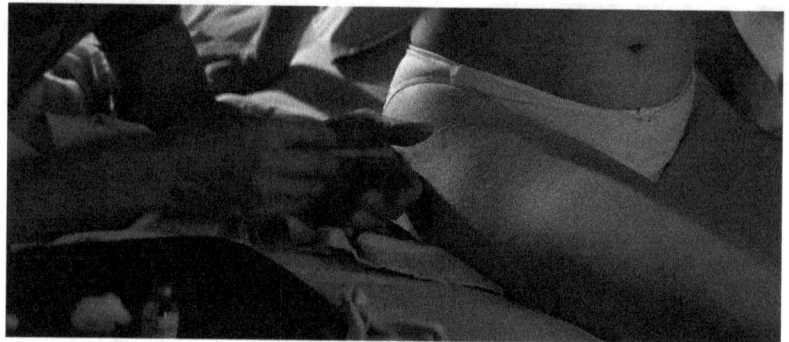

FIGURE 3.27

This kind of repetition aims at exposing the focalized nature of these images and, therefore, unsettling our hypotheses about his past. Overall, the break from the standard rule of representing each action only once is a purely functional device in *Memento* and not in the least decorative. The manipulation of temporal frequency as an expression of mediated time corroborates fully the intricate narrative logic of the film.

3.5 Conclusion

As these analyses have revealed, the system of narrative time in the post-classical mode encompasses a set of consistent creative choices for the articulation of temporal qualities. Despite the lack of tenses in the linguistic sense, the post-classical images are capable of expressing time through a configuration of visual, aural, and graphic elements in a particularly pronounced fashion. Time, in these films, cannot go unnoticed. Unlike other historical modes, the post-classical promotes the notion of mediated time as the governing principle of its temporal axis and relies on the power of complex chronology and elastic duration to materialize it. These norms, however, do not function autonomously from the other systems. Temporal devices collaborate with spatial ones in order to fulfill the purposes of a complex and multi-faceted narrative logic. The episodic plot structures, the multiple characters, and, above all, the hypermediated realism necessitate an overt manipulation of order, duration, and frequency. The privilege to explore these temporal possibilities in favor of a complex storytelling act opens up the creative freedom of the post-classical filmmakers to an immense degree, prompting them to extend and challenge the limits of the cinematic language.

Notes

1 For a comprehensive overview on the phenomenon of mediated time in the digital age, see Hartmann et al. (2019).
2 The story always contains more events than those portrayed on the screen. They are recounted through character dialogue or nondiegetic sources, such as intertitles. For the distinction between recounting and enacting story events, see Chatman (1990).
3 Also known as *8½*.
4 Some notable exceptions in classical Hollywood include films like *It's a Wonderful Life* (1947) and *All About Eve* (1950), which make an evocative use of the freeze-frame to focus the viewer's attention on the main characters.
5 See Introduction.
6 For a detailed textual analysis, see Ghislotti (2009).

4

Post-classical Narration

4.1 Introduction

The storytelling process can be studied according to different sets of principles, each with its own investigative focus. The construction of the historical modes relied primarily on David Bordwell's story/plot/style distinction as well as the narrational analysis of the filmic text on three levels—i.e., devices, systems (narrative logic, time, and space) and the relations between those systems.[1] Thanks to the conceptual rigor of these terms and categories, the paradigmatic options of the post-classical mode were systematically charted, while its distinguishing features came to prominence. Yet there is an additional analytical layer in each mode, one that pertains to the means by which the filmic narration shares story information. According to Edward Branigan, narration can be defined as "the overall regulation and distribution of knowledge which determines when and how a reader acquires knowledge from a text" (Branigan 2002: 106). From the first frame to the last, the film presents elements that are directly or indirectly related to the characters and the storyworld combined with other extratextual aspects that engage the viewer into an activity of comprehension and interpretation. In order to assess how the post-classical mode shapes the narration as a vehicle for the transmission of information, I will deploy two complementary narrative theories that are best suited to the task: 1) Meir Sternberg's three categories of self-consciousness, knowledgeability, and communicativeness; and 2) Branigan's eight levels of narration. As both approaches will testify, post-classical narration is characterized by a distinctively high degree of self-consciousness and communicativeness, while it explores an unusually wide range of narrative levels for its storytelling purposes.

KEY CONCEPTS

4.2 Self-consciousness, Knowledgeability, and Communicativeness

Meir Sternberg's narrative theories were extensively embraced by Bordwell in his effort to formulate a comprehensive narrative theory and to elucidate the differences between the various historical modes (Bordwell 1985: 57). Specifically, the three qualities of self-consciousness, knowledgeability, and communicativeness provided him with yet another interpretive tool for the description of the narrational process. Let us see what they mean and how they can be applied in a filmic analysis. First, a narration can be *self-conscious* to varying degrees, depending on how much it acknowledges that it hails an audience and presents them with information. The more aware the spectators become of the narrating act, the more self-conscious the narration is. Thus, to evaluate the self-consciousness of a film we ask the question: to what extent does the narration reveal its own performance? Secondly, a narration can be more or less *knowledgeable* in relation to how much information it possesses regarding the story. The knowledge of the narration may reach a specific range and depth, both of which are regulated by the function of the characters as sources of information. For instance, when a narration exceeds the awareness of the characters, it displays a wide range and becomes omniscient. When, on the other hand, it enters the consciousness of a character, it acquires great depth. The question to investigate the knowledgeability is: how much does the narration know? Finally, a narration can be *communicative* depending on how much information it communicates to the viewer. Regardless of how much the narration knows, its communicative aspect depends solely on how much of its knowledge it is willing to share with us; it may know little and tell us all (communicative) or it may know it all and tell us little (suppressive). Thus, the question becomes: how willing is the narration to give away its knowledge?

Every historical mode has handled the process of story transmission differently, codifying in distinctive ways the degrees of self-consciousness, knowledgeability, and communicativeness in the narration of their films. The classical Hollywood film opens with a series of sequences that may be moderately self-conscious and fairly omniscient, as they intend to provide key information about the storyworld, namely the setting and the characters. Gradually, the narration phases itself out and communicates information only through the characters' dialogues and interactions. The cornerstone of the classical narration is the creation of a compact diegetic world that effaces the narrational act, maintains a potentially high level of knowledgeability and gradually communicates all the secrets of the story. By the time we reach the closing moments, all the gaps have been filled and the clarity of the resolution builds a feeling of certainty (Bordwell 1985: 57).

The art film, on the other hand, often leaves the viewer baffled and ambivalent about the state of things. Besides, ambiguity is the trademark of art cinema, according to Bordwell, and this may be the result of all three narrational qualities in question. First, a high degree of self-consciousness stems from the authorial intervention, which blatantly interferes with the plot or style construction. The increased self-consciousness may be coupled with an omniscient narration that overtly plays with spectatorial expectations (225). For instance, a flashforward, a common device in this mode, indicates a wide range of knowledge that is not accessible to the characters but reveals the power of the narrator. Yet full story knowledge is rarely disclosed to the audience, as art films consistently resort to a limited communicativeness that obstructs the pleasure of filling the narrative gaps. Art cinema narration suppresses key information in order to deny access to the secrets of the characters and the outcomes of their actions.

Post-classical narration differs considerably from the previous two modes when it comes to the transmission of information and the regulation of self-consciousness, knowledgeability, and communicativeness. Admittedly, this is justified, given the differences at the level of narrative logic, space, and time, which were thoroughly discussed in the previous chapters.[2] Post-classical options produce a different balance among the three qualities and refashion the films' storytelling capacity. The most emblematic feature of a post-classical narration is its impressive self-consciousness. And there are a number of reasons for this significant transformation in the development of this new mode. First, the hypermediated form of realism that characterizes the realistic motivation dictates a filmic representation favoring a discontinuous depiction of time and space, distinctly in contrast to the seamless diegetic world of the classical narration. Its take on reality foregrounds the narrational process, even if the purpose is not that of estrangement but rather that of immersion. Second, the generic motivation also carries along a sense of knowingness in relation to the generic formulas, whether it adheres to the hybrid or the archaeological approach. Post-classical films embed generic tropes in a playful fashion that contributes to the increased self-consciousness of the narration. Finally, the flagrant artistic motivation in the form of parody raises the degree of reflexivity even higher. The intention of artistically motivated elements is, by definition, to foreground the storytelling act and to directly address the audience. The parodic references that abound in post-classical films invite us to acknowledge the power of an extratextual presence that deliberately highlights the historicity of other art forms and engages in a dialogue with other cultural products. Overall, from the opening to the closing moments, a post-classical narration maintains a high degree of self-consciousness that emanates from almost all the facets of the narrative logic.

The creative freedom that results from this self-consciousness also affects the aspect of knowledgeability, which becomes explicitly high. Unlike the classical omniscience that was constrained by continuity editing and the limited spatiotemporal movement within the storyworld, post-classical narration can travel openly in all directions, while the reliance on the characters for the transmission of information is no longer necessary. Post-classical films contain a series of narrational devices that far exceed the consciousness of single individuals and allow the narration to display omniscience as well as omnipotence. Apart from the wide range, however, the knowledge is also distinguished by great depth, as the subjective realism regularly allows the narration to penetrate the characters' inner worlds and access their most intimate thoughts and feelings.

Finally, the post-classical mode is distinctively communicative, as it shares abundant information about the characters, the progression of the action and the outcome of the story, ensuring the filling of the narrative gaps by the time we reach the end credits. As noted previously, post-classical compositional motivation maintains an essential chain of causality, even if looser or more episodic, demanding the constant communication of information. In fact, the multiplicity of the characters and the complexity of the plot structures compel the narration to meticulously inform the viewers, offering them multiple entry points to the story. The high level of communicativeness ensures a necessary level of coherence and intelligibility in a way that manifestly separates the post-classical mode from the art cinema. In the latter, the elevated self-consciousness works *against* the communicativeness of the narration obstructing access to key information regarding the characters and the story. On the other hand, post-classical communicativeness differs from the classical as well. Although both classical and post-classical narrations are fairly communicative types that increasingly transmit more information as the plot develops, the flaunted post-classical self-consciousness releases more daringly the forces of communicativeness, disclosing crucial secrets of the story even from the very beginning.

To conclude, the post-classical mode develops its own combination of self-consciousness, knowledgeability, and communicativeness that separates it from the older historical modes. Post-classical self-consciousness stands out for the way it collaborates with the other two categories in order to produce highly complex, fragmented and nevertheless entertaining films that challenge the viewers' activity without denying them the pleasure of solving their puzzles. This kind of self-consciousness, instead of thwarting the knowledgeability and communicativeness for the sake of obscurity and ambiguity, reinforces them to such a degree that results in an intricate form of storytelling that "knows" too much and "shares" it all with its audience.

4.3 Levels of Narration

The idiosyncrasies of post-classical narration in terms of its transmission of story information can be further elucidated through the theory of narrative "levels" put forward by Branigan in his book *Narrative Comprehension and Film* (1992). Given that a considerable number of post-classical films feature ostentatious voice-over narrators, the question of who is telling/showing us the story comes center stage. In fact, this has been one of the most vexed questions among film narratologists for almost a century, and the many answers proposed on the concept of the "narrator" vary.[3] The value of Branigan's narrative approach, however, lies in its capacity to account for all kinds of filmic narrations, from the most straightforward cases to the most perplexing ones. According to his theory of "levels," "a text is composed of a hierarchical series of levels of narration, each defining an epistemological context within which to describe data" (Branigan 1992: 87). These include the following:

1. *Historical author*: the director as a biographical person, a brand name, or a public persona.
2. *Extra-fictional narrator*: the information that comes from the outer limit of the narration at a transitional level between non-fiction and fiction. It could be an intertitle or even a sequence that comments on the fiction while still being on the threshold.
3. *Nondiegetic narrator*: a device that gives information *about* the storyworld from within the fiction but outside the diegesis. This includes voice-overs, intertitles, or music that can only be accessed by the audience.
4. *Diegetic narrator*: the film gives us information that is limited by the laws of the storyworld and could be potentially accessed by anyone within it.
5. *Character (non-focalized narration)*: the film presents the characters as agents, showing us what they say and do. We acquire information by watching them speak and act.
6. *External focalization*: the film presents us information within the characters' awareness. We see or hear what they know or perceive.
7. *Internal focalization (surface)*: the film shows us exactly what they see.
8. *Internal focalization (depth)*: the film enters the characters' mind and visualizes what transpires in their inner world.

As Branigan explains, a film "may define any number of levels to any degree of precision," ranging from the more historical/contextual to the more individual/personal (Branigan 1992: 87). At the top four levels, he designates the role of the "narrator" (historical author, extra-fictional narrator, nondiegetic narrator, and diegetic narrator) that intentionally communicates information about the story, while at the bottom four he identifies the characters as narrative agents who transmit information either as actors (non-focalized narration and external focalization) or as focalizers (surface and depth internal focalization). These three nominal agents (the narrator, actor, and focalizer) are what he calls "convenient fictions, which serve to mark how the field of knowledge is being divided at a particular time" (106). In other words, he emphasizes the conceptual value of these three categories for describing the distribution of knowledge within the narrational process. Tracing the narrative agency in every scene in a film, or more simply, understanding "who tells us what and in what way" in every moment may be an exercise that is not consciously undertaken by the average viewer. Yet it is the workings of the narrative agents that determine the direction of their assumptions and inferences. And this becomes explicitly evident in cases of complex storytelling, where the mystery derives from the intricate play among these levels, as the filmmakers strive to mislead the audience and frustrate their hypotheses.

Historically, each mode has utilized the potential of these levels of narration quite differently. The classical narration opens with a credit sequence that quickly gives way to a diegetic narrator who locates us within the storyworld via establishing shots and analytical editing. Soon, the large bulk of story information comes from the characters as agents who speak, pursue goals, and interact with the world around them, while the external focalization regularly ensures that we find out what they know and perceive. For instance, we learn about their personalities by witnessing their external behavior and we discover their views or intentions through their conversations. More rarely, a classical narration will embed the level of the nondiegetic narration in the form of a voice-over or an intertitle, while the lower levels of internal focalization (either surface or depth) will be reserved for moments of high drama. The combination of these levels maintains a low degree of self-consciousness and guarantees the seamlessness of the narrational process.

On the other hand, the arrangement of the levels in art cinema is more erratic. The directors as historical authors exercise their power more overtly in art films, where we witness several configurations of the levels. The increased self-consciousness stems from the abrupt and unpredictable switch of narrative levels that may at one moment give prominence to the higher narrators (historical, extra-fictional, nondiegetic), and in another to the focalized images of the characters' inner visions. The authorial commentary and the subjective realism, the two cornerstones of the art mode, result from the transmission of information through the higher and lower levels respectively. However, those levels are not always signaled with precision.

The overarching ambiguity of these films results from the fact that the viewers are not able to unequivocally discern whether an image comes from a higher or lower level, while their hypotheses are hardly ever confirmed. Determining the narrative levels in the average art film may prove to be an arduous task, as the narration transmits little story information and refuses to fill in the gaps.

Finally, the post-classical mode contains its own unique pattern of narrative levels that achieve the high degrees of self-consciousness, knowledgeability, and communicativeness discussed above. On the one hand, there is a systematic exploration of the upper levels of narration and, particularly, the level of the nondiegetic narrator. From the opening moments, a dominating voice may openly address the audience and explain the setting of the story. The voice may belong to someone entirely outside the diegesis, as in *Europa* or *500 Days of Summer*, it may belong to one of the leading characters, as in *The Big Short* or *Deadpool*, and in some cases, there may be more than one voice heard in the soundtrack, as in *Chungking Express* and *Sidewalls* (2011). The purpose of these narrators is to introduce the characters in a flaunted fashion and initiate the plotlines. Due to the complexity of the compositional setup of these stories, the nondiegetic narrators seek to transmit as much information as necessary to sufficiently orient the viewers. Their presence may subsequently allow the middle levels to take over the narrational process, but they always return to reiterate their authority and organize the multiple threads of the story. The role of these narrators is key in the post-classical mode, as they ensure the combination of self-consciousness and communicativeness that renders these films both intriguing and accessible. On the other hand, there is an extensive use of the lower levels, using the characters as focalizers whether on the surface or, even more frequently, in depth. The narration visualizes their mental images or their inner lives in a sustained manner, shedding light on their emotions, thoughts, and motivations. In some cases, the switch from the upper to the lower levels is abrupt and provocative without becoming unintelligible. The provenance of some shots may not be entirely clear in the beginning, especially when there are plot twists or generically motivated mysteries, but by the end of the film the viewer will be able to interpret those images in retrospect and recognize the level of narration in play.

All in all, Branigan's narrative schema of levels has a remarkable explanatory value for scrutinizing the storytelling process in all types of films, whether ordinary or idiosyncratic. It is an analytical tool that complements Sternberg's categories in the effort to map the dissemination and regulation of story information throughout the entire narrational act. Finally, it helps us identify the paradigmatic options within each historical mode and bring out their distinguishing features. As the film analyses will illustrate, post-classical films formulate their own systematic patterns of information transmission and exhibit a consistent strategy for balancing the forces of self-consciousness and communicativeness, allowing them to tell highly complex and compelling stories in an accessible and pleasurable way.

ANALYSIS

CASE STUDY A: *TRISTRAM SHANDY: A COCK AND BULL STORY* (2005)

Michael Winterbottom's film is an intriguing adaptation of Lawrence Sterne's novel *The Life and Opinions of Tristram Shandy, Gentleman* (1759), which is legendary for its highly self-reflexive narration and its ample dose of parody. The post-classical mode is, indeed, the most fitting choice for adapting this long and complex literary work to the screen, preserving several of the narrational and thematic devices of the source text. The plot contains two fairly distinct threads: the shooting of a film adaptation of Tristram Shandy (plotline A), and the actual film that is being shot (plotline B). The presentation of these two plotlines is anything but straightforward, as Winterbottom opts for an overly complex chronology with multiple flashbacks-within-flashbacks that render the timeline of the events rather modular. The two plotlines intertwine in an irregular fashion, constantly pressing the viewer to adjust their hypotheses to two diverse filmic planes, i.e., the film and the film-within-the-film.

The opening starts with plotline A, showing us the two protagonists, Steve Coogan (Steve Coogan/Tristram Shandy) and Rob Brydon (Rob Brydon/Uncle Toby), who discuss their roles in the dressing room while having their makeup applied (Figure 4.1). The scene gives us information on the level of the characters (non-focalization), showing their personalities and their competitive relationship. The next sequence switches to plotline B, showing us the opening of the film with Coogan introducing himself as Tristram Shandy by talking directly to the camera (Figure 4.2). The credits roll while he knowingly acquaints us with the setting of the story and the main characters, such as his Uncle Toby, his mother, and himself at an early age. Within this plotline, Coogan's physical presence as a narrator incessantly interrupts the flow of the diegesis. His address to the audience becomes overwhelming, while his interference with the reenactment of his life's story knows no limit. For instance, after we witness a traumatic scene from his childhood that entails his penis being injured, he scolds the child actor for not being able to convey the pain and shock of such an event (Figure 4.3).

FIGURE 4.1

FIGURE 4.2

FIGURE 4.3

Apart from this physical intrusion to the storyworld, plotline B also contains a series of nondiegetic interventions that persistently remind the viewer that they are watching a film. One of the recurring devices is the freeze-frame that pauses the diegetic exposition and allows the nondiegetic level to take over the screen, pivoting to a different moment in the story or transmitting further information. For instance, in Figure 4.4. Tristram speaks in front of a freeze-frame from a scene that takes place shortly before his birth and shows Dr. Slop (Dylan Moran) demonstrating the use of forceps with the help of a melon. Tristram freezes the action to explain why his father allowed the forceps to be used, despite the utter failure of the demonstration. The acknowledgement of the narrating act is further signalled by stylized shot transitions and split screens. The former can be glimpsed in Figure 4.5 where a horizontal wipe accompanied by a relevant sound effect gives away the filmic material of the shots and unites the two images (a black-and-white image of Alexander the Great and the previous freeze-frame) in a visually obtrusive manner.

The split screens, on the other hand, complement or replace the traditional cross-cutting in several scenes in both plotlines (Figures 4.6–4.7).

FIGURE 4.4

FIGURE 4.5

Finally, the use of nondiegetic material in black-and-white is another way to transmit story information through the higher levels of narration, as the material in question does not derive from the storyworld but instead reflects or comments upon it. For example, during the scene of Tristram's conception, the homonymous narrator is inclined to explain the situation by drawing a comparison between his parents' habitual lovemaking and Pavlov's experiment, using a series of shots from archival material (Figures 4.8–4.9).

FIGURE 4.6

FIGURE 4.7

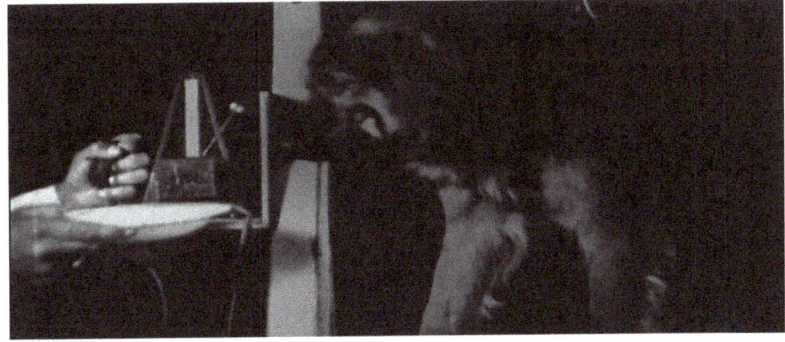

FIGURE 4.8

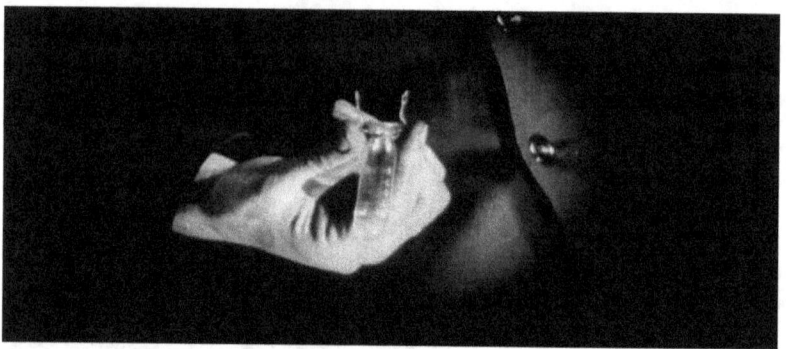

FIGURE 4.9

The demarcation of the two plotlines is relatively clear thanks to Winterbottom's stylistic signposting of the two separate threads, with plotline A bookending the film and plotline B dominating the first half. There are, however, several notable moments when the filming style deceptively merges the two threads to create internally focalized sequences. The first comes around the fortieth minute during a car ride scene with Coogan and his assistant Jennie, who talks about her own preferred section of the book, the Tristrampedia, i.e., an encyclopaedia that Tristram's father was planning to create for his son. Her description visually takes the form of a scene from plotline B, even though those images exist only in her mind. Similarly, a nightmare experienced by Coogan merges the styles of the two plotlines, beginning as a scene from the film-within-the-film and ending as a part of the shooting. Yet the entire segment clearly takes place in his imagination and amounts to a focalization in depth. Finally, the closing minutes of the film craft an intricate mingling of the two plotlines as the editing of the shots below attests:

Figure 4.10: Coogan as Tristram's father who faints as soon as he sees his son coming out of his wife's womb. (Diegetic shot within Plotline B)

Figure 4.11: The shot of Coogan screened in a movie theatre. (Diegetic shot within Plotline A)

Figure 4.12: A title indicating the end of the film. (Diegetic shot within Plotline A)

Figure 4.13: The audience of the screening with the cast and the crew in attendance. (Diegetic shot within Plotline A. The two previous shots can be reinterpreted as externally focalized since the viewers were watching them.)

FIGURE 4.10

FIGURE 4.11

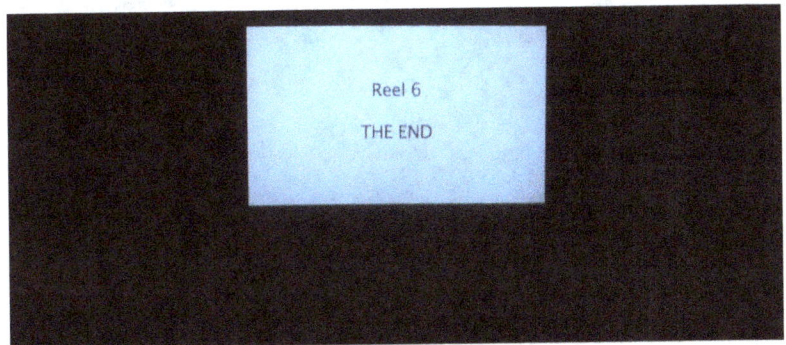

FIGURE 4.12

FIGURE 4.13

198 A GUIDE TO POST-CLASSICAL NARRATION

With these four shots, Winterbottom interweaves the two plotlines for the last time, indicating the ending of the finished film. The other thread, however, continues a little longer, showing a group of viewers discuss with the director and the screenwriter the ending of the book in relation to the ending of the adaptation. Then, Joe (Ian Hart) delightfully responds "The book has got a great ending!" and an iris-in takes us to another focalized sequence (depth) that depicts that conclusion, which was never filmed (Figures 4.14–4.15).

This last sequence can be viewed as a scene in Joe's mind, a version of how he could have visualized the ending of the book, even though he chose not to. Finally, the closing shots mirror the opening with the two protagonists teasing each other, as the end credits roll on the side (Figure 4.16).

All things considered, *Tristram Shandy: A Cock and a Bull Story* flaunts a highly intricate plot structure that resorts both to the higher and the lower levels of narration to tell the story of an effort to adapt this historic novel into a film. It combines multiple competing levels of narration that maintain an exceptionally high level of self-consciousness throughout. Yet

FIGURE 4.14

FIGURE 4.15

FIGURE 4.16

the aspect of knowledgeability and communicativeness are not obstructed, despite the inherent difficulty of the actual story—i.e., Tristram's failed attempt to narrate his entire life being mirrored by the filmmakers' failed attempt to turn this into a film that pleases its audience. Deploying the options of the post-classical mode, Winterbottom comes the closest to Sterne's problematics described most aptly by Patrick, curator at Shandy Hall, as follows:

> The theme of Tristram Shandy is a very simple one: life is chaotic. It's amorphous. No matter how hard you try you can't actually make it fit any shape. Tristram himself is trying to write his life story, but it escapes him—because life is too full, too rich to be able to be captured by art.

By exploring the creative potential of post-classical norms on all narrative axes (causality, time, space) and on all narrative levels, Winterbottom succeeds in telling a complex, digressive, and yet pleasurable story that transposes all the literary concerns into the filmic discourse and offers a provisional but rich answer to the problem of artistic representation.

CASE STUDY B: *SIDEWALLS* (2011)

Sidewalls is a romantic comedy directed by Argentinian filmmaker Gustavo Tarreto, who explores the issue of romantic love in contemporary Buenos Aires. In fact, the city and its buildings' architecture are the key protagonists alongside the two main characters, Martin (Javier Drolas) and Mariana (Pilar López de Ayala), who lead their solitary lives in small one-room apartments located on opposite sides of a busy street. Taretto crafts an interesting case of episodic plot structure that combines the "boy-meets-girl" story with the "boundary situation" of people experiencing urban alienation and existential crisis in the age of cyberlife. Filled with accidental encounters, mirroring events, and missed opportunities, *Sidewalls* flaunts a very loose but enjoyable plot that reconfigures several classical and art cinema tropes through the new dominant principles of post-classical storytelling.

The opening sets the tone of the narrational process that comes center stage from the first to the last minute. Images of buildings in Buenos Aires are accompanied by the voice-over of a male character who muses on the relation between urban architecture and the human condition (Figures 4.17–4.19).

FIGURE 4.17

FIGURE 4.18

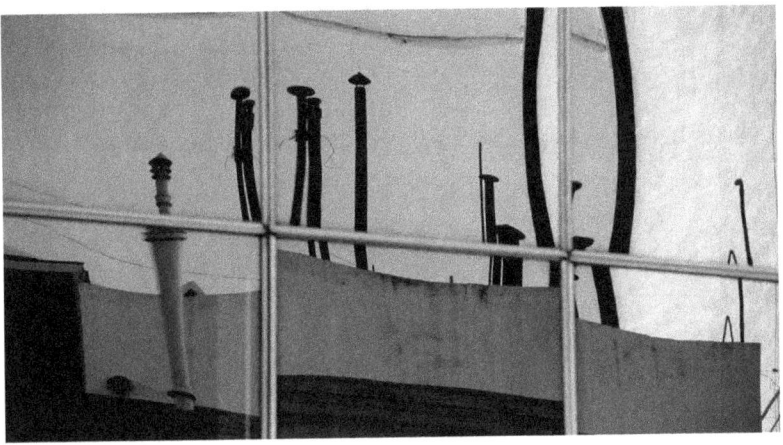

FIGURE 4.19

We feel that we have entered the filmic world but not necessarily a storyworld, as those images cannot be anchored on any individual or any specific time and place, i.e., all the necessary ingredients of a story. For four minutes, the narrator shares his views on the city's architectural features as symptoms of social life, as if he is making a documentary. Eventually, the voice is linked to a person who sits in front of his computer (Figure 4.20), an image that seems to be part of a diegesis. Yet the nondiegetic narrator returns to introduce himself as the main character from the higher levels of narration, listing in detail his personality traits, his past experiences, and his daily routine. The material he uses combines nondiegetic images with diegetic moments of his everyday life. For instance, he shows us a floor plan of his apartment (Figure 4.21), its exact location in a four-way split screen (Figure 4.22), a visit to the psychotherapist (Figure 4.23) and his taking up photography (Figure 4.24), among other things.

FIGURE 4.20

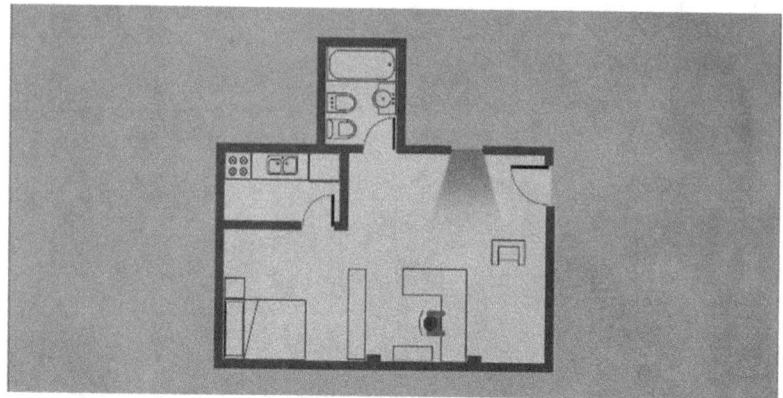

FIGURE 4.21

FIGURE 4.22

FIGURE 4.23

At one point, the narration is taken over by the female character, who presents herself in a symmetrical fashion, describing her relation to architecture, her backstory, her apartment, and her favorite activities. Again, the images blend nondiegetic elements with scenes that could be part of a storyworld (Figures 4.25–4.26). This typically post-classical character exposition flaunts an exceedingly high degree of self-consciousness, knowledgeability, and communicativeness at the same time.

FIGURE 4.24

FIGURE 4.25

FIGURE 4.26

Following this ten-minute introductory segment, a nondiegetic intertitle with the words "A Short Autumn" opens (what appears to be) a separate chapter. It plunges us into the diegetic world, into the streets of Buenos Aires, where the two characters cross paths while witnessing a strange accident involving the death of a dog and the injury of two people. Subsequently, the narration shows us a string of events that are indicative of the characters' "boundary situation," i.e., their emotional distress and their disconnectedness from their social environment. For instance, Martin is diagnosed with a mild case of discarthrosis while Mariana mourns the end of her four-year relationship. These scenes are mostly presented from the middle levels of narration with the characters acting as agents (non-focalization) with occasional focalized moments that stem from eyeline matches and brief point-of-view shots. However, the voice-over narration does not disappear, as Martin and Mariana continue to share their intimate thoughts. At this point, we could interpret them as internally focalized elements, as aural expressions of their inner lives, instead of nondiegetic pieces of information. Either way, the degree of self-consciousness, knowledgeability, and communicativeness remains elevated.

The next episode is called "A Long Winter" and lasts for forty-three minutes. Here, the two characters go on dates that leave them even more disillusioned and lonely. Interspersed with these loosely connected incidents are more musings on the cityscape and the meaning of life. These segments resort to the higher levels once more, deploying the screen as an illustration board. The most impressive sequence is Mariana's presentation of the Kavanagh Building, her favorite skyscraper in Buenos Aires. Combining drawings, photographs, and diegetic shots, she confesses to the audience her fascination with the building's architectural design as well as the history of its owners (Figures 4.27–4.28).

FIGURE 4.27

FIGURE 4.28

The demonstrative powers of the nondiegetic narrator become exceptionally flaunted when the screen circles elements on an old photograph to accompany Mariana's recounting (Figure 4.29). The same principle is applied in another key scene, when the two protagonists cross paths again and momentarily stand close to each other. In Figure 4.30 we see how an intervention from outside the diegesis addresses the audience and highlights part of the action, foreshadowing their eventual romantic coupling.

FIGURE 4.29

FIGURE 4.30

Finally, the episode "Spring at Last" brings the two characters closer and closer together, as they accidentally coincide several times in real and virtual spaces, before meeting face-to-face in the film's final scene. It is striking that after we have waited so long for them to meet, the film does not give them a chance to exchange one word at a diegetic level. Their encounter is filmed through brief shot/reverse-shots (Figures 4.31–4.32) before rising higher to frame them from above one last time (Figure 4.33).

Yet, right after the end credit, the characters return through a video. Someone types in the words "Martin and Mariana" on YouTube and then

FIGURE 4.31

FIGURE 4.32

plays the first hit. The two lovers appear in a home-made video singing *Ain't No Mountain High Enough* (Figure 4.34). Once more, the narration informs us about the characters and the happy ending of their story in a highly mediated fashion that betrays the presence of a nondiegetic narrator.

On the whole, *Sidewalls* is another representative example of post-classical storytelling that succeeds in striking a balance between fragmentation and unity by taking advantage of all the levels of narration and combining an extremely high degree of self-consciousness, knowledgeability, and communicativeness. The narrational act stands out from the first to the last frame of the film, but never diminishes our engagement with the story. Tarreto experiments with a variety of narrative levels while granting us the pleasure of watching two young people fight their emotional struggles and end up happy together.

FIGURE 4.33

FIGURE 4.34

CASE STUDY C: *THE LAWS OF THERMODYNAMICS* (2018)

Mateo Gil's film is a romantic comedy that seeks to examine the emotional life of a series of characters from the point of view of science. It is a thought-provoking project that pulls from numerous discourses, encompassing fiction, documentary, and modern scientific research. The paradigmatic options of the post-classical mode facilitate this filmic experiment, as they allow the use of multiple—and often incongruous—levels of narration while they imbue the narrational process with an exceptional degree of self-consciousness, knowledgeability, and communicativeness. The story's premise is the following: Manel (Vito Sanz) is a PhD candidate in astrophysics who studies the laws of thermodynamics in complex systems. His interest in physics, however, is not limited to his academic research but expands on and, in fact, overwhelms his personal life. His current relationship with fellow scientist Raquel (Irene Escolar) ends abruptly when he falls in love with Elena (Berta Vázquez), a model and aspiring actress. Despite their different personalities, Elena also develops an interest in Manel. Their turbulent affair is depicted from start to finish, as if it were governed by several laws of physics. This "boy-meets-girl" story is contained in a highly intricate and episodic plot structure, as the emotional trajectories of the protagonists are incessantly interrupted by scientists who explain relevant scientific phenomena. The temporal order of the plot takes on a modular form because the purpose of the film is to investigate each episode in the life of the characters as an illustration of a particular law of physics.

A closer look at the opening of the film will be illuminating. After the credits, a series of stock images of nature (volcanos, wild forests, oceanic waves, glaciers) take over the screen while a male voice-over says: "Nature, the universe, our own existence, are ruled by laws that are well known. Laws that nothing and no one can escape." Then, a series of scientists explicate how the laws of nature are so precise that they can be expressed through the language of mathematics. In Figure 4.35 we see how the intervention of the experts is staged throughout the film with a medium shot of their figure and graphs complementing their explanations.

Both kinds of images—the nature and the talking heads—may initially confound the viewer since they do not seem to belong to a typical fictional storyworld. The first diegetic scene comes after a minute and a half, when a physics professor is seen in the classroom introducing the students to the concept of thermodynamics (Figure 4.36). In this brief segment we are acquainted with Manel, who assists the professor with an experiment that goes awry. Soon, the storyworld recedes again, as a title "The laws of thermodynamics, a documentary by Manel Suarez" appears, opening a new section structured as an expository documentary (Figure 4.37).

FIGURE 4.35

FIGURE 4.36

FIGURE 4.37

A voice-of-God commentary navigates the viewer through archival material that illustrates the significance of thermodynamics in universal and historical phenomena. Eventually, the commentator transfers us back into the storyworld from the nondiegetic level. He shows us Manel crossing paths with Elena and urges us to view the characters as particles that belong to the "system of humanity," arguing that their interactions will be affected by the laws of thermodynamics.

From here on, the narration of the film establishes the following pattern: 1) brief diegetic scenes portray the actions of the characters; 2) the nondiegetic narrator replays and manipulates the diegetic moments to explain how these actions are governed by a certain law of physics; and 3) the experts explain in scientific terms the workings of the said law. Sometimes the voices of the scientists accompany diegetic images, mixing the formula even further. For instance, the first law of thermodynamics that refers to the conservation and transformation of energy in isolated systems is portrayed through the reaction of the characters to their partners' rejection. With a unique cross-cutting technique, the narration alternates between two scenes that occur one year apart: in the first, Manel breaks up with Raquel; in the second, Elena breaks up with Manel. In Figure 4.38 we have a deceptive image that shows Raquel and Manel exiting the same café. Thanks to the nondiegetic intervention that indicates the time of the incident, we realize that these two characters do not leave that place simultaneously. The voice of a physicist explains the law of physics while the narration presents a split screen of the characters as they walk away in frustration (Figure 4.39). Soon, their anger brings them back to the same café to continue their argument. In Figure 4.40 we see a freeze-frame on an intriguing spatial montage of the two characters whose superimposed bodies create a spectral effect.

By now, the narration has established its intrinsic norms fairly clearly; the story information will predominantly emanate from the higher levels, and the degrees of self-consciousness, knowledgeability and communicativeness will reach the maximum.

FIGURE 4.38

FIGURE 4.39

FIGURE 4.40

In fact, the opening of the film is relatively moderate compared to what follows. The introduction of more individuals and the explanation of more complex laws of thermodynamics will regularly transform the screen into a drawing board. The key event of Manel and Elena's first encounter as well as the presentation of the secondary characters, Pablo (Chino Darín) and Eva (Vicky Luengo), take place in a series of microsegments presented though overhead shots, replays, slow motion, and reverse action that render the narrator's demonstration even more spectacular. For instance, in Figure 4.41 we see Pablo and Eva's accidental collision, while Figures 4.42–4.43 show the configuration of bodies that were involved in the same scene. The purpose of this segment is to portray the characters' movements and activities as the result of specific laws, such as the laws of motion, the action-reaction principle, and the law of gravity. Later on, the narration reaches an apex when it seeks to visualize the laws of planetary orbits through the dancing bodies in a disco scene (Figure 4.44).

FIGURE 4.41

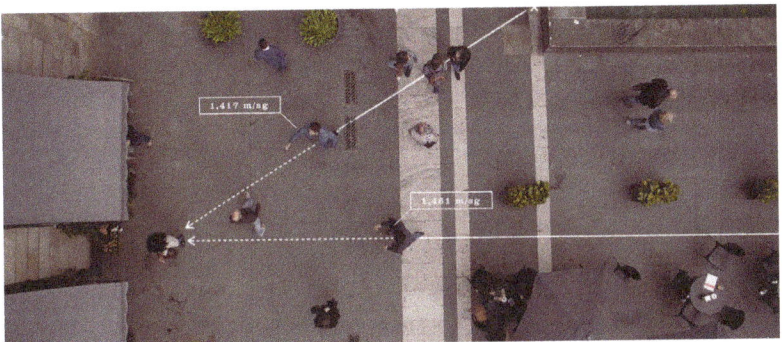

FIGURE 4.42

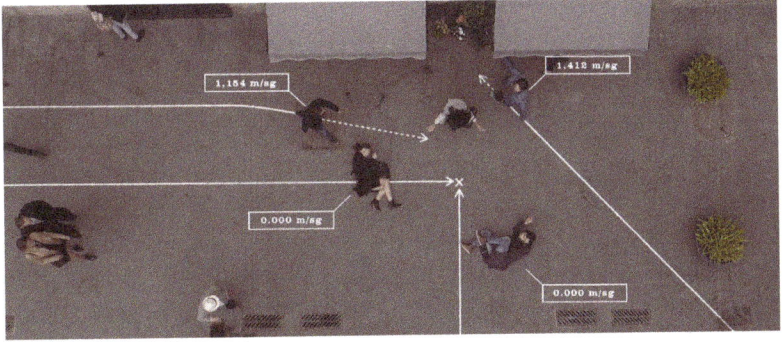

FIGURE 4.43

FIGURE 4.44

All in all, when it comes to demonstrating various scientific phenomena, the nondiegetic narrator in this film knows no boundaries. Gil blatantly manipulates the audiovisual elements in a way that constantly renders the act of narration visible to the audience, openly acknowledging a stunning omnipotence. *The Laws of Thermodynamics* is a multi-layered narration that transmits information from different sources, mixes fictional with factual material, and deploys self-conscious narrators throughout. Once again, it is the constructional principles of the post-classical mode that allow for this type of blending without estranging the audience and without, ultimately, failing to tell the story of people who fall in love and then fall apart.

4.4 Conclusion

The intricate structure of the post-classical mode of narration, previously discussed at the level of narrative logic, space, and time, has been further substantiated with the help of Sternberg and Branigan's theories. As a vehicle of story information, post-classical narration differs from the previous historical modes in the way it reshapes the qualities of self-consciousness, knowledgeability, and communicativeness and handles the eight narrative levels. Specifically, as the case studies have shown, post-classical films opt for an exceptionally high degree of self-consciousness that foregrounds the act of narration in every opportunity, playfully revealing the process of knowledge regulation and distribution. The element of self-consciousness, however, does not oppose the quality of knowledgeability and communicativeness. Instead, it allows the narration to maintain a wide and deep range of knowledge and share it with the audience in a steady—if sometimes audacious—pace. This sort of balance among Sternberg's three narrational qualities can only be achieved through a narrative pattern that explores the higher and the lower levels of narration in a consistent and fairly unambiguous fashion. Post-classical narration combines imaginative nondiegetic narrators with characters as focalizers, spreading and regulating information from the highest and the lowest levels. This type of interplay between the extreme entry points of the storyworld ensures the delicate balance between complexity and accessibility that characterizes post-classical storytelling.

Notes

1 See Introduction.
2 As Bordwell explains: "As categories of information transmission, knowledgeability, self-consciousness, and communicativeness all bear on how film style and syuzhet construction manipulate time, space, and narrative logic to enable the spectator to construct a particular unfolding fabula" (Bordwell 1985: 61).
3 For the long-standing debates on the function of the narrator, see Thanouli (2013b).

5

The Post-classical Auteur: Quentin Tarantino

5.1 Introduction

Before there are auteurs, there are constraints; before there are deviations, there are norms.

BORDWELL et al. 1985: 3[1]

Thus far, post-classical narration has been described as a historical mode, i.e., as a set of creative norms of narrational construction. These norms contain a range of paradigmatic options for the formation of the axes of narrative logic, space, and time, on the one hand, and for the arrangement and distribution of story information, on the other. The historical modes are elaborate constructions characterized by internal coherence and stability, transcending individual filmmakers, genres, or even national cinemas. And yet, of these three antagonistic parameters, it is the role of the filmmaker that stands out the most, nearly opposed to the notion of the mode. For instance, how can one appreciate the brilliance of Wes Anderson if his works are viewed as mere reiterations of the post-classical mode? Or how can one argue for Scorsese's signature style in *The Wolf of Wall Street*, if his creative choices are anticipated in the inventory of post-classical devices? A similar concern was previously voiced in relation to classical Hollywood cinema and Bordwell's position on the matter is quite illuminating. As he writes,

> Classical narration, in other words, was not a recipe but a range of choice, a paradigm. It seems possible, therefore, to identify various auteurs' work by their characteristic narrational strategies and patterns. Hitchcock's and Fuller's films are more self-conscious than, say, those of Hawks and Preminger.
>
> BORDWELL 1985: 204

Of course, historically, the role of the auteur within Hollywood was only acknowledged in retrospect, first by the French critics of the *Cahiers du Cinéma* in the 1950s and later by their American colleagues, gradually constituting what has been known as the auteur theory (Crofts 1998). In art cinema, on the other hand, the presence of the filmmaker as auteur was identified as a built-in element of the narrational mode from the start. As previously noted, Bordwell classified the authorial commentary within the narration as one of the three driving forces of the art film, alongside objective and subjective realism. Thus, the different industrial and institutional contexts of the Hollywood movies and the art films nurtured divergent approaches to the role of the filmmaker vis-à-vis the narrational act. Between the "genius of the system"[2] that privileges the power of the cinematic tradition and the unique vision of the artist that prioritizes individual creation, the historical study of norms can offer a better understanding of how these two poles, the production practices and the filmmakers, engage in a power play that sustains and reinvigorates the creative process. The function of the narrative mode is not to thwart creativity but to offer solutions to artistic problems that have been posed numerous times before. Each historical mode possesses a different array of options that can be deployed for the storytelling purposes with an extensive range of variations. In fact, the notion of variation and the example of music composition through Leonard Meyer's words describe the creative potential quite aptly:

> For any specific style there is a finite number of rules, but there is an indefinite number of possible strategies for realizing or instantiating such rules. And for every set of rules there are probably innumerable strategies that have never been instantiated.
>
> Quoted in BORDWELL et al. 1985: 81

In addition to the concepts of "style" and "rule," the notion of the "norm," defined by Jan Mukařovský as "a regulating energetic principle," allows us to grasp the degree of freedom in relation to the narrational norms. It is worth quoting him at length:

> To the acting individual a norm makes its presence felt as limitation on the freedom of his action. For the evaluating individual the guiding force is his own judgement; however, the individual has the right to decide whether to subordinate his judgement to the constraint of this pressure. Therefore, whether a norm is applied *consciously or unconsciously*, it is in essence energy rather than a rule. Because of this dynamic nature, a norm is subjected to continuous changes.
>
> MUKAŘOVSKÝ 1978: 49–50

In this light, the filmmaker is guided by their own expressive and creative needs while also succumbing—knowingly or not—to trends that develop within their production framework or even within the wider cultural environment. The case of post-classical narration is no different from the other historical modes when it comes to the relation between the norms and the authorial potential for originality. A post-classical filmmaker is a figure that deploys the norms of the post-classical mode and the degree of authorial status that will be granted to them is determined predominantly—although not exclusively—by extratextual factors. In fact, James Naremore's prescient observation on the "paradoxical survival of the author" in the 1990s is greatly felt even today (Naremore 1990). The bulk of film criticism still revolves around the notion of the auteur as an inspired artist while the industry and other institutional factors continue to rely on the-name-of-the-author as important currency.

What may be different today, however, is the freedom of each filmmaker to switch narrational modes from film to film. Contemporary auteurs are not tied to the established cinematic practices in the same way as their predecessors. Hitchcock, Fuller, Hawks and Preminger, to stay with Bordwell's examples, remained throughout their careers within the classical boundaries just as Antonioni, Bergman, and Resnais clung to those of art cinema. This is hardly the case with many of the auteurs of recent years. For instance, Lars von Trier began with post-classical works such as *The Element of Crime* (1984), *Epidemic* (1987), and *Europa* before experimenting with other formulas that seemed closer to art cinema, such as *The Idiots* (1998) or *Dogville* (2003). Several years later, he returned to post-classical storytelling with two exemplary instances: *Nymphomaniac Vol. I & II* (2013) and *The House That Jack Built* (2018). Others started with more classical works and gradually subscribed to the post-classical tenets. For instance, Baz Luhrmann's *Strictly Ballroom* (1992) was fairly classical before he developed his own variation of post-classical narration in a series of films, such as *Romeo + Juliet* (1996), *Moulin Rouge!*, *The Great Gatsby* (2013), and *Elvis* (2022). On the other hand, Danny Boyle took the opposite direction. After delivering a tour de force of post-classicism with *Trainspotting*, *Slumdog Millionaire*, and *127 Hours*, he returned to a rather classical formula in *Yesterday* (2019). From the older generation of American filmmakers, such as Oliver Stone, Francis Ford Coppola, and Martin Scorsese, Coppola opted for post-classical options only once in *Bram Stoker's Dracula*, whereas Stone and Scorsese have done so several times, as the films *Natural Born Killers* (1994), *U Turn* (1997), *Goodfellas* (1990), *Casino* (1995), and *The Gangs of New York* (2002) attest. From the younger breed, on the other hand, one can single out David Leitch, Adam McKay, and Zack Snyder from the United States and Edgar Wright, Michael Winterbottom, Guy Ritchie, Joachim Trier, and Michel Hazanavicious from Europe as filmmakers who regularly adapt post-classical devices to their own expressive needs.

Of all these creators, however, the one who is most flagrantly related to the post-classical mode is Quentin Tarantino. Tarantino has created textbook post-classical narratives, such as *Pulp Fiction*, *Kill Bill I & II* (2003–04), and *Inglourious Basterds*, showcasing the post-classical options to such a degree that his name became synonymous with some of the most emblematic post-classical strategies. In fact, given that the term "post-classical narration" is hardly well-known within film criticism, most reviewers characterize many post-classical films as Tarantino-esque, often accusing their directors of mimicry. "As if we needed more proof of the Tarantinization of contemporary cinema," notes the reviewer of Leitch's *Bullet Train* (2022) in *The Washington Post*, before arguing that ever since *Pulp Fiction*, "we've been awash in imitators who have sought to master QT's branded elixir of sadistic violence punctuated by expository flashbacks, deep-cut needle drops and grandiloquent pronouncements on pop-culture arcana" (Hornaday 2022). Hopefully, this guide to post-classical narration has sufficiently illustrated that narrational strategies, such as blatant character exposition and complex chronology (expository flashbacks), on the one hand, and parodic motivation (deep-cut needle drops and grandiloquent pronouncements on pop-culture arcana), on the other, are not unique moments of inspiration of a single individual. Instead, they are constructional norms that regulate the storytelling process in such a coherent and consistent manner that allows them to constitute their own distinct historical mode.

In the following pages, I would like to analyze four Tarantino films in order to examine the extent to which they adhere to post-classical principles. Reading Tarantino's oeuvre through the prism of post-classical narration is an intriguing enterprise that may illustrate the complex relation of individual creation and the influence of the norms, demonstrating the limitations of auteur theory vis-à-vis the power of the historical poetics.

5.2 *Pulp Fiction* (1994)

One of Tarantino's most influential films, *Pulp Fiction* has been hailed as a turning point in contemporary cinema across the literature for reasons that I laid out in my introduction. In terms of the principal characteristics of its narration, it combines several of post-classical options along all three narrative axes, as my brief analysis will illustrate.

Starting with the narrative logic, the compositional motivation relies on a modified character-centered causality that presents a series of characters woven into an episodic plot structure. The film consists of the following episodes:

1 A couple of petty criminals, Yolanda/Honey Bunny (Amanda Plummer) and Ringo/Pumpkin (Tim Roth), have a casual discussion in a diner before deciding to rob it.

2. Vincent Vega (John Travolta) and Jules Winnfield (Samuel L. Jackson) enter an apartment and violently retrieve a briefcase for their boss, the gangster Marsellus Wallace (Ving Rhames).
3. Following the title "Vincent Vega and Marcellus Wallace's wife," we are introduced to boxer Butch Coolidge (Bruce Willis) who takes a bribe from Marsellus to lose a forthcoming bout. Then, Vincent takes Mia (Uma Thurman) out for dinner and things go awry.
4. A dream/memory sequence tells us how Butch got hold of his father's gold watch before going out to fight.
5. The title "The gold watch" shows Butch's escape to a motel room after disobeying Marcellus' orders and winning the fight. Alas, he has to return to his apartment to retrieve his father's watch. There, he runs into Vincent and kills him. Later on, he accidentally runs into Marsellus and they have an adventure that reconciles them.
6. The title "The Bonnie situation" takes us back to the apartment in episode 2 and picks up the story from there. Jules experiences a miracle and Vincent accidentally kills a hostage in the car. This episode depicts in painstaking detail the operation to clean up the car and return the suitcase to Marcellus.
7. After cleaning the car, Vincent and Jules go to the diner for breakfast. As Pumpkin and Honey Bunny try to rob the customers, they confront Vincent and Jules, who manage to protect their possessions and allow the robbers to walk away with their gains.

The plot is extremely fragmented, featuring a string of individuals whose paths intersect either intentionally or more often by sheer coincidence. Despite the intentionality driving their various missions, the characters are constantly thwarted by the actions of adversaries, or by the miraculous interventions of fate and luck (good or bad). One of the most striking incidents, for instance, is Vincent's unexpected and unheroic death in the toilet (episode 5) followed by his reappearance later in the film during the second diner scene (episode 7) where his actions in the toilet again play an important role in the unfolding of the story. Apart from the compositional motivation, the narrative logic is dominated by generic elements and a heavy dose of parody in the form of references, both explicit and more nuanced, to other genres, film titles, scenes, and lines of dialogue, among other things. Even though Tarantino's penchant for homage to his own favorite moments from film history is often cited as his trademark tactic, it is widely known that these maneuvers have been observed in American and European filmmakers from the 1970s onwards (Carroll 1998).

In terms of its spatial construction, *Pulp Fiction* is relatively constrained. Its cutting rate is relatively slow with an ASL of 7.7 seconds. Nevertheless, it relies heavily on the principles of intensified continuity, utilizing tight close-ups, the distorting effects of the extreme lens lengths, and a prowling camera. Moreover, Tarantino occasionally resorts to a graphic framing of the scene, deploying shallow focus (Figure 5.1), special effects (Figure 5.2), and black-and-white back projections reminiscent of von Trier's *Europa* (Figures 5.3–5.4).

FIGURE 5.1

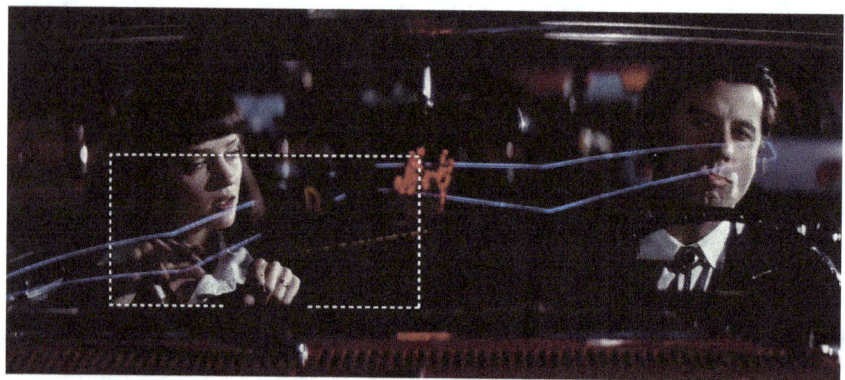

FIGURE 5.2

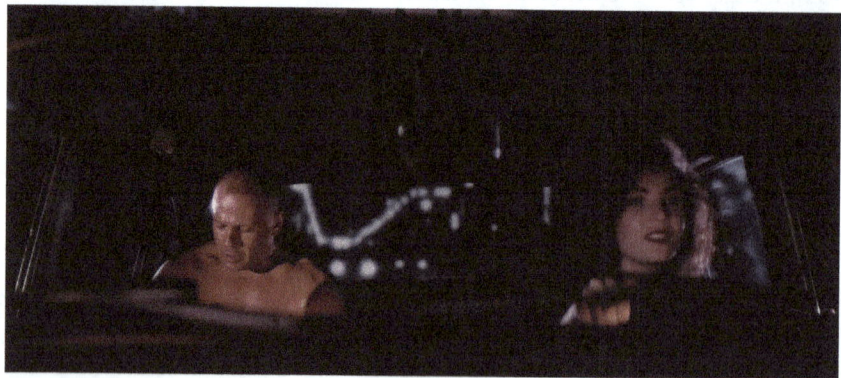

FIGURE 5.3

THE POST-CLASSICAL AUTEUR: QUENTIN TARANTINO 223

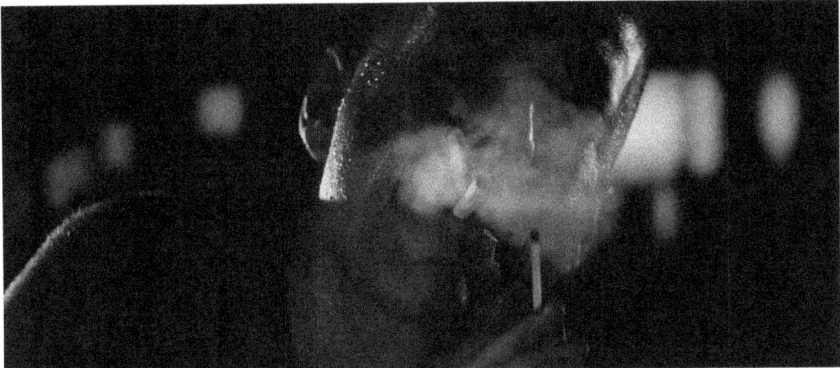

FIGURE 5.4

The overall hypermediacy, however, is limited and the narrative space amounts to the least obtrusive element in the narrational act. In fact, in *Pulp Fiction* the limelight falls on its plot structure and the temporal order of the events, both of which feel entirely unmotivated. The complex chronology, or rather the modular logic of the plotting, highlights the aspect of randomness and contingency, as there is no clear causal justification.

Finally, regarding the process of transmission of information, the aspect of self-consciousness is explicitly high throughout the narrational act, while the gap filling is eventually completed, despite the achronological exposition. As Allan Cameron aptly observes, "unlike *Lost Highway*, it does not connect its non-linear structure to character psychology and rewards the attentive viewer with a secure vantage point overlooking the entire narrative action" (Cameron 2008: 45). In other words, Tarantino balances his self-reflexive techniques with communicative devices that render his playful narration accessible to the viewers, even if he offers multiple entry points to the storyworld and layers his compositional elements with multiple levels of signification.

5.3 *Kill Bill: Vol. I* (2003)

Kill Bill was designed and produced as one complete work but was distributed in two volumes due to its long running time. Both parts were major commercial and critical successes, sharing the same stylistic and constructional premises. Here, I will focus on *Vol. I.* to present its key narrational characteristics and to demonstrate how this film takes the post-classical formula to extremes.

Like *Pulp Fiction*, *Kill Bill: Vol. I* breaks down the plot in multiple chapters. This time, however, there is a very clear mission plainly established by the title itself: to kill Bill. Specifically, the film portrays the story of a female protagonist, the Bride (Uma Thurman), who seeks revenge on the

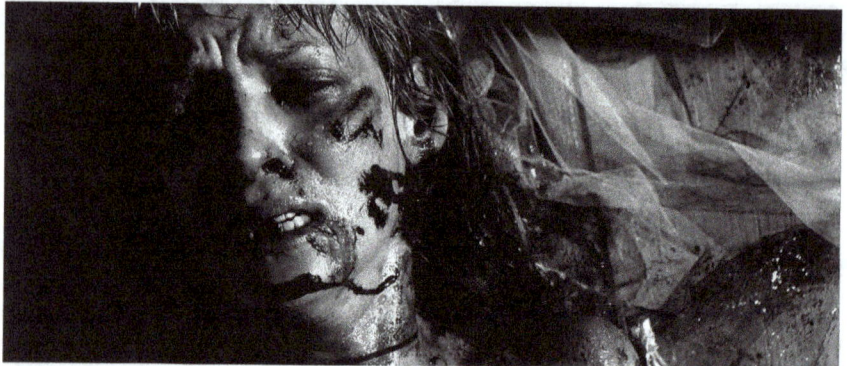

FIGURE 5.5

people who attacked her on her wedding day, killing several guests and leaving her wounded (Figure 5.5).

The perpetrators of this massacre are Bill (David Carradine) and his group of assassins, the Deadly Vipers, who include the following: O-Ren Ishii (Lucy Liu), Vernita Green (Vivica A. Fox), Budd (Michael Madsen), and Elle Driver (Daryl Hannah). The compositional motivation in the narrative logic depends on a modified character-centered causality that sets the Bride at the center of the plot while populating the action with numerous characters that appear in multiple threads. The plot is exceedingly episodic not only because it is structured literally into five chapters signposted with intertitles, but also because each chapter contains numerous further digressions. One such digression occurs with the blatant character exposition that pauses the progression of the action to present the protagonists' backstory as well as their main personality traits through voice-over recounting or graphic material (Figure 5.6).

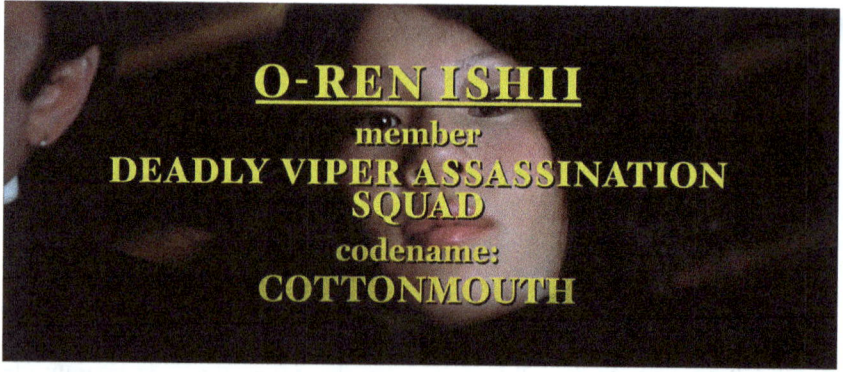

FIGURE 5.6

Yet what is constantly vying for our attention throughout the film is the hypermediated sense of realism. Tarantino opts for a hypermediated depiction of the storyworld, hoping not to disengage the audience but rather the opposite. Through an extreme degree of hypermediacy, the bloodsplattered confrontations are transformed into utterly engrossing scenes, while the characters' feelings of resentment and animosity are rendered impressively palpable. Additionally, a recurrent use of subjective realism visualizes the Bride's painful memories, dedicating shots or even entire sequences to the physical experience of pain, not only during her initial wounding but also during other moments of trauma. Furthermore, the narrative logic imbues the compositional elements with explicit generic qualities, juxtaposing genres as diverse as anime and spaghetti westerns, while layering every part of the storyworld, from the characters to the *mise-en-scène*, with references to Tarantino's favorite cinematic moments.

This level of complexity in the narrative logic could not have been achieved without the collaboration of post-classical options in the spatial and temporal construction of the plot. Regarding the axis of space, *Kill Bill: Vol. I* deploys an extensive array of techniques that render the story space highly obtrusive and self-conscious. Apart from the standard devices of intensified continuity that persist throughout (fast cutting rate, extreme lens lengths, tight framing, and intense camera movement), Tarantino explores the graphic qualities of the frame as well as the power of spatial montage to a degree that he had never done before or since. One of his regular stylistic tricks is the play with color. For instance, in the relentless showdown at the House of Blue Leaves, the Bride's battle is portrayed with abrupt changes from black-and-white images to color (Figures 5.7–5.8) as well as with entirely graphic compositions (Figures 5.9–5.10).

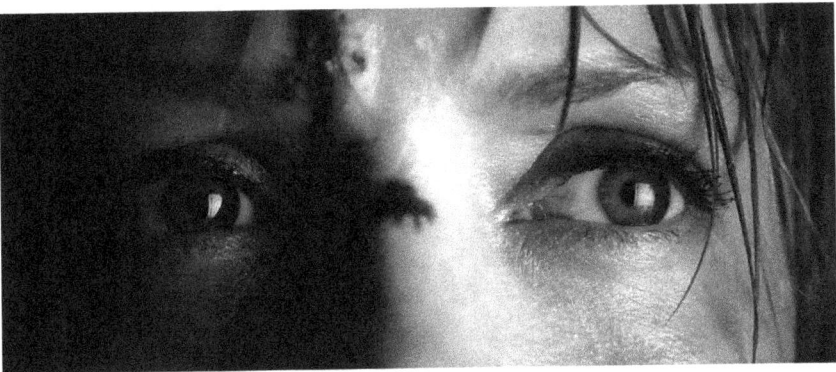

FIGURE 5.7

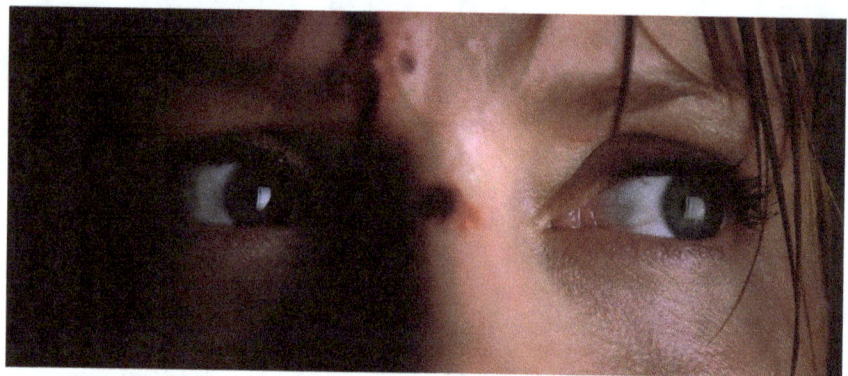

FIGURE 5.8

FIGURE 5.9

FIGURE 5.10

FIGURE 5.11

FIGURE 5.12

Moreover, in Chapter Three an interesting combination of live-action and animation in a three-way split screen (Figure 5.11) opens a segment that consists entirely of anime footage presenting O-Ren Ishii's backstory. In fact, the device of the split screen is used several times in an imaginative manner that matches vividly the two frames (Figure 5.12). Finally, the graphic elements of the screen are accentuated with superimpositions, overhead shots, the use of print and other visual effects (Figures 5.13–5.15).

Needless to say, the axis of time as well as the arrangement of story information undergo all the necessary post-classical transformations to serve this exceedingly intricate story and to keep the viewer oriented and informed about the action. The complex chronology allows Tarantino to complicate the rather classical trope of the revenge mission with flaunted movements in the timeline of the events, revealing the characters' motivations and allowing them to acquire the necessary depth that facilitates the viewers' engagement. One of the strengths of *Kill Bill: Vol. I* is that, despite the caricature-like

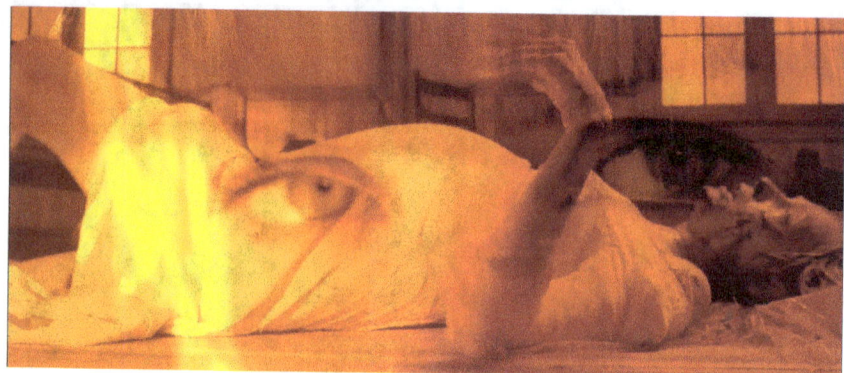

FIGURE 5.13

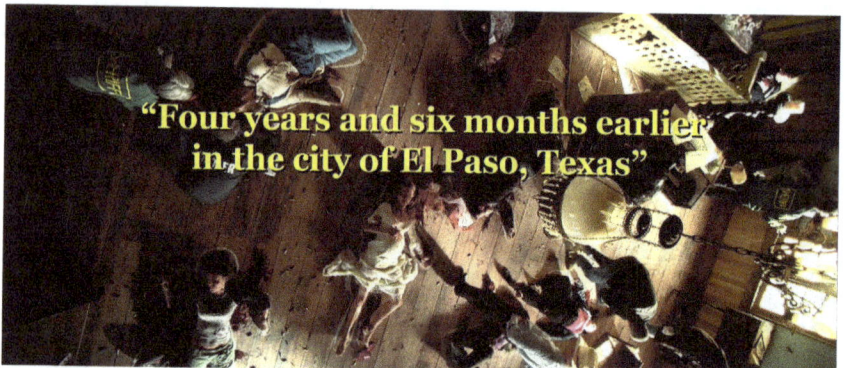

FIGURE 5.14

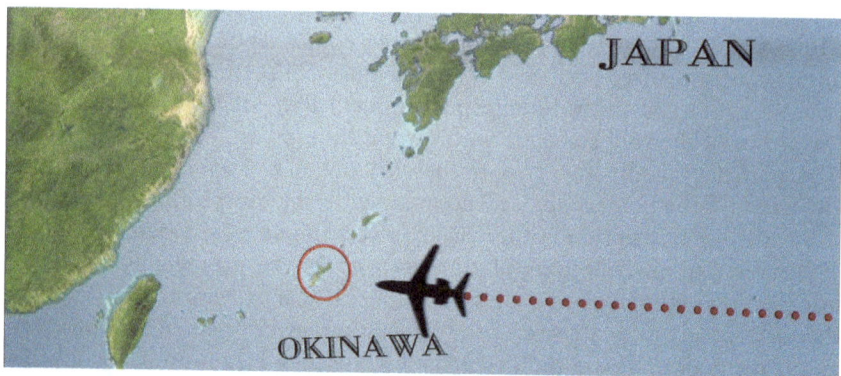

FIGURE 5.15

action sequences, the female protagonist possesses such emotional depth that even the most preposterous confrontations seem justified. One of the technical parameters that generate this type of psychological realism is the use of extreme levels of narration that either render the heroine omniscient and omnipotent through the voice over (higher levels) or penetrate her innermost thoughts though focalization (lower levels). In addition, the role of elastic duration in the form of fast and slow motion, particularly in action sequences, gives away the presence of a nondiegetic narrator that seeks to transmit the energy of the scene or to allow the necessary time for the audience to grasp specific information. In both cases, the narration in *Kill Bill: Vol. I* exhibits an extraordinary degree of self-consciousness combined with increased knowledgeability and communicativeness that eventually fill in all the narrative gaps and advance the story.

5.4 *Inglourious Basterds* (2009)

Tarantino's seventh feature is a counterfactual account of the Second World War, which recasts Jews as violent avengers of Nazi persecution. Like the two previous case studies, *Inglourious Basterds* boasts an episodic plot structure comprising five chapters with specific titles like "German night in Paris" and "Operation Kino." Across these episodes, we follow two separate tales of Jewish revenge: 1) the story of Shosanna (Melanie Laurent) who seeks to avenge her family's execution by SS officer Hans Landa (Christoph Waltz); and 2) the activity of the Basterds, a group of Jewish American soldiers led by Lt. Aldo Raine (Brad Pitt) whose purpose is to kill and scalp Nazis. These two threads converge in the last episode called the "Revenge of the Giant Face," where Shosanna and the Basterds inadvertently collaborate to exterminate Adolf Hitler and other high-ranking Nazi officials attending a film premiere. As in most post-classical works, the episodic structure of *Inglourious Basterds* allows for the presentation of numerous idiosyncratic characters, such as Archie Hicox (Michael Fassbender), Bridget von Hammersmark (Diane Kruger), Hugo Stiglitz (Til Schweiger), and Fredrick Zoller (Daniel Brühl), some of which are given blatant expositions that introduce their key traits and condense their backstory (Figure 5.16).

The compositional motivation relies on a modified character-centered causality that presents individuals in pursuit of dangerous missions, the outcome of which, however, is contingent upon several other forces, including chance. For instance, Archie's un-German "three-finger" gesture blows his cover and results in the entirely accidental bloodshed that exterminates the Basterds' most prominent members and severely challenges Operation Kino.

In terms of realism, Tarantino maintains a hypermediated approach, although significantly toned down compared to *Kill Bill: Vol. I*. He regularly resorts to subjective flashbacks and memories of the characters in an effort to

FIGURE 5.16

clarify their motivations and justify the intensity of their vindictive emotions. In addition, the narrative logic adheres to a series of flaunted generic elements drawn from the repertoire of Tarantino's favorite genres. In fact, what stands out most in *Inglourious Basterds*, even more than his previous works, is the role of parody. From start to finish, the characters, dialogue, and acting style seem to be governed not only by the mandates of the story but also by Tarantino's extratextual concerns. The excessive use of parody blatantly coats every moment with several additional layers of signification. As Eyal Peretz aptly puts it, "every frame and gesture in *The Inglourious Basterds* are marked as belonging to *cinema* rather than to a supposedly representational, natural reality" (Peretz 2010: 65 (emphasis in the original)). Thus, what appears to be motivated compositionally or realistically is simultaneously motivated artistically, i.e., as a self-conscious reference to other cultural works. This unique blend of realism and self-reflexiveness that so characterizes the post-classical narrative logic reaches its zenith in *Inglourious Basterds*.

The construction of narrative space, on the other hand, is the least obtrusive element in the narrational act. There are several long sequences with classically balanced compositions (Figure 5.17), albeit interspersed with graphic shots, as in Figures 5.18 and 5.19. The presence of intensified continuity is persistent throughout the film, whereas the use of spatial montage and graphic elements is evidenced only sporadically. For instance, in Figure 5.20 there is a split screen combining images of two very diverse origins; on the left, there is celluloid film that may belong to the storyworld and could be located in Shosanna's projection room, while on the right there is an extradiegetic scene from a different film. This composite shot functions as illustration to the argument of a nondiegetic voice-over narrator who explains that "At that time, 35-millimeter nitrate film was so flammable that you couldn't even bring a reel onto a streetcar." Later on, the nondiegetic narrator reappears with another graphic intervention to identify Herman Göring in the crowd (Figure 5.21).

FIGURE 5.17

FIGURE 5.18

FIGURE 5.19

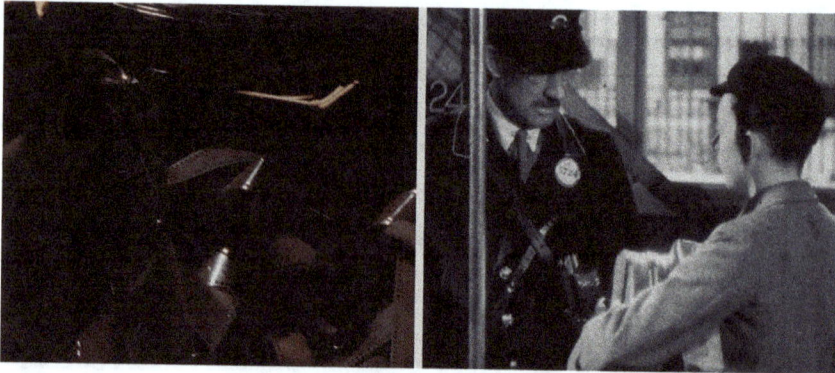

FIGURE 5.20

FIGURE 5.21

These graphic tricks in *Inglourious Basterds* are limited, however. Tarantino chooses to experiment, instead, with the axis of narrative time, adopting a complex chronology and an elastic duration that renders the temporal dimension of the story exceptionally self-conscious. Regarding the temporal order of the events, the plot makes regular breaks in the chronology intertwining past and present scenes in an abrupt fashion. Some flashbacks are motivated realistically, as in the scene with the German soldier and the Führer in Chapter Two, whereas others seem to derive from the playful spirit of an extra-textual authority. In addition to the blatant movements on the timeline of the story, Tarantino deploys freeze-frames, slow motion, and a few replays of shots to remind the viewers of some key story elements. In fact, what holds together this complex mix of characters and pursuits is the combination of self-consciousness with omniscience and communicativeness. Like all post-classical filmmakers, Tarantino wishes to complicate the narrative logic of his tales while keeping them accessible and pleasurable to his fans.

Overall, *Inglourious Basterds* continues the tradition of *Kill Bill: Vol. I* and *Vol. II* by weaving a rich tapestry of individuals into a story of revenge, despite scaling down the degree of hypermediacy, particularly at the level of spatial construction. This tendency will also persist in Tarantino's subsequent works, namely *Django Unchained* (2012) and *The Hateful Eight* (2015), which explore further the theme of revenge through the paradigmatic options of post-classical storytelling.

5.5 *Once Upon a Time in Hollywood* (2019)

Episodic plotlines, multiple protagonists, chance encounters, allusions to other films and TV shows, and an elaborate play between fact and fiction are some of Tarantino's recurrent creative options that have been established by now as emblematic of his own variation of post-classical filmmaking. In *Once Upon a Time in Hollywood*, however, these options extend and bifurcate even further in a narration that runs for 161 minutes. The story opens on February 8, 1969, introducing the two main lines of action via cross-cutting: 1) the career of Hollywood actor Rick Dalton (Leonardo DiCaprio), a fictional TV star, and his friendship with his stuntman Cliff Booth (Brad Pitt); and 2) events that befall the real-life actress Sharon Tate (Margot Robbie) and her husband, Roman Polanski (Rafał Zawierucha), who arrive in Los Angeles and move next door to Rick. The connecting thread of these plotlines is not only their neighboring residences, but also the members of the Manson Family that appear in various scenes before ultimately breaking into Rick's house—instead of Sharon Tate's[3]—where they encounter a very violent death. The impressive mélange of fictional and historical characters, as well as the counterfactual account of Sharon's fate, craft a highly episodic structure that brings center stage the forces of contingency and the loose causality of the story events. Unlike the protagonists of the two previous case studies, these characters hardly qualify as highly motivated agents with a specific purpose in life. For instance, Rick struggles to find meaning in his acting career while Cliff and Sharon drift casually from one situation to another. Their trajectories, however, are not portrayed from an art cinema perspective. On the contrary, the forces of hypermediacy, generic hybridity, and relentless parody meticulously construct a multi-layered narrative logic typical of the post-classical mode. The hypermediated realism stems from the constant blending of different types of images, the varied film stocks as well as the self-conscious play with the diegetic screens at the level of *mise-en-scène* (Figures 5.22–5.26). The characters and their surroundings feel constantly double-encoded; they belong to the storyworld and, at the same time, perform a parodic dialogue with countless cinematic and TV moments of the past.

FIGURE 5.22

FIGURE 5.23

FIGURE 5.24

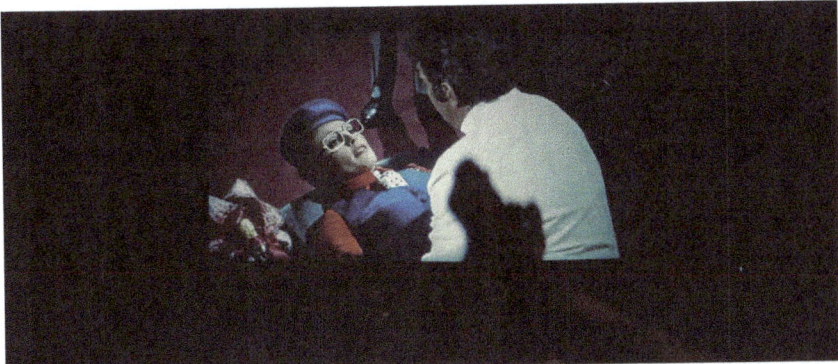

FIGURE 5.25

FIGURE 5.26

The axis of narrative space relies heavily on the dynamics of intensified continuity with impressive crane shots, close framing of dialogue scenes and a recurrent play with lens focal lengths (Figures 5.27–5.28).

FIGURE 5.27

FIGURE 5.28

In addition, Tarantino occasionally demonstrates his graphic spirit by using titles, split screens, and marker signs on the frame to render the filmic image opaque (Figures 5.29–5.31).

FIGURE 5.29

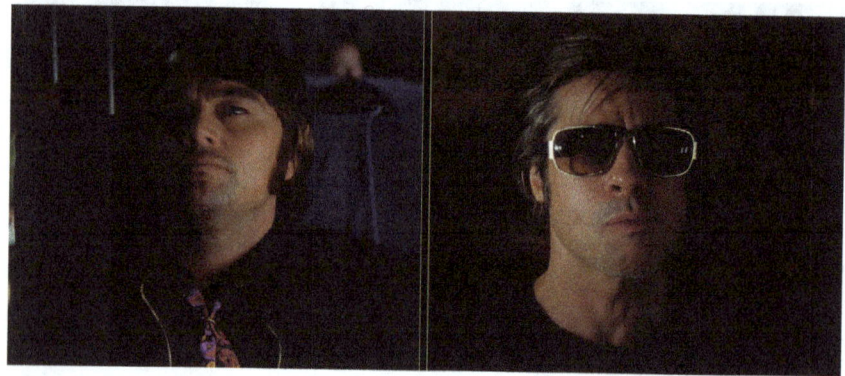

FIGURE 5.30

FIGURE 5.31

Yet once again, his interventions become significantly more prominent on the axis of narrative time and the levels of narration. Regarding the former, the plot flaunts a complex chronology that moves back and forth in time without any realistic justification, merely adding more incidents to an already episodic exposition. Moreover, the duration often becomes elastic thanks to slow motion or jump cuts, while a couple of freeze-frames give the opportunity to the nondiegetic narrator to come forward and distribute more information about the characters and the story. Twice in the plot—the beginning and the middle—there are segments with an extreme level of self-consciousness, omniscience, and communicativeness, thus performing the post-classical paradox, i.e., the simultaneous estrangement from and engagement with the characters and the storyworld. For instance, in the middle part, a voice-over narrator condenses the necessary information regarding Rick's career in Italy. This self-conscious nondiegetic narrator shows the posters of the Spaghetti Westerns he starred in, tracking and zooming in on their details. Furthermore, he presents some of their scenes, providing commentary on Rick's performance. This treatment of the story from a higher level may initially create a distance from the action, but the hypermediacy of the presentation and the abundance of knowledge shared with the audience build a very pleasurable experience. In fact, the voice-over remains in charge of the plot for several minutes in order to explicitly weave together the two threads before the members of the Manson Family arrive in Rick and Sharon's neighborhood. In addition to the traditional cross-cutting between Rick and Cliff, on the one hand, and Sharon and her friends, on the other, Tarantino meticulously signals the temporal coordinates of the story and deploys the voice-over to elucidate causal links or even the characters' state of mind. For instance, as the voice tells us that Sharon was "experiencing a touch of pregnancy-induced melancholy," we see the actress perform accordingly.

All in all, *Once Upon a Time in Hollywood* constitutes another significant contribution to Tarantino's cinematic universe, rehearsing once again a series of quintessentially post-classical narrative tropes. Unlike other filmmakers who are creatively promiscuous when it comes to their narrational choices, Tarantino has remained consistent in his use of the post-classical repertoire to such an extent that many critics may consider it to be his own.

5.6 Conclusion

The four films discussed above have plainly demonstrated that, over the course of twenty-five years, Tarantino has consistently relied on post-classical devices for telling his stories. Despite the changes and variations within his oeuvre, especially regarding the degree of hypermediacy, the iconic American filmmaker has remained faithful to episodic plots, multiple protagonists, a modular temporality, and a rampant use of parody, creating his own Tarantinian mix of post-classicism. Is this a paradox? Quite the contrary. Filmmakers who are granted the status of the auteur, thanks to a series of artistic but also institutional parameters, are free to explore their imagination and creativity to a significant extent without ignoring, however, the artistic norms at play within their profession. As other formalist studies on auteurs have shown,[4] historical poetics and auteur theory can be ingeniously combined to situate a filmmaker's work within a specific historical and creative context and to illuminate the complex process of creativity that entails the collaboration of personal talent with constructional norms as energetic principles.

Yet the *bras de fer* between the individual agency and the cinematic tradition in understanding the poetics of film narration can only be meaningful if our concepts and, specifically, the modes of narration that we consider as pertinent are fully updated. For analysts who are not aware of or do not acknowledge the existence of the post-classical mode, the narrative inquiry into Tarantino's works is bound to result in contradictions, such as those, for instance, found in William Roche's recent study. The following statement is emblematic of this predicament: "In other words, Tarantino's films usually rely on a classical structure within which they integrate an art cinema approach. To put it another way, they are essentially classical films subjected to an art cinema treatment" (Roche 2018: 159). Throughout his analysis of Tarantino's narrational strategies, Roche is trapped between the two dominant paradigms, the classical and the art cinema, as neither of them can sufficiently account for the films' characteristics. Because no matter how much one stretches the boundaries of each mode, *Pulp Fiction* or *Inglourious Basterds* are neither classical nor art films nor something in between. Their constructional principles belong to the post-classical mode of narration, which may have historically drawn elements from both the classical and the art cinema tradition but has also molded them into a solid new formula, as the previous chapters have amply demonstrated. Adopting the post-classical mode as frame of reference allows us to do justice to the narrational features of these films while helping reinforce the historical poetics research.

On the whole, Tarantino's filmmaking is an illuminating case on the issue of authorship and post-classicism, as his films reflect not only his personal sensibilities but also an array of creative norms that have become mainstream in contemporary filmmaking from the 1990s onwards. They are brazen examples of post-classical storytelling that give us the opportunity to observe the transformation of the narrational modes through time. Not all films fit so clearly into the mold, however. There will always be cases that may be considered borderline or that may stress the limits of the established categories. Thus, the next chapter will discuss the boundaries of difference within each paradigm and the problem of "betweenness" when it comes to classifying films according to the historical modes.

Notes

1 *The Classical Hollywood Cinema Film Style and Mode of Production to 1960*, Bordwell, Staiger, Thompson (© 1985). Reproduced by permission of Taylor & Francis Group.

2 Paradoxically enough, it is André Bazin, the most prominent critic of *Cahiers du Cinéma*, who wrote the following: "The American cinema is a classical art, but why not then admire in it what is most admirable, i.e., not only the talent of this or that filmmaker, but the genius of the system, the richness of its ever-vigorous tradition, and its fertility when it comes into contact with new elements" (quoted in Bordwell et al. 1985: 3).

3 In reality, Sharon Tate and four other people were brutally murdered on the night of August 8, 1969, by members of the Manson Family.

4 David Bordwell's studies on individual filmmakers, such as Carl-Theodor Dreyer, Yasuhiro Ozu, Theodoros Angelopoulos, and Hou Hsiao-hsien, to name just a few, have brilliantly shown how formalist analysis can address the quandary "uniqueness vs. norm" by historicizing both the filmmakers as agents and their creative environment as a system of regulating norms and practices (Bordwell 1981; 1998; 2005).

6

Conclusion: On Modes and Boundaries

A historical mode of narration is a distinct set of paradigmatic options that inform the narration of films in specific historical and geographical junctures. Alongside the classical, the art cinema, the historical-materialist, and the parametric mode, I argued for the emergence of a fifth kind—the post-classical. Taking root in the 1990s and growing increasingly popular by the 2020s, this mode encompasses a wide spectrum of geographical and cultural realms, even though the prominence of the United States and Europe in this new type of storytelling should not be understated. Post-classical norms have been laid out meticulously and summarized in the previous chapters, so there is no need to rehash them here. What *is* necessary, however, is the return to a series of methodological issues concerning the concepts and terms of historical poetics that perform the narrational mapping.

Starting with the question of range, it is essential to note that the boundaries within a narrative mode cannot be demarcated definitively. Each mode contains a certain level of elasticity when it comes to the application of its norms. In the case of the classical, Bordwell has aptly tackled the balance between the notion of uniformity and deviation, when discussing "radical moments" within the Hollywood paradigm, such as the exuberance of the musicals and the melodramas, the experimental music or the expressionist techniques of lighting and camerawork in the film noirs (Bordwell et al. 1985: 72–80). For instance, *His Girl Friday* (1940), *All That Heaven Allows* (1955), and even *Psycho* (1960) can be classified within the classical mode, despite the different blend or dosage of the classical norms in their narrations. Similarly, post-classical films exhibit a significant variety in terms of how they implement the post-classical options. From *Europa* and *Moulin Rouge!* to *Deadpool* and *Once Upon a Time in Hollywood*, one can trace a wide range of creativity in the way their directors apply the norms of episodic structures, parodic motivation, graphic frame construction, or complex temporality. In addition, there are films that exhibit varying degrees of post-classicism. There is no doubt, for instance, that *Scott Pilgrim vs. the World* is a more extreme illustration of post-classical storytelling than *The Trial of the Chicago 7* or *Army of the Dead*. Yet these variations do not jeopardize the consistency of the post-classical mode as a historically distinct narrative paradigm. In fact, the terms "mode" and "paradigm" can complement each other in the effort to map narrational principles and forms that coalesce into separate and historically distinct categories.[1] In this light, historical modes are repositories of narrational and stylistic options that develop in particular historical circumstances and continue to fuel the creative imagination of the filmmaking community for shorter or longer periods, depending on the conditions that nurture them. For instance, the historical-materialist mode is evidently the most short-lived, while the classical is, without a doubt, the most enduring one.

The second key issue pertains to the boundaries not within but among the various modes. In his initial mapping, Bordwell delineated the art cinema, the historical-materialist, and the parametric modes as territories containing narrational principles that oppose the classical norms. The influences and the exchanges among the different modes were not deemed a reason for concern, and rightly so. For instance, when introducing the historical-materialist mode, Bordwell notes: "Although this tradition has influenced both classical and art cinema norms, it possesses a distinct set of narrational strategies and tactics" (1985: 234). Specifically, the Soviet films of the period 1925–33 share with art films the aspect of the overt narration, while holding strong generic motivations that resemble the classical genres, despite the obvious thematic disparities. Moreover, the parametric narration is distinguished by the prominence of style, which is also present in the art cinema and the Soviet tradition, though it serves different purposes in each mode. Along the same lines, I would argue that the techniques of intensified continuity are shared by contemporary classical and post-classical narratives, even though their overall spatial system is governed by a distinct logic, namely the photographic and the graphic respectively. Viewed as constellations of creative norms, the historical modes may share narrational devices that are embedded, however, in different overarching principles.

This free-ranging approach to mode-building would enable the poeticians to expand on Bordwell's initial mapping and to continue the meticulous charting of the narrational choices across time and space. Yet the historical poetics project did not follow this course. As I explained in the Introduction, Bordwell maintained his interest in formalist analysis, investigating the style and narration of numerous films and filmmakers, both old and new, without considering the idea of adding new modes in his taxonomy. Instead, he chose to expand the boundaries of the two predominant ones, the classical and the art cinema, in a persistent effort to contain all the contemporary examples therein. Thus, these two paradigms began to be viewed not as historical classifications open to revision and expansion but, rather, as fixed reservoirs that could hold all film production, past, present, and future.

The impact of Bordwell's theory of the classical and art cinema in the film studies community has been enormous, often entrapping the recent narratological research between these two powerful pillars. As William Roche's analysis of Tarantino's films showed in the previous chapter, it is impossible to account for the narrational characteristics of these works, if the two modes are the sole points of reference. The same applies to the *Sixth Sense* or the *Eternal Sunshine of the Spotless Mind* that I mentioned in the Introduction. The notion of betweenness or hybridity may initially provide an easy way to avoid coining new terms, but they do not amount to an adequate response to the narratological questions posed by the heterogeneous and multifaceted storytelling terrain of our times. The addition of the post-classical mode to Bordwell's schema is an essential step for accommodating a significant number of films in a category that can do justice to their narrational features. Yet it is not enough. As I will explain shortly, the mapping of the historical modes and the refinement of our theoretical concepts should remain an ongoing process characterized not only by rigorous thinking but also by self-reflection. In fact, the very process of classification is not such an objective activity as one may tend to think. Compared to other approaches like psychoanalysis or feminism, narratological or formalist analyses may seem more empirical and data-driven. Indeed, the freedom of interpretation is fairly limited when it comes to describing formal devices or narrative strategies. And yet, there is always considerable leeway in the process of evaluation and classification of the narrational elements and, above all, there are always underlying principles and schemata that guide the theorist's research activity. Despite the bottom-up process of investigation that historical poetics professes, the hidden assumptions of each scholar can lead to different analyses of the same filmic narration. Bordwell's and my analyses of *Dunkirk* (2017) below are a testament to this phenomenon.

Dunkirk: Two Readings

Entitled "The art film as event movie," Bordwell's piece on Christopher Nolan's *Dunkirk* appeared on his blog on August 7, 2017, shortly after the film's American premiere. The characterization of *Dunkirk* as an "art film" in the title sets an important tone in the discussion, which progresses by investigating Nolan's narrational idiosyncrasies. The following statement is emblematic: "Like Resnais, Godard, and Hong Sangsoo (a strange crew, I admit), Nolan zeroes in, from film to film, on a few narrative devices, finding new possibilities in what most directors handle routinely" (Bordwell 2017).

Evidently, Nolan is treated as an auteur who expresses a personal approach to cinematic narration through "labyrinthine formal designs," lack of classical war genre tropes, curtailed story exposition and laconic character development (Bordwell 2017). Yet the contradictions are bound to surface, as Bordwell is far from eager to classify *Dunkirk* as an example of art cinema. In fact, it is classical Hollywood filmmaking that remains a key point of reference throughout the essay due to the film's production values and popular appeal. On the one hand, there is an explicit appreciation of Nolan's boldness in the way he handles subjectivity and breaks away from the classical norms, while on the other, *Dunkirk*'s narrational principles are constantly measured against the classical features, whether it is cross-cutting, the war genre, the suspense thriller, or the four-part structure. As a result, Bordwell's analysis reads like a pendulum; one moment the film is considered a variation of classicism and the other an extraordinary authorial achievement.

Regarding the choice of terminology, Bordwell deploys his own narrative terms only selectively. He refrains from discussing the broader concepts, such as the modes, the narrational systems or the motivations, opting for lower-scale devices, such as characters, genres, plots, and editing techniques. For instance, he keenly identifies the film's episodic structure, but avoids addressing its impact on the overall narrative logic. Instead, he deflects to the topic of literature, writing "It's very fragmentary. But then, so is a lot of war fiction" (Bordwell 2017). Similarly, his account of the choppy plot construction does not raise the issue of chronology but remains at the level of technique, and specifically the innovative use of cross-cutting. He writes, "But Nolan avoided block construction and went for braiding. He splintered his story lines and crosscut them. Events that are mostly taking place at different times are, as it were, laid atop one another and offset. Cross-cutting *en décalage*, we might say. I'm struck by how bold this is" (Bordwell 2017). Another term that comes up is the "puzzle film," which appears here to be fully domesticated by the classical mode. He admits that three viewings were not enough for him "to catch all the alignments, shifts, and echoes, the glimpses of things that take on importance only retrospectively," as the very fast cutting pace (an ASL of 3.3 seconds) allows little time to grasp all the details of the action (Bordwell 2017). And yet, not even this is sufficiently unclassical. Instead, his reading of *Dunkirk* concludes in the traditional Bordwellian spirit of "business as usual." The closing paragraph is worth quoting in full:

> In all, Nolan has taken the conventions of the war picture, its reliance on multiple protagonists, grand maneuvers, and parallel and converging lines of action, and subjected it to the sort of experimentation characteristic of art cinema. (As, in a way, Bowman's time-grid in *Beach Red* anticipates the rigor of the Nouveau Roman.) Nolan exploits one feature of cross-

cutting: that it often runs its strands of action at different rates. He then lets us see how events on different time scales can mirror one another, or harmonize, or split off, or momentarily fuse. As a sort of cinematic tesseract, *Dunkirk* is an imaginative, engrossing effort to innovate within the bounds of Hollywood's storytelling tradition.

BORDWELL 2017

As the quote makes evident, falling "within the bounds of the Hollywood tradition" is the inescapable fate of any mainstream film. All forms of innovation and experimentation may draw from art cinema but will ultimately fail to break loose from the classical constraints. No matter how much one deviates from the classical norms and no matter how they dilute the formula, the end result is bound to be a variation of the classical.

Contrastingly, there is my own way of looking at *Dunkirk*'s narrational act. I analyzed Nolan's depiction of Operation Dynamo in my book *History and Film: A Tale of Two Disciplines* (2018), investigating the historical representation of the heroic evacuation of the British armed forces from Dunkirk in 1940. I argued that, despite Nolan's admiration for *The Thin Red Line*, he opted for a post-classical narration that is equally distanced from art cinema's penchant for subjectivity and ambiguity, on the one hand, and from Hollywood cinema's linear and goal-oriented portrayal of a historic mission, on the other. In my reading, the classification of the film in one of the historical modes was the starting point before moving downwards to the axis of narrative logic, which is key for understanding the form of history that the film suggests. Thus, I highlighted the multi-thread plot construction that consists of three distinct segments: 1) the Mole, which depicts the events of the evacuation from the beach over the course of a week; 2) the Sea, which focuses on a single day on one of the boats that sailed to Dunkirk to rescue British soldiers; and 3) the Air, which depicts an hour of dogfights between three RAF Spitfires and German planes. Each plotline contains its own protagonists, missions, and story arcs that transform the unity and linear progression of the story beyond the classical norms. As I noted, "Like all post-classical narrations, *Dunkirk* does not cancel out character-centered causality but it chooses to complicate it considerably through the deployment of a fragmented plot structure and the multiplication of the protagonists" (Thanouli 2018: 147). The modified character-centered causality acknowledges that history is the result of a complex web of forces, human and nonhuman, that interact both by purpose and by chance. By creating an intricate tapestry of human action and fate, Nolan openly defies the dominant principles of both the classical and the art cinema tradition. As I pointed out, "*Dunkirk* is neither a classical tale of heroism nor an abstract exploration of the human psyche" (148). Instead, it is "an elaborate and complex portrayal of a military enterprise in multiple layers and from a wide range of perspectives" that is made possible only through the norms of the post-classical mode (148).

Apart from the post-classical compositional motivation, I also observed a hypermediated approach to realism. Specifically, I argued that "The relentless change of focus at the plot level, from land to sea and air and back, as well as the intensified continuity built through the editing and the camerawork create in tandem a hypermediated sense of realism. This type of realism, instead of effacing the traces of representation, chooses to multiply them for a heightening effect" (147). In my view, Nolan's masterful cross-cutting is not merely a deviation from the classical use. Rather, it is a blatant defiance of the classical realist mandate for invisibility and coherence, establishing a level of hypermediacy that places the viewer at the heart of the action not by hiding the technical devices but by thrusting them in their face. This form of cross-cutting renders the narrative systems of space and time more prominent, serving the complex narrative logic through an equally complex chronology.

My reading also addresses the issue of complexity through the terms of "self-consciousness" and "communicativeness," along with Branigan's levels of narration. Despite the fragmentation and the intricacies of all three narrational systems, I argue that Nolan successfully keeps the viewer informed about the progression of the story by maintaining consistently high levels of self-consciousness and communicativeness—a unique combination found only within the post-classical mode. The recurrent intervention of the nondiegetic narrator connects the three episodes through cross-cutting, choosing a different thread each moment. The initial nondiegetic intertitles help clarify that the switch from one plotline to the other will serve not the temporal relation of simultaneity, as was the case in classical Hollywood, but, rather, the temporal principle of mediated time, as is typical in post-classical storytelling. Unlike Bordwell, who approaches all the nonclassical elements as deviations that ultimately stretch the boundaries of the classical tradition even further, I argue that these nonclassical elements are proof that the classical mode can no longer contain films like *Dunkirk*.

The direct comparison of Bordwell's reading with mine brings center stage two interrelated issues regarding the research within historical poetics: 1) the impact of our underlying schemata with respect to the poetic history; and 2) the severe consequences of the infinite stretching of the boundaries. Starting with the former, it has become manifest that both readings hide a top-down logic, despite the close analysis of the narrational features. Bordwell's point of departure is that there have only been two main modes— the classical Hollywood and the art cinema—and therefore any formal device can be explicated in relation to these two options. My approach, on the contrary, is informed by the argument that the post-classical mode is a consistent paradigm that can account for the narrational developments in a section of contemporary cinema, freeing us from the classical/art cinema binary. As a result, I investigate the narrational parameters comparing *Dunkirk*'s characteristics to those exemplified in other post-classical works and I find that they correspond to a significant extent. The divergent hypotheses of the two readings regarding the historical modes are bound to generate conflicting interpretations of the formal elements. Thus, it is evident that formalist analysis is never really an entirely empirical process that produces objective and falsifiable knowledge.

The second issue is the concrete realization that if we stretch the boundaries of a mode too much, then the films included therein are inevitably going to look less and less alike. For instance, if one juxtaposes Nolan's *Dunkirk* with Leslie Norman's *Dunkirk* (1958), a homonymous film from the late 1950s, their differences speak volumes. Indeed Norman's depiction of Operation Dynamo comprises all the classical norms that craft a traditional portrait of heroism and victory. How could Nolan's film also be classical? In fact, comparing the two versions of the same historical event helps one realize the astonishing changes that took place in the storytelling process over the intervening fifty-nine years. These changes cannot be sufficiently explained through Bordwell's arguments about the bounds of difference and the persistence of classicism that I laid out in the Introduction. Even if we accepted films like *The Conversation* or *Taxi Driver* as classical, we could not possibly extend the same characterization to Nolan's *Dunkirk*, or to any of the numerous films that I examined in the preceding chapters. The modes of narration need to retain their historical resonance as well as their conceptual value by defining narrational principles and describing films in a way that creates distinctions. The introduction of the post-classical mode into the history of the narration in the fiction film is a step towards that direction. It is a useful addition to the existing categories, and it should constitute a point of reference for the narrational analysis of any film, especially from the 1990s onwards.[2]

Evaluating Principles: The Dominant and the Necessary/Sufficient Conditions

Apart from a well-informed poetic history of the narration in the fiction film, the evaluation and classification of each case requires a careful assessment of the narrational act, investigating the similarities with and differences from the paradigmatic options within the historical modes. As we have seen so far, every narration is a complex edifice that contains three key systems: narrative logic; narrative space; and narrative time. Each system is further divided into smaller units: motivations (narrative logic); space in and out of frame (narrative space); and order, duration, and frequency (narrative time) (Chart 6.1).

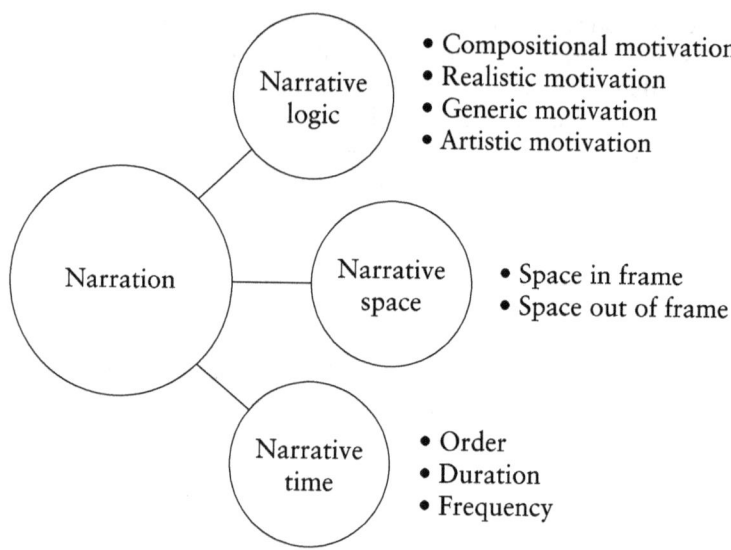

CHART 6.1

In order to assess the type of narration in a specific film, an analyst should examine all these parameters, comparing them to the creative norms that govern each historical mode. The value of historical poetics and Bordwell's narrative theory lies in their comprehensive approach to narration, offering essential terms for scrutinizing the narrational process in its entirety, and at various levels of generality. As a result, no film can be classified unless all its narrational features have been examined. But even then, there are two guiding principles that should determine our final classification, namely the concept of the "dominant" and the method of the "necessary and sufficient conditions."

The dominant as a tool for formalist analysis has been aptly described by Kristin Thompson who delved into the works of the Russian formalist critics to draw out concepts and methods for analyzing form in the cinema (1981; 1988). Starting with the observation that each work has one "dominant structuring principle" around which "other structures in the work cluster," she seeks to understand the function of the hierarchy among the formal elements in any given film. She regularly resorts to Juri Tynianov to elucidate the meaning of the dominant and its application in specific examples. Tynianov observes that every literary work can be viewed as a system, comprising various factors that are foregrounded in varying degrees. As he notes, "A system does not mean coexistence of components on the basis of equality; it presupposes the preeminence of one group of elements and the resulting deformation of other elements" (quoted in Thompson 1988: 89). Similarly, Boris Eichenbaum underlines the power struggle among diverse formal elements that vie for our attention. Ultimately, there is a kind of compromise, as "this or that element acquires the role of the organizing dominant governing all the others and subordinating them to its needs" (1988: 90). Defined by Thompson as "a guide to determining saliency, both within the work and in the work's relation to history," the dominant can prove useful in the narrational analysis of a film and its classification in a historical mode (1988: 92). If we look closely at each shot or each sequence of a film, we will encounter a series of creative choices that build up a whole. Not every choice matters to the same degree, however. For instance, if we scrutinize the frame composition of Luhrmann's *Moulin Rouge!*, we will discover many classically staged shots. But this type of composition is not the dominant in this film. Instead, it is the graphic frame, the spatial montage and the techniques of intensified continuity that dominate the spirit of the narration promoting a graphic articulation of filmic space. *Moulin Rouge!* offers a typical example of a post-classical system of space, which coupled with numerous other post-classical norms in the narrative logic and time, allows us without any hesitation to classify the film within the post-classical mode. The opposite is also possible, nevertheless. Many contemporary Hollywood films, such as most superhero movies from the Marvel Cinematic Universe, for instance, remain remarkably classical, despite some occasional stylistic flourishes. These narrations combine various graphic elements with a mostly traditional approach to photographic space. In these cases, the dominant form is the classical and not anything else.

Yet how precisely can we measure the dominant? Is there an objective way to tell which forms dominate and which remain subordinate? Another Russian critic, a relatively lesser-known figure, Boris Yarkho, claimed the following:

> Synthesizing is above all *a battle with the plurality* of impressions. Man tries to penetrate to the "essential," to separate out from the infinite mass the "main things" and to reject what is "secondary." In our science that "main thing" (which from now on I will call the dominant) is defined at a glance, intuitively; there is no need to prove why precisely it is the "main thing."
>
> YARKHO 1977: 64 (emphasis in the original)

I have found this to be largely true. Being fairly acquainted with the variety of norms of each paradigm, it usually takes a glance to tell which ones are the dominant in any given film. At the same time, however, film analysis should seek more measurable criteria than intuition. To that end, a version of "the necessary and sufficient conditions" method could complement a researcher's insight, facilitating historical poetics' goal for falsifiable evidence. Noel Carroll introduces the method of necessary and sufficient conditions from analytical philosophy to the study of art, hoping to reach an essential definition. Knowing upfront the impossibility of the task, he emphasizes the following: "Attempted analysis of concepts in terms of necessary and sufficient conditions, even where they fail, abet discovery. They systematically flush out data and distinctions that enrich our understanding of art. They awaken us to the breadth and diversity of the world of art, while also charting its boundaries" (Carroll 1999: 10–11). In a similar vein, providing an essential definition of the post-classical film may not be possible, but the notions of necessary and sufficient conditions may allow us to carve-up a method for identifying some possible requirements for membership into this category.

Some examples will be illuminating. The post-classical narrative logic contains the option of multi-thread plotlines. If we consider this element as a necessary and sufficient condition, then all films that contain multiple plotlines should fall under the category of the post-classical. This is not the case, however. Films like *Sliding Doors* (1998), *Crash* (2004), or *Love Actually* (2003) may contain episodic plots but those plots are mostly constructed through the classical norms.[3] Similarly, the device of parody as part of the artistic motivation may be deployed in almost all the films of the Coen Brothers without them qualifying for the label of the post-classical either. In fact, these films adhere closely to the classical devices, while the widespread use of parody may well be considered as a deviation within the bounds of difference of the classical mode. Moreover, Steven Spielberg makes recurrent use of intensified continuity, like most American contemporary filmmakers, but his films sit comfortably among the classical counterparts of the last century. In other words, multi-thread plots, parody, and intensified continuity cannot function individually as necessary and sufficient conditions, but, accumulatively, they can. Of the inventory of the post-classical options, some of them are bound to be necessary, but the level of sufficiency cannot be determined in an absolute degree. The more paradigmatic options we identify in a narration the safer its classification will be.

On the other hand, there are always going to be borderline cases. For instance, Park Chan-wook's films after *Oldboy* are idiosyncratic productions that I find difficult to categorize. Neither the dominant nor the necessary/sufficient criterion allow for a definitive classification. And the same difficulty arises when it comes to many contemporary action movies. *The Gray Man* (2022), for instance, features several graphic tricks and temporal manipulations, such as fast/slow motion and complex chronology, and yet, these elements do not seem sufficient for describing it as post-classical. Borderline cases are fascinating to study, as they may not only reveal weaknesses in the construction of the existing modes, but also point to developments that will eventually lead to the formulation of new modes in the future. And this is an exciting prospect, as I will argue below.

Towards More Historical Poetics

One of the many goals of this book has been to show that the general research platform of historical poetics, and David Bordwell's all-encompassing approach to the narrational process, remain the fundamental tools for formalist analysis to this date. All types of films, whether popular or more obscure, whether complex or straightforward, can be fully dissected through the principles and the categories provided by Bordwell with occasional additions from other narratologists, such as Edward Branigan (levels of narration), or other scholars like Lev Manovich (spatial montage) and Linda Hutcheon (parody). The overall toolkit of analytical terms and concepts that has been presented here through the numerous case studies illustrates that historical poetics is an invaluable research platform that could form the basis for any interpretation of a filmic text. Understanding and historicizing the process of narration should be the starting point for exploring the multiple levels of meaning that can be unearthed in any given film through other cultural theories, from psychoanalysis to semiotics and beyond.[4]

On the other hand, the mapping of the constructional principles in contemporary filmmaking is far from over. Looking at the vast terrain of film production across the world, it becomes evident that the research into poetics has considerable ground to cover. To some extent, the established historical modes can still accommodate several segments of the cinematic territory. For instance, the classical mode endures as the dominant option not only in Hollywood but also in various international cinemas that continue to produce what Bordwell has dubbed "the ordinary film" (Bordwell et al. 1985: 620). Moreover, the emergence of the post-classical mode in the early 1990s and its expansion to more mainstream film practices in the period 2005–22 is a significant development on the poetic map. An increasing number of mainstream Hollywood filmmakers experiment with post-classical norms, even if they remain a secondary preference.

The status of the art cinema mode in the current moment is a more complicated case. From the outset, the construction of this paradigm was fairly problematic.[5] Its purpose was to host all those options that were alternative to the classical, casting, as a result, too wide a net. Bordwell was able to bring together films as diverse as *Eclipse* (1962), *Wild Strawberries* (1957), or *Rashomon* (1950), resorting to the concept of "ambiguity" as an explanation for formal elements that could not be easily accounted for. Yet what these films truly had in common were not so much textual but, rather, extratextual parameters; they shared the same production, distribution, and consumption framework, which was distinct from the Hollywood system and addressed a different film community. In terms of narration, however, their diversity was remarkable. And when we look at the contemporary art film, the problem becomes even graver. If we follow Bordwell's line of thought, i.e., a top-down approach that starts with institutional factors (production practices, festivals, etc.) before selecting films that qualify for the art cinema category, then we are bound to add to the mix films as disparate as those of Béla Tarr, Park Chan-wook and Lars von Trier. Thus, in terms of consistency the art cinema mode has been led to a dead-end. The solution is clear: more historical poetics. We need more narrational analyses that can identify the patterns in the vast filmography around the world, acknowledging the particularities of contemporary storytelling in different sectors of global film production.

To that end, we need to adopt my suggested reformulation of the primary historical poetics' questions[6] and to separate "what the constructional principles are" from "how and why have they arisen." By disconnecting the study of form from the issue of causation, the poetic analysis can be conducted freely and independently in the bottom-up manner that historical poetics professes. Specifically, it is important to differentiate the historical modes of narration from the institutional settings that nurture them; not because they are not connected but because, when viewed as two sides of a coin, they constrain each other and end up imposing a top-down logic. For example, Hollywood as an industry may persist but the films that it spawns may be either classical or post-classical. On the other hand, festival films do not necessarily belong to the art cinema mode. Some of them are fairly classical or, at least, fall within the boundaries of the classical. Above all, we need to maintain a fresh look towards storytelling as an open and evolving process that may take different shapes at different times at different places in the world.

A Guide to Post-classical Narration not only presented the key constructional principles of a new mode, but also sought to highlight the theoretical and methodological stakes in formalist analysis. Historical poetics is one of the most fascinating research traditions and its impact should continue to grow. The analysis of film form and narration should become the cornerstone within film studies, providing a solid foundation for any further discussions in film theory. Whether we wonder what cinema is, or whether we investigate gender issues and ideological mandates in films, the understanding of formal principles is nothing short of indispensable. In fact, the most insightful writings in the history of film theory, whether they come from André Bazin, Thomas Elsaesser, or Robert Ray, have always demonstrated a fine grasp of the nuances of the filmic form. Their exploration of cinema's connections to external reality would always pass through a deeper appreciation of the formal properties of the cinematic medium and its storytelling function. In this respect, the contribution of historical poetics to the entire field of film studies should not be underestimated. As cinema will continue to change and evolve, the process of storytelling will provide a fundamental entry point for understanding how the world around us also changes. In a way, one could rephrase Roland Barthes' famous aphorism to argue that "a little formalism may take one away from Reality, but that a lot brings one back to it."[7]

Notes

1 See also Introduction.
2 The post-classical mode of narration could also be useful for evaluating narrational principles in older periods, especially when one seeks to trace the origins of certain norms. For instance, Rouben Mamoulian's *Love Me Tonight* (1932) features several devices, such as elastic duration and spatial montage, that illustrate the existence of divergent approaches to storytelling in the heart of classical Hollywood cinema. See Thanouli (2008b).
3 Bordwell has developed the term "network narratives" for such cases, offering an overview of their key narrative features, without, however, unsettling the classical/art cinema binary. See Bordwell (2008: 189–250).
4 In *History and Film: A Tale of Two Disciplines* (2008), I argued that the interpretation of any historical film should begin with the identification of its mode of narration, as each mode shapes a specific range of historical explanations.
5 For a detailed critique of this mode, see Thanouli (2009b).
6 For a discussion of these questions and my suggested reformulation, see Introduction.
7 Roland Barthes' exact words are "I shall say that a little formalism takes one away from History, but that a lot brings one back to it" (1972: 112).

APPENDIX A: A LIST OF SUGGESTED POST-CLASSICAL FILMS

Annie Hall (1977), Dir. Woody Allen, USA: Jack Rollins & Charles H. Joffe Productions.
Element of Crime (1984), Dir. Lars von Trier, Denmark: Det Danske Filminstitut.
Epidemic (1987), Dir. Lars von Trier, Denmark: Elementfilm S/A.
Goodfellas (1990), Dir. Martin Scorsese, USA: Warner Bros. Pictures.
JFK (1991), Dir. Oliver Stone, USA/France: Warner Bros.
Reservoir Dogs (1992), Dir. Quentin Tarantino, USA: Live America Inc.
Casino (1995), Dir. Martin Scorsese, USA/France: Universal Pictures.
Nixon (1995), Dir. Oliver Stone, USA: Hollywood Pictures.
Romeo + Juliet (1996), Dir. Baz Luhrmann, USA/Mexico/Australia: Twentieth Century Fox.
Deconstructing Harry (1997), Dir. Woody Allen, USA: Sweetland Films.
Jackie Brown (1997), Dir. Quentin Tarantino, USA: Miramax.
U Turn (1997), Dir. Oliver Stone, USA/France: Phoenix Pictures.
Lock, Stock and Two Smoking Barrels (1998), Dir. Guy Ritchie, UK: Summit Entertainment.
Rushmore (1998), Dir. Wes Anderson, USA: Touchstone Pictures.
Velvet Goldmine (1998), Dir. Todd Haynes, USA/UK: Zenith Productions.
All About My Mother (1999), Dir. Pedro Almodóvar, Spain/France: El Deseo S.A.
Any Given Sunday (1999), Dir. Oliver Stone, USA: Warner Bros.
Being John Malkovich (1999), Dir. Spike Jonze, USA: Gramercy Pictures.
Election (1999), Dir. Alexander Payne, USA: Paramount Pictures.
Human Traffic (1999), Dir. Justin Kerrigan, UK/Ireland: Fruit Salad Films.
Nowhere to Hide (1999), Dir. Lee Myung-se, South Korea: Taewon Entertainment.
Three Kings (1999), Dir. David O. Russell, USA: Warner Bros.
Bamboozled (2000), Dir. Spike Lee, USA: New Line Cinema.
Battle Royale (2000), Dir. Kinji Fukasaku, Japan: Toho Company.
Charlie's Angels (2000), Dir. McG, USA/Germany: Columbia Pictures.
The Royal Tenenbaums (2001), Dir. Wes Anderson, USA: Touchstone Pictures.
24 Hour Party People (2002), Dir. Michael Winterbottom, UK: Revolution Films.
Confessions of a Dangerous Mind (2002), Dir. George Clooney, USA/Germany/Canada: Miramax.
Full Frontal (2002), Dir. Steven Soderbergh, USA: Miramax.
Gangs of New York (2002), Dir. Martin Scorsese, Italy/USA: Miramax.
Hero (2002), Dir. Zhang Yimou, Hong Kong/China: Edko Films.
Big Fish (2003), Dir. Tim Burton, USA: Columbia Pictures.
Reconstruction (2003), Dir. Christoffer Boe, Denmark: Nordisk Film Production.

A Very Long Engagement (2004), Dir. Jean-Pierre Jeunet, France/USA: 2003 Productions.
Casshern (2004), Dir. Kazuaki Kiriya, Japan: Tatsunoko Production.
Kill Bill: Vol. 2 (2004), Dir. Quentin Tarantino, USA: Miramax.
The Life Aquatic with Steve Zissou (2004), Dir. Wes Anderson, USA: Touchstone Pictures.
Breakfast on Pluto (2005), Dir. Neil Jordan, Ireland/UK: Pathé Pictures.
Lady Vengeance (2005), Dir. Park Chan-wook, South Korea: CJ Entertainment.
Sin City (2005), Dir. Frank Miller/Robert Rodriguez, USA: Dimension Films.
The Constant Gardener (2005), Dir. Fernando Meirelles, UK/Germany/Kenya/France/USA/Switzerland: Focus Features.
The Promise (2005), Dir. Chen Kaige, China/South Korea/USA: Beijing 21st Century Shengkai.
300 (2006), Dir. Zack Snyder, USA/Canada/Bulgaria: Warner Bros.
Exiled (2006), Dir. Johnnie To, Hong Kong: Milkyway Image.
I'm a Cyborg, But That's OK (2006), Dir. Park Chan-wook, South Korea: Joy Fund.
Triad Election (2006), Dir. Johnnie To, Hong Kong: China Star Entertainment.
World Trade Center (2006), Dir. Oliver Stone, Germany/USA: Paramount Pictures.
The Baader Meinhof Complex (2008), Dir. Uli Edel, Germany/France/Czech Republic: Constantin Film.
W. (2008), Dir. Oliver Stone, USA/Australia/Hong Kong/Switzerland/China: Lionsgate.
Sherlock Holmes (2009), Dir. Guy Ritchie, USA/Germany/UK/Australia: Warner Bros. Pictures.
Thirst (2009), Dir. Park Chan-wook, South Korea/USA: CJ Entertainment.
Easy A (2010), Dir. Will Gluck, USA: Screen Gems.
Submarine (2010), Dir. Richard Ayoade, UK/USA: The Weinstein Company.
Wall Street: Money Never Sleeps (2010), Dir. Oliver Stone, USA: Twentieth Century Fox.
Hugo (2011), Dir. Martin Scorsese, USA/UK/France: Paramount Pictures.
Django Unchained (2012), Dir. Quentin Tarantino, USA: The Weinstein Company.
No (2012), Dir. Pablo Larraín, Chile/France/Mexico/USA: Participant.
Nymphomaniac Vol. I & II (2013), Dir. Lars von Trier, Denmark/Germany/Belgium/UK/France/Sweden: Zentropa Entertainments.
The Fifth Estate (2013), Dir. Bill Condon, USA/India/Belgium: Dreamworks Pictures.
The Great Gatsby (2013), Dir. Baz Luhrmann, USA/Australia: Warner Bros.
Kingsman: The Secret Service (2014), Dir. Matthew Vaughn, UK/USA: Twentieth Century Fox.
Lucy (2014), Dir. Luc Besson, France/Germany/Taiwan/Canada/USA/UK: EuropaCorp.
Me and Earl and the Dying Girl (2015), Dir. Alfonso Gomez-Rejon, USA: Fox Searchlight Pictures.
The Hateful Eight (2015), Dir. Quentin Tarantino, USA: The Weinstein Company.
La La Land (2016), Dir. Damien Chazelle, USA/Hong Kong: Summit Entertainment.

Snowden (2016), Dir. Oliver Stone, UK/France/Germany/USA: Endgame Entertainment.
Atomic Blonde (2017), Dir. David Leitch, USA/Germany/Sweden/Hungary: Focus Features.
Dunkirk (2017), Dir. Christopher Nolan, UK/Netherlands/France/USA: Warner Bros.
I, Tonya (2017), Dir. Craig Gillespie, USA/UK: AI-Film.
Molly's Game (2017), Dir. Aaron Sorkin, USA/Canada/China: STX Entertainment.
Mr & Mme Adelman (2017), Dir. Nicolas Bedos, France/Belgium: Les Films du Kiosque.
1968 (2018), Dir. Tassos Boulmetis, Greece: Onion Films.
Deadpool 2 (2018), Dir. David Leitch, USA: Twentieth Century Fox.
The House That Jack Built (2018), Dir. Lars von Trier, Denmark/France/Sweden/Germany/Belgium/Tunisia: Zentropa Entertainments.
Vice (2018), Dir. Adam McKay, USA: Annapurna Pictures.
Bombshell (2019), Dir. Jay Roach, Canada/USA: Lionsgate.
Booksmart (2019), Dir. Olivia Wilde, USA: Annapurna Pictures.
Hustlers (2019), Dir. Lorene Scafaria, USA: STX Films.
The Gentlemen (2019), Dir. Guy Ritchie, UK/USA: STX Films.
The Laundromat (2019), Dir. Steven Soderbergh, USA: Netflix.
The Two Popes (2019), Dir. Fernando Meirelles, UK/Italy/USA: Netflix.
Birds of Prey (2020), Dir. Cathy Yan, USA: DC Entertainment.
Enola Holmes (2020), Dir. Harry Bradbeer, UK: Netflix.
The Glorias (2020), Dir. Julie Taymor, USA: Artemis Rising Foundation.
Don't Look Up (2021), Dir. Adam McKay, USA: Hyperobject Industries.
The Worst Person in the World (2021), Dir. Joachim Trier, Norway/France/Sweden/Denmark: Oslo Pictures.
Zack Snyder's Justice League (2021), Dir. Zack Snyder, USA: Warner Bros. Pictures.
Bullet Train (2022), Dir. David Leitch, Japan/USA: Columbia Pictures.
Elvis (2022), Dir. Baz Luhrmann, USA/Australia: Warner Bros.
Barbie (2023), Dir. Greta Gerwin, USA/UK: Warner Bros.

REFERENCES

Altman, R. (1999), "A Semantic/Syntactic Approach to Film Genre," in L. Braudy and M. Cohen (eds), *Film Theory and Criticism: Introductory Readings*, 630–41, New York: Oxford University Press.
Andrew, D., and H. Joubert-Laurencin, eds (2011), *Opening Bazin: Postwar Film Theory and its Afterlife*, New York: Oxford University Press.
Barthes, R. (1972), *Mythologies*, New York: Hill and Wang.
Bazin, A. (1967), *What is Cinema? Vol. I.*, Berkeley: University of California Press.
Bazin, A. (2018), *Écrits Complets*, 2 Vols., Paris: Macula.
Berg, C. R. (2006), "A Taxonomy of Alternative Plots in Recent Films: Classifying the 'Tarantino Effect'," *Film Criticism*, 31(1/2): 5–61.
Bolter, J. D., and R. Grusin (1999), *Remediation: Understanding New Media*, Cambridge: MIT Press.
Bordwell, D. (1979), "The Art Cinema as a Mode of Film Practice," *Film Criticism*, 4(1): 56–64.
Bordwell, D. (1980), *French Impressionist Cinema: Film Culture, Film Theory and Film Style*, New York: Arno Press.
Bordwell, D. (1981), *The Films of Carl-Theodor Dreyer*, Berkeley: University of California Press.
Bordwell, D. (1985), *Narration in the Fiction Film*, London: Routledge.
Bordwell, D. (1989a), *Making Meaning: Inference and Rhetoric in the Interpretation of Cinema*, Cambridge: Harvard University Press.
Bordwell, D. (1989b), "Historical Poetics of Cinema," in R. Barton Palmer (ed.), *The Cinematic Text: Methods and Approaches*, 369–98, New York: AMS Press.
Bordwell, D. (1994), "Toto le Moderne: la Narration dans le Cinéma Européen d' après 1970," *Revue Belge du Cinéma*, 36–7: 32–9.
Bordwell, D. (1997), *On the History of Film Style*, Cambridge: Harvard University Press.
Bordwell, D. (1998), *Ozu and the Poetics of Cinema*, London: BFI.
Bordwell, D. (2000a), *Planet Hong Kong: Popular Cinema and the Art of Entertainment*, Cambridge: Harvard University Press.
Bordwell, D. (2000b), *Visual Style in the Cinema*, Munich: Verlag des Autoren.
Bordwell, D. (2002), "Film Futures," *SubStance*, 31(1): 88–104.
Bordwell, D. (2005), *Figures Traced in Light: On Cinematic Staging*, Berkeley: University of California Press.
Bordwell, D. (2006), *The Way Hollywood Tells it: Story and Style in Modern Times*, Berkeley: University of California Press.

Bordwell, D. (2007), "Shot-consciousness," *David Bordwell's Website on Cinema*, 16 January. Available online: http://www.davidbordwell.net/blog/2007/01/16/shot-consciousness/ (accessed January 10, 2023).

Bordwell, D. (2008), *Poetics of Cinema*, New York: Routledge.

Bordwell, D. (2014), "THE GRAND BUDAPEST HOTEL: Wes Anderson Takes the 4:3 Challenge," *David Bordwell's Website on Cinema*, March 26. Available online: http://www.davidbordwell.net/blog/2014/03/26/the-grand-budapest-hotel-wes-anderson-takes-the-43-challenge/ (accessed January, 10 2023).

Bordwell, D. (2017), "DUNKIRK Part 2: The Art Film as Event Movie," *David Bordwell's Website on Cinema*, August 9. Available online: http://www.davidbordwell.net/blog/2017/08/09/dunkirk-part-2-the-art-film-as-event-movie/ (accessed January 10, 2023).

Bordwell, D. (2018), "Lessons with Bazin: Six Paths to a Poetics," *David Bordwell's Website on Cinema*, October. Available online: http://www.davidbordwell.net/essays/lessonswithbazin.php (accessed December 28, 2022).

Bordwell D., and K. Thompson (1993), *Film Art: An introduction*, New York: McGraw-Hill.

Bordwell D., J. Staiger, and K. Thompson (1985), *The Classical Hollywood Cinema: Film Style and Mode of Production to 1960*, New York: Routledge.

Branigan, E. (1992), *Narrative Comprehension and Film*, London and New York: Routledge.

Branigan, E. (2002), "Nearly True: Forking Plots, Forking Interpretations: A Response to David Bordwell's *Film Futures*," *SubStance*, 31(1): 105–14.

Buckland, W., ed. (2009), *Puzzle Films: Complex Storytelling in Contemporary Cinema*, Malden: Wiley-Blackwell.

Buckland, W. (2014a), "Introduction: Ambiguity, Ontological Pluralism, and Cognitive Dissonance in the Hollywood Puzzle Film," in W. Buckland (ed.), *Hollywood Puzzle Films*, 1–14, New York: Routledge.

Buckland, W. (2014b), "*Source Code*'s Video Game Logic," in W. Buckland (ed.), *Hollywood Puzzle Films*, 185–97, New York: Routledge.

Cameron, A. (2008), *Modular Narratives in Contemporary Cinema*, London: Palgrave.

Campora, M. (2009), "Art Cinema and New Hollywood: Multiform Narrative and Sonic Metalepsis in Eternal Sunshine of the Spotless Mind," *New Review of Film and Television Studies*, 7(2): 119–31.

Campora, M. (2014), *Subjective Realist Cinema: From Expressionism to Inception*, New York: Berghahn Books.

Canby, V. (1992), "Coppola's Dizzying Vision of Dracula," *New York Times*, November 13.

Cardwell, S. (2003), "About Time: Theorizing Adaptation, Temporality, and Tense," *Literature/Film Quarterly*, 31(2): 82–92.

Carroll, N. (1998), "The Future of Allusion: Hollywood in the Seventies (and Beyond)," in N. Carroll (ed.), *Interpreting the Moving* Image, 240–64, Cambridge: Cambridge University Press.

Carroll, N. (1999), *Philosophy of Art: A Contemporary Introduction*, London and New York: Routledge.

Chatman, S. (1990), *Coming to Terms: The Rhetoric of Narrative in Fiction and Film*. Ithaca: Cornell University Press.

Chitwood, A. (2016), "'Suicide Squad': David Ayer on Shooting on Film, Directing The Joker, and Working in the DC Universe," *Collider*, July 11. Available online: https://collider.com/suicide-squad-david-ayer-interview/ (accessed January 10, 2023).

Collins, J. (1989), *Uncommon Cultures: Popular Culture and Post-Modernism*, London: Routledge.

Corrigan, T. (1991), *A Cinema Without Walls: Movies and Culture after Vietnam*, New Brunswick: Rutgers University Press.

Cowie, E. (1998), "Storytelling: Classical Hollywood Cinema and Classical Narrative," in S. Neale and M. Smith (eds), *Contemporary Hollywood Cinema*, 178–190, London and New York: Routledge.

Crofts, S. (1998), "Authorship and Hollywood," in J. Hill and P. Church Gibson (eds), *The Oxford Guide to Film Studies*, 310–24, Oxford: Oxford University Press.

Degli-Esposti, C., ed. (1998), *Postmodernism in the Cinema*, New York: Berghahn Books.

Denzin, N. (1991), *Images of Postmodern Society: Social Theory and Contemporary Cinema*, London: Sage.

Ebert, R. (2001), "Snatch," Rogerebert.com, January 19. Available online: https://www.rogerebert.com/reviews/snatch-2001 (accessed January 10, 2023).

Eichenbaum, B. (1965), "The Theory of the 'Formal Method'," in L. T. Lemon and M. Reis (eds), *Russian Formalist Criticism*, 99–139, Lincoln: Nebraska University Press.

Elsaesser, T. (1971), "Why Hollywood?," *Monogram*, 1: 4–10.

Elsaesser, T. (1975), "The Pathos of Failure: American Films in the 70s: Notes on the Unmotivated Hero," *Monogram*, 6: 13–19.

Elsaesser, T. (1991), "Tales of Sound and Fury: Observations on the Family Melodrama," in M. Landy (ed.), *Imitations of Life: A Reader on Film & Television Melodrama*, 68–91, Detroit: Wayne State University Press.

Elsaesser, T. (2005), *European Cinema: Face to Face with Hollywood*, Amsterdam: Amsterdam University Press.

Elsaesser, T. (2009), "The Mind-Game Film," in W. Buckland (ed.), *Hollywood Puzzle Films*, 13–41, New York: Routledge.

Elsaesser, T. (2012), *The Persistence of Hollywood*, New York: Routledge.

Elsaesser, T. (2016), *Film History as Media Archaeology: Tracking Digital Cinema*, Amsterdam: Amsterdam University Press

Elsaesser, T. (2018), "Contingency, Causality, Complexity: Distributed Agency in the Mind-game Film," *New Review of Film and Television Studies*, 16(1): 1–39.

Elsaesser, T., and W. Buckland (2002), *Studying Contemporary American Film*, London: Arnold.

Fehrle, J. (2015), "Leading into the Franchise: Remediation as (Simulated) Transmedia World. The Case of Scott Pilgrim," *Image: Zeitschrift für interdisziplinäre Bildwissenschaft*, 11(1): 4–16.

Fuller, G. (2001), "Strictly Red," *Sight and Sound*, 11(6): 14–16.

Ghislotti, S. (2009), "Narrative Comprehension Made Difficult: Film Form and Mnemonic Devices in *Memento*," in W. Buckland (ed.), *Hollywood Puzzle Films*, 87–106, New York: Routledge.

Goldman, M. (2013), "Boom and Bust: *The Wolf of Wall Street*," *American Cinematographer*, 94(12): 38–53.

Hartmann, M., E. Prommer, K. Deckner, and S. O. Görland, eds (2019), *Mediated Time: Perspectives on Time in a Digital Age*, London: Palgrave Macmillan.

Heath, S. (1986), "Narrative Space," in P. Rosen (ed.), *Narrative, Apparatus, Ideology: A Film Theory Reader*, 379–420, New York: Columbia University Press.

Henderson, B. (1983), "Tense, Mood, and Voice in Film," *Film Quarterly*, 36(3): 4–17.

Hill, J. (1986), *Sex, Class and Realism: British Cinema, 1956–63*, London: BFI.

Hornaday, A. (2022), "'Bullet Train': A Chaotic Trip to Nowhere, with Brad Pitt on Board, *Washington Post*, August 2. Available online: https://www.washingtonpost.com/movies/2022/08/02/bullet-train-movie-review/ (accessed January 10, 2023).

Huhtamo, E. (1995), "Encapsulated Bodies in Motion: Simulators and the Quest for Total Immersion," in S. Penny (ed.), *Critical Issues in Electronic Media*, 159–86, Albany: State University of New York Press.

Hutcheon, L. (1988), *A Poetics of Postmodernism: History, Theory, Fiction*, London: Routledge.

Hutcheon, L. (1990), "An Epilogue: Postmodern Parody: History, Subjectivity and Ideology," *Quarterly Review of Film and Video*, 12(1–2): 125–33.

Hutcheon, L. (2000), *A Theory of Parody: The Teachings of Twentieth-Century Art Forms*, Chicago: University of Illinois Press.

Jameson, F. (1983), "Postmodernism and Consumer Society," in H. Foster (ed.), *The Anti-Aesthetic: Essays on Postmodern Culture*, 111–25, Seattle: Bay Press.

Jameson, F. (1991), *Postmodernism, or the Cultural Logic of Late Capitalism*, London: Verso.

Jenkins, H. (1995), "Historical Poetics," in J. Hollows and M. Jancovich (eds), *Approaches to Popular Film*, 100–22, Manchester: Manchester University Press.

Jousse, T. (1994), "Les tueurs de l'image," *Cahiers du Cinéma*, 484: 50–3.

Kiss, M., and S. Willemsen (2017), *Impossible Puzzle Films: A Cognitive Approach to Contemporary Complex Cinema*, Edinburgh: Edinburgh University Press.

Klecker, C. (2010), "Fascination for Confusion: Discontinuous Narrative in Tarantino's Pulp Fiction," in P. Eckhard, M. Fuchs and W. Hölbling (eds), *Landscapes of Postmodernity. Concepts and Paradigms of Critical Theory*, 113–28, Münster: LIT-Verlag.

Klecker, C. (2013), "Mind-tricking Narratives: Between Classical and Art-cinema Narration," *Poetics Today*, 34(1–2): 119–46.

Kracauer, S. (1960), *Theory of Film: The Redemption of Physical Reality*, New York: Oxford University Press.

Kramer, P. (1998), "Post-classical Hollywood Film: Concepts and Debates," in J. Hill and P. Church Gibson (eds), *The Oxford Guide to Film Studies*, 289–309, Oxford: Oxford University Press.

Kubler, G. (1970), *The Shape of Time: Remarks on the History of Things*, New Haven: Yale University Press.

Landy, M. and L. Fischer (1994), "Dead Again or A-live Again: Postmodern or Post-mortem?," *Cinema Journal*, 33(4): 3–22.

Lavik, E. (2006), "Narrative Structure in The Sixth Sense: A New Twist in 'Twist Movies'?," *The Velvet Light Trap*, 58: 55–64.
Manovich, L. (2001), *The Language of New Media*, Cambridge: MIT.
Martin, A. (1992), "Mise en scène is Dead, or the Expressive, the Excessive, the Technical and the Stylish," *Continuum*, 5(2): 87–140.
Morson, G. S. (1989), "Parody, History, and Metaparody," in G. S. Morson and C. Emerson (eds), *Rethinking Bakhtin: Extensions and Challenges*, 63–86, Evanston: Northwestern University Press.
Mukařovský, J. (1978), "The Aesthetic Norm," in *Structure, Sign and Function*, 49–56, New Haven and London: Yale University Press.
Munz, P. (2006), "The Historical Narrative," in M. Bentley (ed.), *Companion to Historiography*, 833–52, London: Routledge.
Murray, T. (1999), "By Way of Introduction: Digitality and the Memory of Cinema, or, Bearing the Losses of the Digital Code," *Wide Angle*, 21(1): 3–24.
Naremore, J. (1990), "Authorship and the Cultural Politics of Film Criticism," *Film Quarterly*, 44(1): 14–23.
Neale, S. (1995), "Questions of Genre," in B. K. Grant (ed.), *Film Genre Reader II*, 157–83, Austin: University of Texas Press.
Olson, C. J. (2018), *100 Greatest Cult Films*, Lanham: Rowman & Littlefield.
Panek, E. (2014), "'Show, Don't Tell': Considering the Utility of Diagrams as a Tool for Understanding Complex Narratives," in W. Buckland (ed.), *Hollywood Puzzle Films*, 72–88, London: Routledge.
Peretz, E. (2010), "What is a Cinema of Jewish Vengeance? Tarantino's *Inglourious Basterds*," *The Yearbook of Comparative Literature*, 56: 64–74.
Petro, P. (2014), "SCMS Oral Histories: Interview with Thomas Elsaesser," *Fieldnotes*, 21 March.
Pizzello, S. (2000), "The Downward Spiral," *American Cinematographer*, 81(10): 50–61.
Poague, L. A. (1985), "A Certain Tendency of the Hollywood Cinema, 1930–1980 by Robert B. Ray," *Film Criticism*, 10(2): 39–47.
Poulaki, M. (2014), "Puzzled Hollywood and the Return of Complex Films," in W. Buckland (ed.), *Hollywood Puzzle Films*, 35–54, New York: Routledge.
Ray, R. (1985), *A Certain Tendency of the Hollywood Cinema*, Princeton: Princeton University Press.
Ray, R. (1995), "The Bordwell Regime and the Stakes of Knowledge," in *The Avant-Garde Finds Andy Hardy*, 29–63, Cambridge: Harvard University Press.
Roche, D. (2018), *Quentin Tarantino: Poetics and Politics of Cinematic Metafiction*, Jackson: University Press of Mississippi.
Salt, B. (1992), *Film Style and Technology: History and Analysis*, London: Starword.
Schatz, T. (1981), *Hollywood Genres: Formulas, Filmmaking and the Studio System*, New York: McGraw-Hill.
Schlickers, S., and V. Toro, eds (2018), *Perturbatory Narration in Film: Narratological Studies on Deception, Paradox and Empuzzlement*, Berlin: de Gruyter.
Schrader, P. (1995), "Notes on Film Noir," in B. K. Grant (ed.), *Film Genre Reader II*, 218–23, Austin: University of Texas Press.

Sesonske, A. (1980), "Time and Tense in Cinema," *Journal of Aesthetics and Art*, 38(2): 419–26.
Sharrett, C. (1990), "No More Going Back and Forth as in the Past: Notes on the Fate of History in Recent European Films," *Persistence of Vision*, 8: 29–44.
Shklovsky, V. (1965), "Sterne's *Tristram Shandy*: Stylistic Commentary," in L. T. Lemon and M. J. Reis (eds), *Russian Formalist Criticism: Four Essays*, 25–57, Lincoln: University of Nebraska Press.
Spielmann, Y. (1999), "Aesthetic Features in Digital Imaging: Collage and Morph," *Wide Angle*, 21(1): 131–48.
Staiger, J. (2006), "Complex Narratives: An Introduction," *Film Criticism*, 31(1/2): 2–4.
Tasker, Y. (1996), "Approaches to the New Hollywood," in J. Curran, D. Morley, and V. Walkerdine (eds), *Cultural Studies and Communications*, 213–28, London: Arnold.
Taylor, R., ed. (1982), *The Poetics of the Cinema*, Oxford: Russian Poetics in Translation Publications.
Thanouli, E. (2008a), "To Be or Not to Be Post-Classical? That is the Question," in P. Pisters, J. Kooijman, and W. Strauven (eds), *Mind the Screen: Media Concepts According to Thomas Elsaesser*, 218–28, Amsterdam: Amsterdam University Press.
Thanouli, E. (2008b), "Orson Welles and Rouben Mamoulian: Dr. Jekyll and Mr. Hyde?," *Kinema*, 30: 79–92.
Thanouli, E. (2009a), *Post-Classical Cinema: An International Poetics of Film Narration*, London: Wallflower Press.
Thanouli, E. (2009b), "'Art Cinema' Narration Today: Breaking Down a Wayward Paradigm," *Scope*, 14: 1–14.
Thanouli, E. (2013a), "Diegesis," in E. Branigan and W. Buckland (eds), *The Routledge Encyclopedia of Film Theory*, 133–7, London: Routledge.
Thanouli, E. (2013b), "Narration," in E. Branigan and W. Buckland (eds), *The Routledge Encyclopedia of Film Theory*, 330–3, London: Routledge.
Thanouli, E. (2018), *History and Film: A Tale of Two Disciplines*, New York: Bloomsbury Publishing.
Thompson, K. (1981), *Eisenstein's Ivan the Terrible: A Neoformalist Analysis*, Princeton: Princeton University Press.
Thompson, K. (1988), *Breaking the Glass Armor: Neoformalist Film Analysis*, Princeton: Princeton University Press.
Thompson, K. (1999), *Storytelling in the New Hollywood: Understanding Classical Narrative Technique*, Cambridge: Harvard University Press.
Tzioumakis, Y. (2006), *American Independent Cinema*, Edinburgh: Edinburgh University Press.
Wu, L. Z. (2016), "Transmedia Adaptation, or the Kinesthetics of *Scott Pilgrim Vs. The World*," *Adaptation*, 9(3): 417–27.
Yarkho, B. (1977), "A Methodology for a Precise Science of Literature (Outline)," trans. L. M. O'Toole, *Russian Poetics in Translation*, 4: 52–70.

FILMOGRAPHY

Europa (1991), Dir. Lars von Trier, Denmark/Sweden/France/Germany/Switzerland: Nordisk Film & TV A/S.
Bram Stoker's Dracula (1992), Dir. Francis Ford Coppola, UK/USA: Columbia Pictures.
Chungking Express (1994), Dir. Wong Kar-wai, Hong Kong: Jet Tone Production.
Natural Born Killers (1994), Dir. Oliver Stone, USA: Warner Bros.
Pulp Fiction (1994), Dir. Quentin Tarantino, USA: Miramax.
Trainspotting (1996), Dir. Danny Boyle, UK: Channel Four Films.
Run Lola Run (1998), Dir. Tom Tykwer, Germany: X-Filme Creative Pool.
Fight Club (1999), Dir. David Fincher, Germany/USA: Fox 2000 Pictures.
Memento (2000), Dir. Christopher Nolan, USA: Newmarket Capital Group.
Requiem for a Dream (2000), Dir. Darren Aronofsky, USA: Artisan Entertainment.
Snatch (2000), Dir. Guy Ritchie, UK/USA: Columbia Pictures.
The Million Dollar Hotel (2000), Dir. Wim Wenders, Germany/UK/USA: Road Movies Filmproduktion.
Amélie (2001), Dir. Jean-Pierre Jeunet, France/Germany: UGC.
Moulin Rouge! (2001), Dir. Baz Luhrmann, Australia/USA: Twentieth Century Fox.
City of God (2002), Dir. Fernando Meirelles, Brazil/France/Germany: O2 Filmes.
Kill Bill: Vol. 1 (2003), Dir. Quentin Tarantino, USA: Miramax.
Oldboy (2003), Dir. Park Chan-wook, South Korea: Show East.
Tristram Shandy: A Cock and Bull Story (2005), Dir. Michael Winterbottom, UK: BBC Films.
Slumdog Millionaire (2008), Dir. Danny Boyle, UK/USA: Fox Searchlight Pictures.
500 Days of Summer (2009), Dir. Marc Webb, USA: Fox Searchlight Pictures.
Inglourious Basterds (2009), Dir. Quentin Tarantino, Germany/USA: Universal Pictures.
Watchmen (2009), Dir. Zack Snyder, USA: Warner Bros.
Scott Pilgrim vs. the World (2010), Dir. Edgar Wright, USA/UK/Canada/Japan: Universal Pictures.
Sidewalls [original title: *Medianeras*] (2011), Dir. Gustavo Taretto, Argentina/Spain/Germany: Eddie Saeta S.A.
The Wolf of Wall Street (2013), Dir. Martin Scorsese, USA: Red Granite Pictures.
The Grand Budapest Hotel (2014), Dir. Wes Anderson, USA/Germany: Fox Searchlight Pictures.
The Big Short (2015), Dir. Adam McKay, USA: Paramount Pictures.
Deadpool (2016), Dir. Tim Miller, USA: 20th Century Fox.
Suicide Squad (2016), Dir. David Ayer, USA: Warner Bros. Pictures.

Godard Mon Amour [original title: *La Redoutable*] (2017), Dir. Michel Hazanavicius, France/Myanmar: Les Compagnons du Cinéma.
The Laws of Thermodynamics (2018), Dir. Mateo Gil, Spain: Zeta Cinema.
Once Upon a Time in Hollywood (2019), Dir. Quentin Tarantino, USA/UK/China: Columbia Pictures.
The Trial of the Chicago 7 (2020), Dir. Aaron Sorkin, USA/UK/India: Dreamworks Pictures.
Army of the Dead (2021), Dir. Zack Snyder, USA: Netflix.
The French Dispatch (2021), Dir. Wes Anderson, Germany/USA: Indian Paintbrush.

INDEX

The letter *f* following an entry indicates a page with a figure.
The letter *t* following an entry indicates a page with a table.

Abre los Ojos (Amenábar, Alejandro) 15
agency 45–54
Ain't No Mountain High Enough (Ashford, Nickolas and Simpson, Valerie) 207
All That Heaven Allows (Sirk, Douglas) 241
Amélie (Jeunet, Jean-Pierre) 39*f*–41, 73
"American Cinema: Why Hollywood, The" (Elsaesser, Thomas) 10, 11
American Graffiti (Lucas, George) 7
American mythology 5
an après, Un (Wiazemsky, Anne) 89
animation 114
archaeology 82–5
Aristotle
    Poetics 22
Army of the Dead (Snyder, Zack) 133*f*–9*f*, 242
Arrival (Villeneuve, Denis) 13, 48
art cinema mode of narration 17–18, 27–8, 242–3, 251–2
    artistic motivation 37
    auteurs 218
    betweenness 17, 18, 243
    character agency 46
    communicativeness 187
    Dunkirk (Nolan, Christopher) 243–7
    hybridity 79
    hypermediated realism 61
    knowledgeability 187
    levels of narration 190–1

narrative space 97
narrative time 160
self-consciousness 187
"art film as event movie, The" (Bordwell, David) 243–5
artistic motivation 37, 85–95, 187
ASL (average shot length) 99
auteurs 217–20; *see also* Tarantino, Quentin
average shot length (ASL) 99

Bazin, André 2–4, 239 n. 2, 252
Beach Red (Bowman, Peter) 244
Being John Malkovich (Jonze, Spike) 15
betweenness 17, 18, 243
Big Short, The (McKay, Adam) 41*f*–3*f*, 47, 191
Blade Runner (Scott, Ridley) 9
Blue Velvet (Lynch, David) 36 n. 28
Body Heat (Kasdan, Lawrence) 7
Bolter, Jay David and Grusin, Robert
    Remediation: Understanding New Media 61–2
Bonnie and Clyde (Penn Arthur) 11
Bordwell, David 2, 3–4, 5, 10, 31, 241, 242–3, 246, 251–2
    "art film as event movie, The" 243–5
    Classical Hollywood Cinema Film Style and Mode of Production to 1960, The 1, 3, 4, 26, 28, 32
    Dunkirk (Nolan, Christopher) 243–5
    historical poetics 21–30

"Historical Poetics of Cinema" 21, 34 n. 7
intensified continuity 98–9
Making Meaning: Inference and Rhetoric in the Interpretation of Cinema 21
Narration in the Fiction Film 25, 27, 159
planimetric framing 131
Poetics of Cinema, The 22, 27
postmodernism 29
Way Hollywood Tells It: Story and Style in Modern Movies, The 29–30
bout de souffle, A (Godard, Jean-Luc) 90
Boyle, Danny 219
  127 Hours 88, 219
  Slumdog Millionaire 77–9, 219
  Trainspotting 54, 165–71f, 219
  Yesterday 219
brain, emphasis on 47–8
Bram Stoker's Dracula (Coppola, Francis Ford) 146–52f
Branigan, Edward 185, 189–92, 251
  Narrative Comprehension and Film 189
Brazil (Gilliam, Terry) 8
Buckland, Warren 14–15
  Hollywood Puzzle Films 14
  Puzzle Films: Complex Storytelling in Contemporary Cinema 14
Bullet Train (Leitch, David) 220

cameras 99
Cameron, Allan 163
  Modular Narratives in Contemporary Cinema 16
Campora, Matthew 18
Carmen (Saura, Carlos) 8
Carroll, Noel 249–50
Casino (Scorsese, Martin) 100, 219
Certain Tendency of the Hollywood Cinema, 1930–1980, A (Ray, Robert B.) 4–5
Chan-wook, Park 250, 252
  Oldboy 104f–9f, 250
chance 46, 47

character (non-focalized narration) 189, 190
character agency 45–54, 73
character presentation 38–45
Chasing Sleep (Walker, Michael) 17
Chinatown (Polanski, Roman) 7
Chinoise, La (Godard, Jean-Luc) 89, 90
chronology 162–4, 166–70, 172–4, 177–9
Chungking Express (Wong Kar-wai) 15, 54, 57–8f, 79–80, 191
cinema 2–21; *see also* Hollywood
  animation 114
  categorizing 19t–21
  classicism 2–5
  contemporary 14–15, 28–30
  Elsaesser, Thomas 10–14
  European 17
  history in 50
  mind-game films 13–14, 48
  narratology 14–21
  nostalgia films 7
  postmodernism 5–9
  puzzle films 14–17
City of God (Meirelles, Fernando and Lund, Kátia) 52–4
Classical Hollywood Cinema Film Style and Mode of Production to 1960, The (Bordwell, David; Staiger, Janet; Thompson, Kristin) 1, 3, 4, 26, 28, 32
classical mode of narration 19t, 26–7, 28–30, 241, 242, 251, 252
  artistic motivation 85
  auteurs 217
  betweenness 17, 18, 243
  boundaries 241
  character agency 45–6
  communicativeness 187
  compositional motivation 37
  Dunkirk (Nolan, Christopher) 244–5
  Elsaesser, Thomas 10–13
  hypermediated realism 61
  intensified continuity 98
  knowledgeability 186
  levels of narration 190

INDEX

narrative logic 37
narrative space 97
narrative time 159–60
self-consciousness 186
"Classical/Post-classical" (Elsaesser, Thomas) 11
classicism 2–5; see also classical mode of narration
Coen Brothers 250
Coherence (Byrkit, James Ward) 17
communicativeness 186–8
complex chronology 162–4, 166–70, 172–4, 177–9
complex narratives 14–18, 48
compositional motivation 37, 38–60, 95
  character agency 45–54
  character presentation 38–45
  plot structures 54–60
compression 164
Conformista, Il (Bertolucci, Bernardo) 7
Conversation, The (Coppola, Francis Ford) 11, 29, 247
Coppola, Francis Ford 219
  Bram Stoker's Dracula 146–52f, 219
  Conversation, The 11, 29, 247
  Cotton Club 8
Cotton Club (Coppola, Francis Ford) 8
Crash (Haggis, Paul) 250

Dark City (Proyas, Alex) 15
Dark Country (Jane, Thomas) 17
Deadpool (Miller, Tim) 87f–9f, 191, 241
Desert Hearts (Deitch, Donna) 8
Die Hard (McTiernan, John) 11, 30
diegesis 95 n. 2
diegetic narrators 189, 190
digital technology 114, 140, 161–2
dilation 164
Django Unchained (Tarantino, Quentin) 233
Dogville (von Trier, Lars) 219
dominant principle 248–9
Donnie Darko (Kelly, Richard) 13, 15, 17, 176

dream lens 133, 137
Dunkirk (Nolan, Christopher) 243–7
Dunkirk (Norman, Leslie) 247
duration 160, 164–5, 170–1, 174–6, 179–81
Durgnat, Raymond 62

Easy Rider (Hopper, Dennis) 11
Eclipse (Antonioni, Michelangelo) 251
editing; see also spatial montage
  rates 98, 99
Eichenbaum, Boris 30–1
elastic duration 164–5
Element of Crime, The (von Trier, Lars) 219
ellipses 164
Elsaesser, Thomas 10–14, 252
  "American Cinema: Why Hollywood, The" 10, 11
  "Classical/Post-classical" 11
  "Pathos of Failure, American Films in the 1970s: Notes on the Unmotivated Hero, The" 11
  Persistence of Hollywood, The 12
Elvis (Luhrmann, Baz) 219
Enemy (Villeneuve, Denis) 17
energy realism 62
Enter Nowhere (Heller, Jack) 17
Epidemic (von Trier, Lars) 219
equivalence 164
Eternal Sunshine of the Spotless Mind (Gondry, Michel) 13, 18, 30, 48, 243
Europa (von Trier, Lars) 38, 47, 83, 141–6f, 191, 219, 222, 241
European cinema 17, 61
expansion 164, 165
external focalisation 189, 190
extra-fictional narrators 189, 190

fabula 24–5
fast motion 165
Ferris Bueller's Day Off (Hughes, John) 88, 89f
Fight Club (Fincher, David) 13, 15, 38, 54, 73, 172f–6
film. See cinema
Five Easy Pieces (Rafelson, Bob) 11

500 Days of Summer (Webb, Marc) 48–50, 83, 191
flashbacks 162–3
flashforwards 162, 163
Foucault, Michel 83
framing. *See* graphic frame
freeze-frames 160, 164, 165
French Dispatch, The (Anderson, Wes) 124f–32f
frequency 160, 171, 176, 181–2
Funny Girl (Wyler, William) 88

gai savoir, Le (Godard, Jean-Luc) 26
Gangs of New York (Scorsese, Martin) 100, 219
generic motivation 37, 79–85, 95, 187
 archaeology 82–5
 hybridity 79–82
Godard, Jean-Luc 89–94
Godard Mon Amour (Hazanavicius, Michel) 89–95
Goodfellas (Scorsese, Martin) 100, 219
Grand Budapest Hotel, The (Anderson, Wes) 43f–5f
graphic frame 113–39
 Army of the Dead (Snyder, Zack) 133f–9f
 French Dispatch, The (Anderson, Wes) 124f–32f
 Natural Born Killers (Stone, Oliver) 115–23f
Gray Man, The (Russo, Anthony and Russo, Joe) 250
Great Gatsby, The (Luhrmann, Baz) 219
Groundhog Day (Ramis, Harold) 16

Hateful Eight, The (Tarantino, Quentin) 233
Hazanavicious, Michel 219
 Godard Mon Amour 89–95
heroes 45–6
higher levels of narration 47, 73, 190, 191
Hiroshima mon amour (Resnais, Alain) 163
His Girl Friday (Hawks, Howard) 241
historical authors 189, 190

historical-materialist mode of narration 27, 242
historical modes of narration 25–8, 217, 241–2, 251, 252
 art cinema. *See* art cinema mode of narration
 betweenness 17, 18, 243
 boundaries 241, 242, 247
 classical. *See* classical mode of narration
 historical-materialist 27, 242
 parametric 27, 242
 post-classical. *See* post-classical mode of narration
historical poetics 21, 31–2, 246, 251–3
 Bordwell, David 21–30
 narrative theory and concepts 24–5
 6 Ps of 22–3
"Historical Poetics of Cinema" (Bordwell, David) 21, 34 n. 7
history 50
History and Film: A Tale of Two Disciplines (Thanouli, Eleftheria) 245
Hollywood 3, 4–5, 10–14, 252
 Bazin, André 239 n. 2
 classical mode of narration 26–7, 28–9, 249
 Elsaesser, Thomas 10–12
 European influence 17
 genre 79
 narrative theories 186–7
 narrative time 159–60
 plot structures 54
 puzzle films 14–15
 realism 61
Hollywood Puzzle Films (Buckland, Warren) 14
Hours, The (Daldry, Stephen) 15
House That Jack Built, The (von Trier, Lars) 219
Hutcheon, Linda 8, 86, 251
hybridity 79–82
hypermediacy 61–2, 73
hypermediated realism 61–72, 73, 187

Idiots, The (von Trier, Lars) 219
immediacy 61–2

impersonal agency 46
Impossible Puzzle Films (Kiss, M. and Willemsen, S.) 16
Inception (Nolan, Christopher) 13
Inglourious Basterds (Tarantino, Quentin) 220, 229–33, 238
Inland Empire (Lynch, David) 15, 17
inner life, emphasis on 47–8
insertion 164
intensified continuity 98–113, 250
 ASL 99
 close framing 98, 99
 extreme lens lengths 98, 99
 free-ranging cameras 98, 99
 high cutting rate 98, 99
 Oldboy (Chan-wook, Park) 104f–9f
 Snatch (Ritchie, Guy) 109–13f
 Wolf of Wall Street, The (Scorsese, Martin) 100f–4
Interiors (Allen, Woody) 29
internal focalization 73, 189, 190
Interstellar (Nolan, Christopher) 13, 48
Invisible Man, The (Whale, James) 88f
Irreversible (Noé, Gaspar) 16

Jameson, Fredric 6–8
 Postmodernism, or, The Cultural Logic of Late Capitalism 6
Jerry Maguire (Crowe, Cameron) 30
Jezebel (Wyler, William) 3
JFK (Stone, Oliver) 30
Jour se lève, Le (Carné, Marcel) 3

Kill Bill: Vol. I (Tarantino, Quentin) 220, 223–9
Kiss, M. and Willemsen, S. 16–17
 Impossible Puzzle Films 16
Klecker, Cornelia
 "Mind-Tricking Narratives: Between Classical and Art-Cinema Narration" 18
knowledgeability 186–8
Kubler, George 1

La La Land (Chazelle, Damien) 83
Lavik, Erlend 18

Laws of Thermodynamics, The (Gil, Mateo) 208–14f
Leitch, David 219
 Bullet Train 220
lenses
 dream 133, 137
 lengths 98, 99
levels of narration 47, 73, 189–92
Life and Opinions of Tristram Shandy, Gentleman, The (Sterne, Lawrence) 192
Lock, Stock and Two Smoking Barrels (Ritchie, Guy) 109
Loop (Madarász, Isti) 17
Lost Highway (Lynch, David) 13, 17, 48, 176, 223
Love Actually (Curtis, Richard) 250
Love Me Tonight (Mamoulian, Rouben) 253 n. 2
lower levels of narration 47, 190, 191
Luhrmann, Baz 219
 Elvis 219
 Great Gatsby, The 219
 Moulin Rouge! 83–5, 98, 219, 241, 249
 Romeo + Juliet 219

McKay, Adam 219
 Big Short, The 41f–3f, 47, 191
Magnolia (Anderson, Paul Thomas) 16, 54
Making Meaning: Inference and Rhetoric in the Interpretation of Cinema (Bordwell, David) 21
Manovich, Lev 114, 140, 251
Marlene (Schell, Maximilian) 8
Matrix, The (Wachowski, Lana and Wachowski, Lilly) 15
mediated time 160–2
Memento (Nolan, Christopher) 13, 14, 16, 30, 176–82f
Mépris, Le (Godard, Jean-Luc) 90
Mildred Pierce (Curtiz, Michael) 80
Million Dollar Hotel, The (Wenders, Wim) 80–2f
mind-game films 13–14, 48

"Mind-Tricking Narratives: Between Classical and Art-Cinema Narration" (Klecker, Cornelia) 18
Miraq (Bollók, Csaba) 17
modes of narration 25; *see also* historical modes of narration
modular narratives 16, 163
Modular Narratives in Contemporary Cinema (Cameron, Allan) 16
montage 140–1
motivation. *See* artistic motivation; compositional motivation; generic motivation; realistic motivation
Moulin Rouge! (Luhrmann, Baz) 83–5, 98, 219, 241, 249
moustache, La (Carrère, Emmanuel) 17
Mukařovsky, Jan 218
Mulholland Dr. (Lynch, David) 15, 17, 48
multi-thread plotlines 250

narration 1–2, 185, 247–51; *see also* narrative logic; narrative space; narrative time; post-classical narration
 analysis 25, 37
 complex 14–21, 48
 complexity categories 16
 dominant principle 248–9
 fabula 24–5
 higher levels of 47, 73, 190, 191
 historical modes of. *See* historical modes of narration
 levels of 189–92
 lower levels of 47, 190, 191
 mode 25
 modular 16, 163
 motivation types 37
 narrative theory 24–5
 narratology 14–21
 necessary and sufficient conditions method 248, 249–50
 network narratives 253 n. 3
 offbeat 30
 style 25

 syuzhet 24–5
 theory and concepts 24–5
Narration in the Fiction Film (Bordwell, David) 25, 27, 159
Narrative Comprehension and Film (Branigan, Edward) 189
narrative logic 37–95, 162, 247–8
 archaeology 82–5
 artistic motivation 85–95, 187
 character agency 45–54
 character presentation 38–45
 compositional motivation 38–60, 95
 generic motivation 79–85, 95, 187
 hybridity 79–82
 hypermediated realism 61–72, 73, 187
 parody 85–95, 187
 plot structures 54–60
 realistic motivation 60–79, 95
 subjective realism 72–9
narrative space 97–157, 162, 247–8
 intensified continuity 98–113
 graphic frame 113–39
 spatial montage 140–57
narrative time 159–82, 247–8
 complex chronology 162–4, 166–70, 172–4, 177–9
 duration 160, 164–5, 170–1, 174–6, 179–81
 elastic duration 164–5
 Fight Club (Fincher, David) 172f–6
 frequency 160, 171, 176, 181–2
 mediated time 160–2
 Memento (Nolan, Christopher) 176–82f
 order 160, 162
 simultaneity 162, 163
 Trainspotting (Boyle, Danny) 165–71f
Natural Born Killers (Stone, Oliver) 54, 79, 115–23f, 219
necessary and sufficient conditions method 248, 249–50
network narratives 253 n. 3
non-focalized narration 189, 190
nondiegetic narrators 189, 190, 191

norms 23, 26, 28, 31, 217, 218–19, 241, 242, 249; *see also* historical modes of narration
nostalgia films 7–8
Nymphomaniac Vol. I & II (von Trier, Lars) 219

objective realism 61
Oh!, Soojung! (Hong Sang-soo) 15
Oldboy (Chan-wook, Park) 104f–9f, 250
Once Upon a Time in Hollywood (Tarantino, Quentin) 233–8, 241
127 Hours (Boyle, Danny) 88, 219
ontological spatial montage 140
order 160, 162
Otto e Mezzo (Fellini, Federico) 163

parametric mode of narration 27, 242
parody 85–95, 187, 250
Passion of Joan of Arc, The (Dreyer, Carl Theodor) 94f
pastiche 7
pathos of failure 46
"Pathos of Failure, American Films in the 1970s: Notes on the Unmotivated Hero, The" (Elsaesser, Thomas) 11
Persistence of Hollywood, The (Elsaesser, Thomas) 12
photographic realism 113–14
Pierrot le Fou (Godard, Jean-Luc) 92
planimetric framing 131
Play it Again, Sam (Allen, Woody) 8
plot duration 164
plot structures 54–60
    multi-thread plotlines 250
Poetics (Aristotle) 22
Poetics of Cinema, The (Bordwell, David) 22, 27
Poetics of Cinema, The (Eichenbaum, Boris) 22
post-classical mode of narration 30–3, 185–215, 217, 241–2, 243, 246–7, 250, 251; *see also* narrative logic; narrative space; narrative time; Tarantino, Quentin

borderline cases 250
Branigan, Edward 185, 189–92
communicativeness 186–8
Dunkirk (Nolan, Christopher) 245–6, 247
Elsaesser, Thomas 12–13
films 255–7
knowledgeability 186–8
Laws of Thermodynamics, The (Gil, Mateo) 208–14f
levels of narration 189–92
multi-thread plotlines 250
self-consciousness 186–8, 214
Sidewalls (Tarreto, Gustavo) 191, 199–208f
Sternberg, Meir 185, 186
Tristram Shandy: A Cock and Bull Story (Winterbottom, Michael) 192–9f
postmodernism 5–9, 29
Postmodernism, or, The Cultural Logic of Late Capitalism (Jameson, Fredric) 6
Predestination (Spierig, Michael and Spierig, Peter) 17
Pretend (Talen, Julie) 16
Prieto, Rodrigo 100
Primer (Caruth, Shane) 17
projection time 164
Psycho (Hitchcock, Alfred) 241
Pulp Fiction (Tarantino, Quentin) 14, 15, 16, 30, 35 n. 13, 36 n. 28, 54, 163, 220–3f, 238
Purple Rose of Cairo, The (Allen, Woody) 8
puzzle films 14–17
Puzzle Films: Complex Storytelling in Contemporary Cinema (Buckland, Warren) 14

Raiders of the Lost Ark (Spielberg, Steven) 7
Rashomon (Kurosawa, Akira) 251
Ray, Robert B. 252
    Certain Tendency of the Hollywood Cinema, 1930–1980, A 4–5
realism 61–2
    photographic 113–14

realistic motivation 37, 60–79, 95
   hypermediated realism 61–72, 73, 187
   subjective realism 72–9
Reality (Dupieux, Quentin) 17
reduction 164
Remediation: Understanding New Media (Bolter, Jay David and Grusin, Robert) 61–2
Requiem for a Dream (Aronofsky, Darren) 74–7f, 79, 98, 152–7
Return of Martin Guerre, The (Vigne, Daniel) 8
Ritchie, Guy 219
   Lock, Stock and Two Smoking Barrels 109
   Snatch 109–13f
Roche, William 238
Romeo + Juliet (Luhrmann, Baz) 219
Royal Tenenbaums, The (Anderson, Wes) 54
Run Lola Run (Tykwer, Tom) 16, 29, 54, 59–60f, 163

Scorsese, Martin 100, 219
   Casino 100, 219
   Gangs of New York 100, 219
   Goodfellas 100, 219
   Shutter Island 14
   Taxi Driver 29, 247
   Wolf of Wall Street, The 100f–4, 217
Scott Pilgrim vs. the World (Wright, Edgar) 67–72, 241–2
screen duration 164
self-consciousness 186–8, 214
Shutter Island (Scorsese, Martin) 14
Sidewalls (Tarreto, Gustavo) 191, 199–208f
Silence of the Lambs, The (Demme, Jonathan) 13
simultaneity 162, 163
6 Ps of historical poetics 22–3
Sixth Sense, The (Shyamalan, M. Night) 18, 243

Sliding Doors (Howitt, Peter) 250
slow motion 164, 165
Slumdog Millionaire (Boyle, Danny) 77–9, 219
Snatch (Ritchie, Guy) 109–13f
Snyder, Zack 219
   Army of the Dead 133f–9f, 242
   300 138
   Watchmen 54, 55–7, 138
Source Code (Jones, Duncan) 16, 17
spatial montage 140–57
   Bram Stoker's Dracula (Coppola, Francis Ford) 146–52f
   Europa (von Trier, Lars) 141–6f
   ontological 140
   Requiem for a Dream (Aronofsky, Darren) 152–7
   stylistic 140
special effects 131–2f
Spielberg, Steven 250
   Raiders of the Lost Ark 7
Stage Fright (Hitchcock, Alfred) 179
Stagecoach (Ford, John) 3
Staiger, Janet 4
   Classical Hollywood Cinema Film Style and Mode of Production to 1960, The 1, 3, 4, 26, 28, 32
Star Wars (Lucas, George) 7
Sternberg, Meir 185, 186
Stone, Oliver 219
   JFK 30
   Natural Born Killers 54, 79, 115–23f, 219
   U Turn 219
story duration 164
style 25
stylistic spatial montage 140
subjective realism 47, 61, 72–9
Suicide Squad (Ayer, David) 63–7f
Sunset Boulevard (Wilder, Billy) 80
syuzhet 24–5

Tarantino, Quentin 220–39
   Django Unchained 233
   Hateful Eight, The 233
   Inglourious Basterds 220, 229–33, 238
   Kill Bill: Vol. I 220, 223–9

Once Upon a Time in Hollywood 233–8, 241
Pulp Fiction 14, 15, 16, 30, 35 n. 13, 36 n. 28, 54, 163, 220–3*f*, 238
Tarr, Béla 252
Taxi Driver (Scorsese, Martin) 29, 247
technology 114, 140, 161–2
temporality 16; *see also* narrative time
themes 47–8
Thin Red Line, The (Malick, Terrence) 245
32 Short Films About Glenn Gould (Girard, François) 16
Thompson, Kristin 4, 36 n. 28, 248–9
  Classical Hollywood Cinema Film Style and Mode of Production to 1960, The 1, 3, 4, 26, 28, 32
300 (Snyder, Zack) 138
Time Code (Figgis, Mike) 16
Timecrimes (Vigalondo, Nacho) 17
Toto le héros (Van Dormael, Jaco) 29
Trainspotting (Boyle, Danny) 54, 165–71*f*
Trial of the Chicago 7, The (Sorkin, Aaron) 50–2*f*, 242
Triangle (Smith, Christopher) 17
Trier, Joachim 219
Tristram Shandy: A Cock and Bull Story (Winterbottom, Michael) 192–9*f*
21 Grams (Iñárritu, Alejandro González) 15, 16
Two-Lane Blacktop (Hellman, Monte) 11
Two Weeks' Notice (Lawrence, Marc) 30
Tynianov, Juri 248

U Turn (Stone, Oliver) 219

Vent d'Est (Godard, Jean-Luc) 90
voice-overs 38, 47
von Trier, Lars 219, 252
  Dogville 219
  Element of Crime, The 219
  Epidemic 219
  Europa 38, 47, 83, 141–6*f*, 191, 219, 222, 241
  House That Jack Built, The 219
  Idiots, the 219
  Nymphomaniac Vol. I & II 219

Watchmen (Snyder, Zack) 54, 55–7, 138
Way Hollywood Tells It: Story and Style in Modern Movies, The (Bordwell, David) 29–30
Who Wants To Be a Millionaire (Briggs, David; Whitehill, Mike; Knight, Steven) 77
Wiazemsky, Anne
  an après, Un 89
Wild Strawberries (Bergman, Ingmar) 251
Winterbottom, Michael 219
  Tristram Shandy: A Cock and Bull Story 192–9*f*
Wolf of Wall Street, The (Scorsese, Martin) 100*f*–4, 217
Wright, Edgar 219
  Scott Pilgrim vs. the World 67–72, 241–2

Yarkho, Boris 249
Yesterday (Boyle, Danny) 219

Zanjeer (Mehra, Prakash) 78
Zed and Two Noughts, A (Greenaway, Peter) 16
Zelig (Allen, Woody) 8